World Food

TURKEY

Dani Valent and
Jim & Perihan Masters

WORLD FOOD Turkey
1st edition

Published by
Lonely Planet Publications Pty Ltd A.C.N. 005 607 983
192 Burwood Rd, Hawthorn, Victoria 3122, Australia

Lonely Planet Offices
Australia PO Box 617, Hawthorn, Victoria 3122
USA 150 Linden Street, Oakland CA 94607
UK 10a Spring Place, London NW5 3BH
France 1 rue du Dahomey, 75011 Paris

Photography
All of the images in this guide are available
for licensing from Lonely Planet Images.
email: lpi@lonelyplanet.com.au

Published
June 2000

Although the author and publisher have tried to make the information as accurate as possible, they accept no responsibility for any loss, injury or inconvenience sustained by any person using this book

ISBN 1 86450 027 1

Printed by
The Bookmaker Pty. Ltd.
Printed in China.

About the Author

Dani Valent was born with a slotted spoon in her mouth and fingers snapping for garcon. She has eaten her way through a bursting baker's dozen of countries and cuisines. She has worked with fiery chefs, a mad pie inventor and sold ice cream in the cone, door to door. Since 1995 she's written travel guides and web fodder for Lonely Planet, typically with a local nibble in one hand, a corkscrew at the ready and a drool down her chin. She is based in Melbourne, Austalia.

About the Linguists

Jim and Perihan Masters (co-authors with Tom Brosnahan of Lonely Planet's *Turkish Phrasebook* – 2nd Edition) are a husband and wife team, living on the Aegean Coast of Turkey just 50 miles south of Izmir. There they savour an idyllic life by the sea – writing, drawing and painting, teaching English, and providing computing service support to local businesses. They also sponsor the MSNBC award-winning Learning Practical Turkish Website (http://www2.egenet.com.tr/mastersj) which has built an enthusiastic international following of devoted Turkophiles and inquisitive language students of all ages. They may be reached by e-mail at: 'mastersj@egenet.com.tr'.

About the Photographer

A predilection for playing with knives and fire led Greg Elms to a lukewarm vocation in catering. His life changed when he saw a black & white photograph of a pepper – now others cook while he eats the props.

He is a fine art graduate (VCA), has a Bachelor of Arts and works out of a disused church in Melbourne where he produces blasphemous Christmas cards – when he's not freelancing for various Australian and international magazines.

From the Publisher

This first edition of *World Food Turkey* was edited by Patrick Witton and Martin Hughes of Lonely Planet's Melbourne office. Joanne Adams and Brendan Dempsey designed. Natasha Velleley mapped and Lara Morcombe indexed. Tim Uden and Andrew Tudor provided technical know-how. Valerie Tellini, Lonely Planet Images, co-ordinated the supply of photographs and Brett Pascoe managed the pre-press work on the images. Peter D'Onghia oversaw the production of the language section, and Kerrie Hickin assisted.

Sally Steward, publisher, developed the series and Martin Hughes, series editor, nurtured each book from the seeds of ideas through to fruition, with inimitable flair.

Acknowledgements

The publisher wishes to thank Allison Jones, London, who made helpful suggestions, and Guy Mirabella for design concepts.

The author thanks Sevgi Boz (Director, Turkish Information Office, Sydney, Australia), Yalcin Manav (Director, Turkish Association of Cuisine Professionals), Bayram Ergun (Alanya Association of Cuisine Professionals), Zekai Ademir and Mesut Önal, Mustafa Kadioğlu (General Manager, Grand Zaman Hotel, Alanya), Haşim Yetkin, Nuh Doğatu, Nurten Erbey, Jim & Perihan Masters, M. Doğan Şahin & İlyas Tunaoğlu (Hacı Bekir Confectionary), Neşet Eren, Turan, Feray, Melis and Tülay Çevik, Zerin, Murat, Sekert, Deniz, İlkay, Aylin, Ally & everyone at Smiley Restaurant, Gümbet. Thanks to Pat Yale, Dawn Köse, Ruth Lockwood, Ömer Tosun, Özgür Çinkay (Gaziantep Tourism Information Office), Hüseyin Uğurlu (owner, Hotel Büyük Veliç, Gaziantep) and family, Şeflerin Yeri (Mazıcıoğlu et lokantası, Gaziantep), Burcu Zor & family, Ridvan Tandogan and family in Amasya, all at Mengen cooking school (but especially Sheyda), Levent Rudar, all at Ipek Yolu in Konya, Richard Naisby, Roni Askey-Doran, Ayberk Yuksel, Amy Valent, Greg Andresen, and Melanie (Paddy Pallin).

Warning & Request

Things change; markets give way to supermarkets, prices go up, good places go bad and not much stays the same. Please tell us if you've discovered changes and help make the next edition even more useful. We value all your feedback, and strive to improve our books accordingly. We have a well-travelled, well-fed team that reads and acknowledges every letter, postcard and email and ensures that every morsel of information finds its way to the appropriate people.

Each correspondent will receive the latest issue of Planet Talk, our quarterly printed newsletter, or Comet, our monthly email newsletter. Subscriptions to both are free. The newsletters might even feature your letter so let us know if you don't want it published.

If you have an interesting anecdote or story to do with your culinary travels, we'd love to hear it. If we publish it in the next edition, we'll send you a free Lonely Planet book of your choice.

Send your correspondence to the nearest Lonely Planet office:
Australia: PO Box 617, Hawthorn, Victoria 3122
UK: 10a Spring Place, London NW5 3BH
USA: 150 Linden St, Oakland CA 94607
France: 1 rue du Dahomey, Paris 75011

Or email us at: talk2us@lonelyplanet.com

5

contents

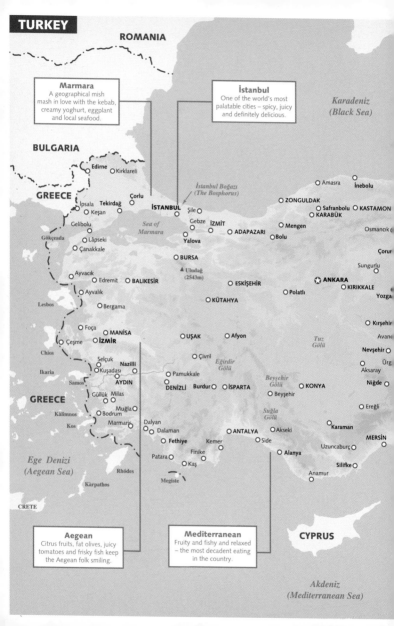

TURKEY

ROMANIA

BULGARIA

GREECE

GREECE

Marmara
A geographical mish mash in love with the kebab, creamy yoghurt, eggplant and local seafood.

İstanbul
One of the world's most palatable cities – spicy, juicy and definitely delicious.

Aegean
Citrus fruits, fat olives, juicy tomatoes and frisky fish keep the Aegean folk smiling.

Mediterranean
Fruity and fishy and relaxed – the most decadent eating in the country.

Karadeniz (Black Sea)

Ege Denizi (Aegean Sea)

Akdeniz (Mediterranean Sea)

CYPRUS

CRETE

Edirne
Kırklareli
İpsala
Keşan
Tekirdağ
Çorlu
İstanbul Boğazı (The Bosphorus)
İSTANBUL
Şile
Gebze
İZMİT
ADAPAZARI
Yalova
Mengen
Bolu
Gelibolu
Gökçeada
Lâpseki
Çanakkale
Sea of Marmara
BURSA
▲ Uludağ (2543m)
ESKİŞEHİR
Amasra
İnebolu
ZONGULDAK
Safranbolu
KARABÜK
KASTAMON
Osmancık
Çorum
Sungurlu
ANKARA
KIRIKKALE
Yozga
Polatlı
KÜTAHYA
Ayvacık
Edremit
BALIKESİR
Ayvalık
Lesbos
Bergama
Foça
Çeşme
MANİSA
İZMİR
Chios
Selçuk
Kuşadası
Nazilli
AYDIN
Samos
Güllük
Milas
Muğla
Bodrum
Marmaris
Ikaria
Kâlimnos
Kos
UŞAK
Afyon
Çivril
Pamukkale
DENİZLİ
Burdur
İSPARTA
Eğirdir Gölü
Beyşehir Gölü
Beyşehir
KONYA
Tuz Gölü
Kırşehir
Avane
Nevşehir
Ürg
Aksaray
Niğde
Ereğli
Karaman
MERSİN
Suğla Gölü
Dalyan
Dalaman
Fethiye
Kemer
Finike
Patara
Kaş
Megiste
ANTALYA
Akseki
Side
Alanya
Uzuncaburç
Silifke
Anamur
Rhodes
Kârpathos

RUSSIA

Elevation

3000 m	10000 ft
2000 m	6500 ft
1500 m	5000 ft
1000 m	3000 ft
500 m	1500 ft
0 m	0 ft

Black Sea
Hazelnuts, rice, saffron, tea and an obsession with salty anchovy.

Eastern Anatolia
Turkey's most isolated people eat the simplest food – yoghurt, meat, cheese and apricots are staples.

GEORGIA

ARMENIA

IRAN

fra ○
SAMSUN ○

○ Ünye ○ Ordu   **TRABZON** ○   ○ Hopa   ○ Artvin   *Çıldır Gölü*

○ Giresun   ○ Rize ○ Yusufeli   ○ Göle

▲ Kaçkar Dağı   Sarıkamış ○   **Kars** ○
(3937m)

○ Amasya   ○ Niksar   Gümüşhane ○   **○ Bayburt**   ○ Tortum   Kağızman ○

Turhal ○   ○ Tokat   Koyulhisar ○   ○ Şebinkarahisar   ○ Horasan   Tuzluca ○   ○ Iğdır

Suşehri ○   **ERZURUM** ○   Pasinler   ▲ Mt Ararat
                                                                    (5137m)

○ Zara   ○ Refahiye   ○ Tercan   Ağrı ○   ○ Doğubeyazıt

○ **SİVAS**   **Erzincan**

○ Divriği   ○ Tunceli   ○ Patnos

Keban   Muradiye ○
Barajı   ○ Bingöl   ○ Muş   *Van*
                                                              Gölü   Özalp ○
KAYSERİ   *Karakaya*   ○ **ELAZIĞ**   ○ Tatvan   **VAN** ○
          Barajı   ○ Bitlis   Gevaş ○   ○ Gürpınar

          ○ **MALATYA**   ○ Çatak

Göksun ○   ○ Elbistan   ○ **DİYARBAKIR**   ○ **Siirt**   Yüksekova ○
                                                        Kurtalan   Hakkari ○ ▲
          Gölbaşı ○   ○ Adıyaman   ○ Siverek   ○ Şırnak   *Cilo Dağı*
          ○ Kahramanmaraş   ○ Hilvan   (4168m)

○ Kozan   *Atatürk*   ○ Viranşehir   ○ Mardin
                Barajı
●ANA   ○ **OSMANİYE**   **ANTEP**   ○ **ŞANLIURFA**
                              ○ Birecik
●NDERUN
   ○ Kırıkhan
●ntakya ○

SYRIA   **IRAQ**

Central Anatolia
Olives, grapes, garlic, wheat and dinky donkey-towed harvests.

Southeastern Anatolia
Middle Eastern influence keeps the food hot and spicy; ice cream and baklava round things off sweetly.

0	100	200 km
0	50	100 mi

Turks are passionate about food – they write love songs to yoghurt, ballads about fish sandwiches and poems that imagine battles between pastry and pilav. Turks have fun with food too. Their ice cream is so supple it can be used as a skipping rope, a to-die-for eggplant dish is called 'the priest fainted' and plump meatballs are dubbed 'woman's thighs'. Food is about being together: tea is dosed out like a communal intravenous drip, and Ramazan (the fasting month) turns into thirty days of night-time feasting. Food is also serious and symbolic – the ram slaughtered because the son was saved, the **helva** (sesame sweet) distributed after death, every mouthful a sign of the generosity and potency of heaven and earth.

The underlying fact is that food is entwined with the joys, cycles and responsibilities of the well-lived life. Eating and drinking aren't merely about servicing the body's needs, and it's a rare Turk who regards food as simple fuel. Whether it's the juicy plums signalling spring or the sherbet which celebrates a newborn child, food is about connecting with nature's rhythms and savouring life in general. As you would expect, the most explicit intertwining of the arts of eating and being occurs during religious festivals and life's major passages, but meaning is attached to just about every eating experience. The traveller silencing a growling bus-trip tummy with a **simit** (bread ring), the shopper staving off pre-dinner pangs with a streetside cob of corn, the farmers augmenting their lunch with freshly-picked cucumbers or the family sitting down to soup and bread, are all engaging with a quintessentially Turkish tradition.

For the visitor, Turkey is a feast even when you're not eating, a banquet of plenty expressed in colours, smells and customs. You might be dazzled by strings of cherries hung at a street stall, charmed by the theatrics of an ice-cream seller, overwhelmed by the smell of mint from roadside fields or moved by the sight of people *not* eating during Ramazan. And when you get down to the actual quaffing, whether as part of a long and lazy night of **meze** (hors d'oeuvres) in a local lokanta, or creating **yayla çorbası** (plateau soup) in your own kitchen, the encounters – culinary and human – will be delightful.

the
culture
of turkish cuisine

Turkey is one of the few countries which can feed itself and have leftovers. This is not hard to believe as there's food being grown, sold and eaten wherever you look. Every Turk is a gourmet – if they don't have a signature dish of their own, their mother makes the best **börek** (pastry dish) in the land, or the red peppers grown near their village are a gift from above.

When purists talk about Turkish food, they mean **saray** (palace) cuisine, developed in the massive, extravagant kitchens of İstanbul during Ottoman times. But even at the empire's height, most Turks didn't have access to the astounding variety and sheer quantity of food available to the wealthy – not everyone was eating whole sheep and buckets of saffron-infused pudding. Eating and drinking in Turkey has always varied according to heritage, wealth and region.

The central principles are the same though, rich or poor, east or west. Food and drink sustain the body and the spirit. Eating should be joyful and celebratory, but it should also be respectful and appreciative. Meats, vegetables and grains are prepared in unfussy ways to foreground their essential nature. Herbs, spices and sauces are partnered with foods without overwhelming them. There is an enthusiasm for seasonal produce but preserved meats, fruits and vegetables can be eaten out of season.

Where saray cuisine revelled in plenty, much village cuisine developed to make more of less. Many dishes make sparing use of meat so it will go further, perhaps by pairing it with chickpeas or other pulses – known as 'poor man's meat'. Regional ingredients supplement core foods or lead to modifications in pan-Turkish dishes. Even today, when domestic trade is extensive, food varies widely from region to region, even from village to village. It doesn't, however, vary much within a household, as individuals don't tend to vary their repertoire. If they've got zucchini, they cook it up with tomato and onion; if they've got artichokes, they fry them in olive oil. This can come across as inflexibility – a vegetarian asking if the börek could be made without meat may be met with bafflement. In the very next village, the recipe may change again, and the cook's recipe will be adhered to with the same rigidity.

The mark of a good traditional cook in Turkey isn't creativity, it's skill: their **yufka** (filo pastry) is a mere membrane, their kebab tender, their **sarma** (roll-up dish) well-formed, their pilav fluffy, their **ayran** (yoghurt drink) smooth and light. You don't experiment with what is perfect, you just enact it to the best of your ability. Though many procedures are delicate, the cook needs to be deft rather than fussy; sometimes elbow grease and grunt is the way to epicurean heaven.

Until recently, cooks tended to absorb cooking techniques and combinations from the people around them, rather than from cookbooks or recipe exchanges. Old recipe books here read more like herbal medicine treatises, prescribing particular foods for various ailments rather than actually teaching how to cook. These days, a concern to preserve old dishes within Turkey and to introduce Turkish food to an international audience has made writing down recipes more common.

Spice display, Spice Bazaar, İstanbul

The historical contempt for recipes is illustrated in a story about Empress Eugenie, wife of Napoleon III. While a guest at İstanbul's Topkapı Palace, the empress fell in love with a lamb & eggplant dish and arranged for her chef to meet with the sultan's chef to learn how to cook it. The French chef duly turned up at the palace kitchen with his notebook and his scales and his measuring spoons. The Turkish chef was outraged. 'A true chef cooks with his feelings and his senses!', he bellowed and threw his colleague's equipment out the window. The empress returned to France with the memory, but no recipe. Today, the dish is known as **hünkar beğendi** (literally, the sultan was pleased) and it's okay to write down the recipe, which you'll find in the Turkish Banquet chapter.

History

The Turkic people became a mighty presence in Central Asia from about the 4th century, influencing the region with their mostly meaty diet. Horse, mutton, goat and beef were salted, sun-dried, grilled on open fires or baked in clay ovens. There's also a story about dashing Turkish nomads hanging steak from their saddles, curing it with sweat, wind and leather – maybe true, certainly a pretty image. Their fleshophilia was toned down with the serendipitous addition of wild vegetables and fruit. Wheat and barley were harvested – though not cultivated – to make flat bread and bulgur; yoghurt was churned in leather bags to make butter and cheese. Also kept in leather was **kımız** (fermented mare's milk), the nomads' party potion.

During the 6th century the Turks began to move into northwestern China. The Chinese and the Turks swapped some ideas and came up with a tiny pasta parcel the Turks know as **mantı** and the Chinese know as won ton. Another joint creation was a concave griddle that the Turks know as a **çin tavası** and the Chinese as a wok.

The Turks then moved slowly westward, some of them pausing to set up an empire based in Tashkent in the 11th century. The first Turkish dictionary was compiled during this period and it includes **şiş kebab** (skewered meat), **börek** (pastry dish) and **sucuk** (spice-cured sausage), so we can be sure that these foods have a long lineage. Selcuk Turks reached Persia in 1055, capturing Baghdad. Here

TALKING TURKEY

The Turkish for 'turkey' is **hindi** (Indian), a confusion of India and the Indies (ie the Americas) where the big blustery bird actually heralds from. The Turks introduced Europeans to the bird, hence the English word 'turkey'.

they stopped, adopted Islam, planted grains, learned about rice and showed the Persians bulgur in exchange. They also discovered dumpling soups, stews and the art of drying fruit which quickly gained favour in both sweet and savoury dishes.

A healthy appetite for land had them looking north, into Anatolia. The Byzantine Anatolians had a foodie heritage bequeathed by the Hittites (1900-1300 BC) and the Romans, both having a wheat and mutton-based cuisine augmented by beans, vegetables and fruits. A reverence for olives and grapes had been passed down from the Hittites.

Within 10 years, the Selcuks had driven out the Byzantine Anatolians and taken over most of Anatolia. By this time they had added **zerde** (rice & nut dessert), **helva** (sesame sweet) and vegetable dishes with garlic and yoghurt to their ever-expanding culinary repertoire. They introduced poultry, eggs and the chilli pepper to the region, and met new friends like olives, cabbage, chickpeas and parsley. Those who made it down to the Mediterranean Sea learned about seafood from the Greeks.

It was a creative time in the kitchen: the Selcuks perfected the preserving techniques required for **pastırma** (pastrami), yoghurt and vegetables. They fortified themselves with **boza** (fermented millet drink) and celebrated with wine. They were well nourished and robust – a lot of their success can be attributed to their skills in stocking the pantry.

But the Selcuk Turks got edgy when the Mongols came calling in the mid-13th century, and they were pushed west. They scattered around the Aegean and Marmara coasts in warrior bands. One group, led by Osman, was more acquisitive than all the others put together and eventually they grew into the Ottoman Empire, seizing İstanbul from the Byzantines in 1453.

Sultan Mehmet the Conqueror built Topkapı Palace in 1453, shortly after his ascension, placing great importance on the kitchens. He installed hundreds of chefs who competed to please the sultan and lesser worthies, their sparring spurring ever greater gastronomy. Such was the status of food, it even became a topic of poetry. A contemporary scribe, Bushak, wrote loving epics with titles such as *Ballad of Pilav with Saffron and Börek* and *Dream of Being in a Tomb Made of Food*.

The Ottoman Empire engulfed a mass of land from North Africa to the Danube, turning the whole region into one big recipe swap meet. French sweet teeth shared their cakes and pastries. Italians introduced pastas and **tavuk göğsü** (chicken breast pudding). The palace chefs seized upon new ingredients for their constantly expanding kitchens. Food from the empire and beyond found its way to İstanbul along trade routes known as 'spice roads' and other routes, if not by land, then by sea. Okra stumbled in from north Africa. Tomatoes, potatoes, peppers, beans and the turkey arrived from the Americas in the 16th century and were happily incorporated into the Turkish larder.

Sultan Süleyman the Magnificent (1520-60) built a six-domed kitchen at Topkapı Palace and placed epicurean indulgence at the heart of İstanbul life. The sultan and his family had all their food prepared in a separate kitchen overseen by 12 specialist cooks and a host of underlings. Some of the extravagance was precautionary – one group tasted the food for poison – but some of it seems pure overkill. One man's sole responsibility was to keep the sultan's napkins in order.

In 1600, there were about 200 staff sweating in the palace kitchens; by 1650, 1300 workers fed up to 10,000 people a day, 5000 of them inhabitants of the palace. Shopping lists for feasts were novella length, including list items like '50,000 chickens' or '60 cows (with horns)'. Cooking guilds emerged with particular specialities: the pilavçı did rice dishes, the çorbaçı was the soup god and the börekçi knew everything there was to know about pastries. Each guild harked back to a saint, instilling reverence for

MEVLÂNA AND THE WHIRLING DERVISHES

Mevlâna was a great 13th-century Sufi mystic and founder of the Whirling Dervishes. He mingled food and spirituality in his teachings, equating the cooking of food with the 'cooking' of a man (ie his path to spiritual knowledge). As understanding grew, the crudite kitchen-hand transformed into the al dente master.

The Sufi dervishes aimed for inspiration within discipline. The strict organisation of the palace kitchens can be traced back to Sufi principles as can the Turkish reliance on cooking by 'feel' rather than measurement and calculation. Many Ottoman chefs were Sufis.

If you've ever snickered at the sight of a chef in a puff pastry hat, consider the whirling dervishes who, as their name suggests, moved toward enlightenment by spinning around until dizziness gave way to godliness. When you consider their inverted ice-cream cone headgear and voluminous capes, it gives a whole other meaning to being a 'whizz in the kitchen'.

Ateşbaz Veli, a 13th century dervish and chef, is the most revered cook in Turkish history. A shrine was erected to his memory and stocked with salt. Cooks came to buy salt from the shrine believing it to have a mega-MSG tasty effect and also because it was thought to make a little food stretch to feed many, even if it wasn't loaves and fishes.

their produce and ensuring that the highest quality was maintained. The breadmakers claimed Adam for inspiration but there were lesser saints for just about everything, even a Saint of Pickles. Each guild had its own uniform and each cook's outfit signalled his speciality and his position within the guild.

A cook's training would take years, mostly in the form of an extended unpaid apprenticeship. After a few years, he received money for coffee and shaving needs but would rely on tips for spending money. Only senior chefs drew a salary. Further specialisation continued over the centuries. By the mid-18th century, separate master chefs were responsible for each of six varieties of helva, each with 100 assistants.

The Janissaries, the elite military corps personally responsible for the sultan, communicated many of their demands with food. If they over-turned their massive **kazan** (pilav cauldron), it was a sign of dissatisfaction and a signal that rebellion was imminent. If they didn't eat all of the baklava presented to them during Ramazan, the civil service (and the pastry chefs) began quaking. (For more on the sulky Janissaries, see the boxed text Lolly Loyalty in the Staples & Specialities chapter.)

During the slow decline of the Ottoman Empire throughout the 18th and 19th centuries, Turkey's culinary trade slackened off. Low level European interpolation continued, particularly from the French, but there was none of the mad scientist creativity which had characterised the empire's high times.

When Turkey's national hero, Mustafa Kemal Atatürk, reshaped the country, he emphasised a national homogeneous identity, and outsider cuisines went out of favour. It wasn't until the last 30 years of the 20th century, when Turkey started courting Europe and styling itself as a bridge between east and west, that foreigners and their food became fashionable once more.

Some foods came to Turkey with returning or visiting emigrants. German schnitzel, French profiteroles, Italian gelati, American burgers – all can be found on otherwise 'Turkish' menus. Eastern Turkey is prone to Middle Eastern culinary incursions, and as eastern Turks move from rural villages to the central and western cities, they bring these flavours with them. The northeast has taken in floods of Georgian and Russian immigrants, making it as easy to get borsch as börek along the eastern Black Sea coast.

Urbanised Turks tend to balance an interest in food from elsewhere with concern for preserving their Turkish traditions – they are happy to be able to get tacos and choc-chip cookies, but they don't want to see them take over.

How Turks Eat

Eating in Turkey is as much about social interaction as sustenance. Definitely, the connection between food and function is strong and meals are deliberately hearty to generate the energy necessary for hard rural work. But the concept of chewing on a muesli bar and slugging back a power drink would be completely alien: food is an occasion before it is a fuel-up.

In Ottoman times Turks ate two meals a day, one in the late morning and one in the evening. Now three meals a day is the norm. The day starts with **sabahları** (morning food) or **kahvaltı** (breakfast). A **Türk kahvaltı** (Turkish breakfast) consists of bread, white cheese and honey or jam at minimum. Usual augmentations are cold boiled eggs, tomato, cucumber, olives and sliced meat. Even though kahvaltı suggests coffee – **kahve** means coffee – tea is normally served. Soup is also a common breakfast food.

The food eaten for the three daily meals regularly cross over. **Öğle yemeği** (lunch) might be the same cold spread as breakfast or it could be the more substantial kinds of foods that are eaten for **akşam yemeği** (dinner). This typically means soup, salad, vegetable dishes, grilled meat, pilav and fruit for dessert. If lunch is a big meal, dinner may revert to breakfast style bread-cheese-olives, probably with the addition of **sarma** (wrapped dish) or some other **meze** (hors d'oeuvre). There is a traditional late afternoon cakes session which includes börek, **poğaça** (buns) and coffee.

Breakfast is eaten between 6 and 8am, lunch is around noon and dinner is eaten between 6 and 9pm. In many households, dinner is whenever dad gets home – the custom of serving cooked dishes lukewarm makes the timing of meals much easier for mum. If people are drinking, they might sit around the meze table from sunset until after midnight.

In Ottoman homes, people sat on cushions and carpets and the food was placed on a **tepsi** (tray) on a low trestle in front of them. The food was eaten directly from communal dishes, scooped up with bread or a spoon. In cities this custom died out during the 19th century but it persists to this day in some village households (see the Home Cooking & Traditions chapter). For the most part, however, you will encounter very little culture shock when eating in a Turkish home. There are no real danger zones that you should be wary of, and the only hard and fast rule is to enjoy both the food and company.

While out and about you'll soon find that Turkey is well set up for snack attacks. Buying a **simit** (bread ring) or a corncob to chew on when in transit or while shopping is routine. Snacks don't replace meals though – eating alone or grabbing a sandwich on the way out the door instead of eating with family or friends is frowned upon. In the cities, though, this kind of latchkey eating is catching on.

Tea drinkers, Old Bazaar, İstanbul

Etiquette

Sitting down to eat in Turkey is mostly about being there and enjoying your time – the demands of etiquette are not particularly onerous. Keep a general attitude of respect for the food and for your fellow diners and you won't go wrong.

This wasn't always the case; there were bucketloads of detailed prescriptive etiquette in Ottoman times. For example, bread had to be picked up with three fingers, everyone had to stop eating when one person paused for a drink of water and food dropped on the floor was kissed and held above the head.

If you're eating in a religious household, the blessing you'll hear before the meal begins **bismillâhirrahmânirrahim** (in the name of God, the Compassionate, the Merciful), recited by the father. At the end of the meal, the father thanks God by saying **elhamdülillah**, the response to which is **elinize sağlık** (health to your hands), which is also said to honour the cook at the beginning of the meal.

Apart from the blessings, there isn't much ceremony. After the food is served and the blessing said, you should dig in. Courses follow hot on each other's heels, partly because it's considered slothful to linger and rude to keep someone waiting. If someone finishes their soup, main dishes will be brought out. If someone finishes their mains, dessert will arrive. The underlying directive seems to be: get it all on the table! Let's eat! Naturally, the cook will appreciate your praise, but the best way to show your enjoyment is by eating. And then eating some more. And then, just a little more.

You may still occasionally find yourself eating soup from a communal bowl. If so, hold a piece of bread under your spoon so it doesn't drip. If you're in a cutlery-less environment, pick up food with a piece of bread, not with your fingers. Unlike in some stricter Muslim societies, holding utensils or food in your left hand is not a grave faux pas in Turkey. It is however best to use your right hand for taking food from shared dishes.

Red peppers, İstanbul street market

Generally, when eating from communal dishes, you eat the food nearest to you. If you spy a juicy morsel in the dish but it's on the opposite side of the table, you have to grin and bear it – it ain't yours.

Shared salad can be eaten straight from shared plates with your fork. Alternatively you can scoop some onto your plate and eat it from there. Most people will enjoy a squeeze of lemon on the salad but it's polite to ask if everyone wants some or to just dose up the salad nearest your plate.

Dipping bread in your soup is okay, though it's more a village custom and might be clucked over by city hens. It's the same with belching and slurping: in urbanised families it might be frowned upon, in the country-side you can go for it. Blowing your nose is considered pretty explicit behaviour, country or city; sniff or excuse yourself to have a good snot. Tipping your head back to have a drink of water is also considered quite intimate because the throat is exposed. You may see older people turn their head away to drink but you won't shock anyone these days by sipping without turning.

MEDITERRANEAN MEZE

Feray and Ayberk live in Bodrum, a town that caters to European beach bunnies on package tours. They both work in travel agencies which, in tourist season, means they don't get home until well into the evening. Right through the summer, they round off their long days with **meze** (hors d'oeuvre). For Feray and Ayberk, the meze spread lends itself to easy, sociable dining. A simple meal of meze can be cobbled together in 10 minutes, making it easy to accommodate last minute ravenous visitors, and letting Feray and Ayberk relax almost as much as their guests.

There's always a steady stream of drop ins: neighbourhood friends, or Feray and Ayberk's university-age kids home from the movies or the bowling alley, perhaps with friends of their own. Anyone who turns up is prompted to pick at the table of meze: olives, cheese, dolmas, cold chicken, boiled eggs, bread and salad. There will always be something to drink as well: wine, beer rakı, or tea. Everyone will pick and sip while dissecting the day, to a background of an Arabesk music (see Music in the Turkish Banquet chapter).

The atmosphere is casual, a combination of exhaustion, satisfaction and the sedative properties of the Mediterranean breeze. There's no protocol – anyone who is tired or has eaten enough can leave or simply move to the couch and stretch out. The stayers sit around chatting, mopping up food with their bread, and perhaps philosophising over a little more rakı.

It's considered bad luck to hand knives or scissors directly to anybody. If you want to pass them to someone, lay them down on the table for the other person to pick up.

If food or drink are passed to you on a plate, don't pass the plate on to someone else. You can assume that it was given to you with the intention that you be the one to eat it. Though it's polite to eat at least a couple of mouthfuls of whatever is offered to you, there's no problem leaving unfinished food on your plate – a Turkish host can't be sure they have filled you up unless it's obvious you can eat no more. In fact, an empty plate will be a matter of consternation, especially if you won't let your host fill it up again for you.

It's not unusual for people to smoke while others are eating, though they may first ask if it's okay with everyone. Abstainers will be offered, indeed urged to smoke cigarettes. The phrase 'hayır teşekkür ederim, sigara içmiyorum' (no thanks, I don't smoke) may come in handy.

Eating out in Turkey, whether a no-frills lokanta or an upscale restoran, isn't a culturally complicated activity. If everyone is making a meal of meze but you want to tuck into a hearty stew, there's no problem ordering it at the same time. It's not considered very important that everyone eats the same courses at the same pace. Similarly, the kitchen will send out dishes as they are ready: it's quite normal for all the chicken dishes to arrive and then, five minutes later, all the lamb. You don't have to wait for everyone's food to arrive to begin eating.

Because most Turkish food comes in bite-size portions, a fork is usually sufficient and simple restaurants may not bother giving you a knife at all. You can hold a piece of bread in the other hand and use it to push food onto the fork if necessary.

Turkish waiters seem to either leave your plate in front of you until you've left the restaurant or snatch it away before you've finished. Sometimes it defies logic: the soup plate that you'd done with 20 minutes ago slowly encrusts on the table, but the waiter snatches the plate that your fork hovers over. Saying 'kalsın' (let it stay) may slow them down. When you have finished, put your knife and fork together to indicate that the waiter can take the plate. If this has no effect (or you don't have a knife), say 'biti, alabilirsin' (finished, you can take it) to the waiter.

Toothpicking should be done behind your hands but you don't need to be particularly discreet. Very few restaurants have a non-smoking section, but outdoor eating can be a good way of avoiding the haze. If common practice is a guide, mobile-phone etiquette is to have an obnoxious loud ring and to talk on the phone incessantly.

staples
& specialities

Many Turkish staples are at their best straight from nature: apples
so crisp they're almost too loud to eat, a simple meat sizzle, herbs
which seem to fling flavour at you from the markets. Some dishes
require a bit of preparation: yoghurt and cheese, fragrant soups,
deftly combined salads. Still others rely on an expert's touch: an
airy pilav or a 40-layer baklava. No matter how complicated it is,
every dish stands and falls on core ingredients that, even when
they're staples, can still be very special.

Bread delivery, Süleymaniye, İstanbul

Ekmek (Bread)

"It is essential to have bread during the meal" is the first principle laid down by Turkey's Association of Cuisine Professionals. That bread be present when eating be done is as binding as a religious commandment. Living on breaded meals in Turkey would be no problem at all. You could have a sesame-studded **simit** (bread ring) for breakfast, crusty bread and cheese for lunch, a spicy meat **lahmacun** (Turkish pizza) drizzled with lemon for dinner and a syrup-soaked, cream-topped rusk of bread for dessert. You could even top it off with a midnight swig of **boza** (fermented millet drink).

When the Central Asian nomads came storming west, they brought unleavened bread with them. **Ekmek** is the general term for bread of any sort but these days spongy white sourdough loaves are ubiquitous; **pide** (flat bread) is basic homemade village fare (see the Home Cooking & Traditions chapter), as well as a pouch for döner and a base for pizza. **Lavaş** (thin crispy bread) is yeast free but it balloons exuberantly when cooking. The chewy **simit** (bread ring) is sold in every plaza and on just about every street corner in Turkey (see the Street Food chapter). Turks are inclined to eat their bread plain, in between mouthfuls of food or with a little salt. Butter isn't usually offered but, as most households will have a pat available, you can probably get some to spread on your slice.

During **Ramazan** (the fasting month), normal loaves are sold in the mornings, but pide with **çörekotu** (black cumin seeds) is sold in the afternoons so hungry people have something special with which to break the day's fast. You can still find this pide for the rest of the year though it's not as plentiful.

Lahmacun is a type of pizza, most often topped with ground meat, onion, chilli and parsley. Other possible toppings include cheese, meat pieces and sausage. The classic lahmacun is oval and as long as a goalie's foot, though restaurants may make palm-sized portions. Each region has its own way of making a lahmacun. For example, in Antep they're made with garlic but no onion and in Samsun they're made in boat shapes, with filling-hugging edges. The best come from big woodfire ovens and are paddled in and out on wooden oars. When you're not doing it dainty, lahmacun is eaten as follows: slice it into strips, drizzle it with lemon, daub it with chunks of tomato, roll it up and eat it with your fingers. Once it's finished, you eat the debris off your hands and arms. It's also possible to eat lahmacun with a knife and fork, but it's not as much fun.

Lahmacun, Turkish pizza

Et (Meat)

Et appears in most main meals, though it's usually itsy bitsy rather than hunka hunka – there isn't much sitting down to a rump steak. More often, it's cut in small pieces or minced and cooked with vegetables. Historically, whole joints or cuts of meat were reserved for the wealthy or for special occasions. As well as the expense of the meat itself, the need to conserve fuel made cooking small chunks of meat a better option. It is also used to flavour soups, rice and bulgur, and to stuff vegetables.

Kuzu (lamb and mutton), **dana** (beef) and **tavuk** (chicken) are used in similar ways around the country, depending on availability. Beef is more common along the Black Sea, lamb along the Aegean and east of the centre. Chicken is popular throughout the country.

Coronary carers will note from the crackle and spit that fatty meat is most prevalent. Sheep's tail was traditionally used to procure frying lard, especially in the east, though these days vegetable oil is more common. People in cities eat more meat than their country cousins, even though villagers are the ones raising animals. Many villagers sell their livestock and live mostly on fruit, vegetables and cereals. Generally, less meat is eaten in summer, when lighter dishes are preferred. Celebrations are an exception: no matter what time of year it is, a table groaning with beast-flesh is essential.

Just about every bit of the animal is eaten: organs, head, feet, nether regions. Economy was the initial reason, but it does seem that Turks have a taste for the spooky bits. Once a nomadic warrior had sucked blood from his cantering horse's jugular for an afternoon tea on the go, it probably didn't seem too adventurous to eat sheep's balls. But you may not want to get that intimate. Innards-lovers and the squeamish should learn the translations for **işkembe** (tripe), **kelle** (head) and **koç yumurtası** (ram's 'eggs') so they can seek or avoid. **Kokoreç** (grilled intestines) are common street food, snapped up by snack-hungry Turks and **işkembe çorbası** (tripe soup) is the drinking man's favourite midnight feast (see the boxed text İşkembe Çorbası later in the chapter).

Kokoreç (grilled intestines), Milas, south Aegean

There are six main ways of cooking meat. Within each of these major streams, there are countless variations:

kebab – cubes of meat ızgara (grilled) on a şiş (skewer) with vegetable chunks of equal size. In its wider sense, kebab can be used to mean just about any meat and vegetable dish.

döner – thin slices of meat stacked on a vertical skewer, then grilled and shaved off. The meat is packed into pide or a bread roll, along with soggy potato chips and green chillies.

köfte – ground meat or bulgur mixed with herbs, chopped vegetables, breadcrumbs and egg yolk, made into meatballs or fingers or wedges, then broiled or grilled

saç kavurma – rapid stirfrying of small cubes of meat (usually beef) on a flat-bottomed pan

STAPLES

Food cooked in a guveç, small clay stewing pot

guveç - meat and vegetables stewed together in a clay pot in their own juices. **Sahan** is another type of stew, where the meat is cooked with **salça** (tomato puree); **yahni** adds vegetables and pulses to the burbling brew. **Mussaka** starts with a vegetable fry up, continues with a mincemeat overlay, and then the whole kaboodle is cooked slowly over a flame or in the oven.

tandır – massive clay woodfire oven traditionally built in a pit and sometimes big enough to cook a whole lamb. It's rare to find a restaurant using an authentic clay oven; any big oven is likely to be dubbed tandır. The similarity both linguistically and stylistically to Indian tandoor cooking is explained by a shared Persian heritage. The Turks – who call it **tandır** – and the Indians are thought to have adopted this ancient technique (and the name) from the Persian word, tennur.

Meat in Turkey is killed **halal**, that is, in accordance with Muslim law – a prayer is said, the beast's throat is cut, rapid death ensues and the blood is drained from the body. When you're ordering a meat dish, you need to specify that you don't want your meat well done by asking for it **az pişmiş** (literally, little cooked). The Turks are loathe to leave meat even a little bit pink because of the Islamic injunction against eating blood.

When using mince, lamb is quite often mixed with beef, especially if health considerations are at the fore: beef is appreciated for its lower fat content while lamb is enjoyed for its flavour. Young lamb is particularly prized. The flesh may be soaked in milk, yoghurt, mineral water or **rakı** (anise alcohol) to soften it. Marinating the meat in oil, onion and herbs is also popular.

Beef is used to make **pastırma**, a cured sausage encrusted with **çemen**, a pungent 15-spice mix which includes pepper, salt, cumin, chilli, fenugreek and a hell of a lot of garlic. Pastırma is sliced wafer thin, and enjoyed fried up with eggs, cooked with dried beans, on lahmacun or as an accompaniment to rakı. **Sucuk** is a spicy beef sausage, sometimes encrusted with pepper or chilli. It's a popular breakfast dish, eaten slightly warmed.

Chicken is usually cooked simply: cubed and skewered, barbecued or boiled. Sometimes, it sees service in some more fussy dishes where it's pounded, rolled, stuffed or coated in a complicated sauce. **Çerkez tavuğu** (walnut chicken) is the most famous of these. If you're at a barbecue, **göğüs** means breast; **kanat** means wing and **but** means thigh.

Islam forbids the eating of pork; just about the only place you'll find it is in awful British bacon & eggs enclaves.

Kebab
Just about anything you can poke a **şiş** (skewer) at will be an essential component of some little Turkish town's proprietary kebab. They're made with cubed meat, minced meat, vegetables, even plums and chestnuts. Kebabs are cooked vertically, horizontally – someone, somewhere probably swears by the diagonal cooking method. Though truly the rightful kingdom of the baa-lamb, cows and chickens are also good mates with the şiş. But kebabs don't even have to be cooked on a skewer – just about anything that's got anything to do with meat and isn't cooked with water can end up labelled a kebab.

Kebab corner, Taksim, İstanbul

The most famous kebabs are İskender (or Bursa) kebabı, Adana kebabı and Urfa kebabı. Also very common is the patlıcan kebabı. The İskender (or Bursa) kebabı is relatively elaborate: it's comprised of döner lamb served on a bed of crumbled pide and yoghurt. Two different sauces, first a tomato and then a burnt butter sauce, are poured on at the table. It's a very rich dish, and though it's available in name throughout Turkey, Bursa locals swear that it's never going to be any good unless you eat it on their turf. This kebab is named after İskender Usta, the chef who invented the vertical grill in the 1860s. He realised that he could avoid charring his meat if the flames came from a different place to that which the fat dripped onto. So, he packed slices of meat onto his sword and fanged it into the ground next to his fire. Even today, you can sometimes see crafted 'sword hilts' on some skewers in celebration of İskender's brainwave. Today, the revolving roast is a better known Turkish symbol than the nation's flag.

The Adana and Urfa kebabs are flip sides of the same coin. Both are made from mincemeat worked into pellets and grilled on a skewer, served with onions, paprika, parsley and pide. The difference is that the Urfa version isn't spicy while the Adana kebab is a real tongue-attacker. Once again, you'll find these at the corner kebab stores all over Turkey, but the home-grown versions are the best. Patlıcan kebab is sometimes made with cubed meat and sometimes with mince. The fixed point is the presence of eggplant discs, glossy-skinned and plump, threaded between the meat.

Köfte (Mincemeat or Bulgur balls)

Köfte is one of the only dishes that men are happy to make, possibly because of the legend of its origin. It is supposedly a throwback to the days when Turkish nomads carried spiced ground meat in their saddle bags, kneading it over a long ride with their muscular, sweaty thighs, glistening, flexing proudly … um, you get the idea, we'll go get a glass of water. The most swooned over meatball is çiğ köfte, spicy mince kneaded with bulgur for three or four hours, wrapped in a lettuce leaf and eaten raw with a squeeze of lemon. Though blokes will dirty their hands with çiğ köfte all over Turkey, it's most fabulous in eastern Anatolia and around Urfa.

Another famous köfte is içli köfte, fist-sized ground lamb and onion köfte with a bulgur coating, a speciality of Antep and Diyarbakır. Tekırdag köfte (ground meat mixed with garlic, cumin, red chilli flakes and black pepper) is more spicy. İnegöl köfte is made with a mixture of beef rib meat, lamb and onion. After being minced and mixed, the köfte is left for up to four days before being seasoned and rapidly cooked on a woodfire grill. They're perfect served with piyaz (white bean salad). A Cappadocian favourite is sulu köfte where the meat is bashed in a wooden mortar, mixed with bulgur and spices, made into tiny meatballs, then boiled in stock.

Deniz Ürünü (Seafood)

Given 8400km of coastline curtsying to four seas and a landscape puddled with lakes and strewn with rivers, water-life is important in the Turkish diet. But seafood didn't turn up much in palace cuisine until the 19th century when fishy French influence was rife. A widely held suspicion was that the fish might come alive inside them when they drank a glass of water.

Even today, Turks haven't fallen for seafood hook, line and sinker. Many never eat it, partly because it's often expensive and partly because of a residual ichthyophobia. Even inhabitants of coastal towns will often steer clear of the fruit of the sea. Indeed, it's only along the **hamsi** (anchovy) ridden Black Sea that seafood occupies a mainstream place in the diet. That said, there are still enough seafood-eating natives and visitors to keep plenty of fisherfolk in business.

Catches are most plentiful in winter. Hamsi clog the northern coastal stretches while their larger cousins scoot away from the chilly Black Sea, through the Bosphorus and into the warmer waters of the Aegean. Summer catches aren't drab though: there are plenty of fish and shellfish along the Aegean and Mediterranean. **Kalamar** (calamari) is a hugely popular northern Aegean dish, and with good reason, as the squid is both fleshy and tender. **Midye** (mussels) are a common cheap snack in Marmara, often deep fried and served on a stick (**midye tavası**). **Karides** (shrimp) are also popular, especially served with a chilli sauce. The pimply **kalkan** (turbot) is a spring bloomer and **lakerda** (sliced and salted tunny fish) can be found all year round. Other common fish are **kılıç balığı** (swordfish), prevalent along the Mediterranean and **çipura** (gilt-head bream), a favourite candidate for the grill, mostly found in the Aegean.

Fish are sold at regular markets and at specialised fish bazaars, usually located right by the fishing dock. You can often choose your fish from a bucket of half-alive gaspers, still slapping and kicking. Just to confuse you, fish are named differently according to their age and size. For example, the popular six-finned Bosphorus **lüfer** (bluefish) is called **çinekop** when it's a little tacker, **sarı kanat** when it's middling and **kofana** when it's a whopper.

Fish is made into **çorba** (soup), **guveç** (stew, cooked in a clay pot), **ızgara** (grilled) whole or in chunks on a **şiş** (skewer) or **tava** (battered and fried). For a fishy version of **pilaki** (a cold stew), onion and garlic are sauteed in oil, and fish is added along with water and salt to be gently poached with vegetables, rice or beans. An elaborate stuffing technique is applied to **ukumru** (mackerel): the bones are removed and the fish stuffed to such careful sleekness that it looks like it jumped straight from the sea onto the plate. On the Black Sea, there's a you-name-it-we-do-it attitude to seafood: omelette, pilav, börek and dessert are all likely to arrive slightly fishy.

Fish market, Eminönü, İstanbul

WEATHERFISH

In İstanbul, the changing of the seasons can be forecast by fish-spotting. **Tekir** (red mullet) is the rosy flag of high summer, but when the **ukumru** (mackerel) swims in, summer swims out. By the time the **lüfer** (bluefish) arrives, it's a sign that things are shivery, while **palamut** (bonito) is the harbinger of snow. Even though it's a weird looking fish, **kalkan** (turbot) is greeted by a happy welcoming committee, for it is the unwitting bringer of spring.

Bitkiler (Vegetables)

Turks are mighty fond of vegetables, eating them fresh in season and preserved through winter, enjoying both the flavours and the vitamins. They love their native produce and have enthusiastically adopted foreign vegetables brought to their attention. Sure, not even the Italians knocked back the tomato or the potato but Turkey went so far as to welcome much-maligned okra with pot-stirring arms. However, even the most inclusive and fair-minded parents tend to have a favourite child they're completely ga-ga about, and when we're talking Turks and vegetables, we're talking **patlıcan** (eggplant). If there's any conceivable way of sneaking eggplant into a dish, it will be there.

The standard treatment for vegetables is to cook them in olive oil, and **zeytinyağlı** is the name given to dishes made this way. All this entails is to saute the chopped vegetable until it is cooked to a succulent mushiness. Sometimes the vegetable will fly solo but more often onions, tomatoes, green chillis, salt and pepper will be on board too. Tougher vegetables, like carrots, may be softened in simmering water before they are fried. Zeytinyağlı dishes are served anything from warmish to room temperature and are eaten with a squeeze of lemon and a dollop of garlic yoghurt.

Vegetables are often filled with rice or meat mixtures. If the vegetable is stuffed it's called **dolma**, such as **kabak dolması** (stuffed zucchini). If the vegetable is wrapped around the stuffing it's called **sarma**, such as **yaprak sarma** (stuffed grape leaves). Candidates for dolma include mushroom, eggplant, tomato and zucchini. Sarma is made with cabbage or grape leaves, and the filling is usually cooked, at least partially, before it's packed or rolled into the vegetables. If a rice stuffing is used, the dish is served at room temperature; if the stuffing is mince, it's served warm with a yoghurt and garlic sauce.

Ubiquitous summer vegetables are tomato, eggplant, green beans, green chilli peppers, corn, potato and onion. Turkish tomatoes are spec-

Sweet green chillies, İstanbul street market

tacular through spring and summer – to the western consumer used to stoplight-red tomatoes that taste of disappointment, the Turkish toms are true misty eye material.

Potatoes, onions and garlic are grown whenever the ground is soft enough to dig them out and a surplus is stored for winter. Potatoes are made into chips and chopped into stews. Onions are added to everything and eaten raw in salads. Turkish garlic reeks gorgeously and is monstrous to boot. The biggest clove we came across (a single clove) was as big as a chestnut. Garlic is a compulsory addition to yoghurt sauce and is also minced into other dishes such as soup, köfte and pilav. Wild greens and mushrooms are an important food source for semi-nomadic Anatolian herders and village dwellers. **Madımak**, a cress-like sprout, is one of the ground plants used in stews and salads.

Summer vegetables are dried and pickled to see them through the winter. Eggplant, okra, capsicum and chilli pepper are dried on strings for winter – you'll even see them on apartment balconies. Before use, they're soaked in warm water for 15 minutes rendering them almost as plump and juicy as when fresh. **Turşu** (pickled vegetables) are made by standing raw vegetables in vinegar, salt and herbs and spices (most commonly garlic, dill and mint) for at least a month. You'll often see turşu sold by the side of the road and they're highly recommended travel munchies.

Rather than use tomatoes when they are not in season, most Turks use **salça** (tomato puree) through the winter. The two main salça varieties are **tatlı** (sweet, made without chillies) and **acı biber** (made with chillies). Some vendors also carry salça made purely from pounded chillies which adds a bit more of bite to dishes (see Salça in the Home Cooking & Traditions Chapter).

Winter vegetables include spinach, carrot, okra, celeriac and cauliflower. Almost invariably, these vegetables will be cooked in olive oil with a spoonful of salça. Pumpkin is not used much as a savoury vegetable; it's most popular as a dessert.

Yaprak Sarma (Stuffed Grape Leaves)

Ingredients

500g drained vine leaves	½ cup olive oil
200g rice	1 cup water
2 large onions, finely chopped	2 lemons
1 cup parsley, coarsely chopped	4 tablespoons pine nuts
1 cup dill, coarsely chopped	
4 tablespoons currants	
salt	
pepper	

If using fresh vine leaves, boil for two minutes, remove carefully and drain. If the leaves are preserved in brine, rinse them in hot water and drain. Heat the olive oil in a large pan. Gently fry the onions and the pine nuts until golden brown. Add the rice and fry another five minutes. Add the currants and water. Stir briefly then cover and simmer for 15 minutes or until the liquid is absorbed (the rice will be undercooked). Stir in chopped parsley and dill. Let cool.

Lay the leaf out, matte side up, stem pointing at you. Place a glob of stuffing near the base of the leaf and fold the stem over. Fold both sides of the leaf in towards the centre then roll it all up, cigar style. Lay your little nuggets stem side down so there's no chance they'll unravel and arrange them in a saucepan. Cover with water and weigh down with a **dolma taşı** (clayweight; see the Home Cooking & Traditions chapter) or a plate. Simmer for about 30 minutes until the rice is tender. Let cool. Decorate with lemon wedges to serve.

PATLICAN (EGGPLANT)

There's a cute story about a visitor to Turkey who was served a long succession of **patlıcan** (eggplant) dishes. Eventually he asked for a glass of water but felt it safest to call after the waiter 'please, make it without eggplant'. It's not too far from the mark. Eggplant is everywhere! It's sauteed, pureed, chopped, stuffed; it's meze, it's main, it's lurking in börek, peeping from kebab, it even sneaks into jam. In fact, about 200 recipes call for this favoured vegetable, so if you don't like it, you might want to learn which dishes *don't* have it, rather than straining your brain cataloguing those that do. The most famous eggplant dishes are **imam bayıldı** (literally, the priest fainted) and **karnıyarık** (literally, split belly).

İmam Bayıldı (The Priest Fainted)
Ingredients

6	long eggplants	3 onions, finely chopped
8	cloves garlic, finely chopped	juice of half a lemon
1	cup parsley, coarsely chopped	salt
1	teaspoon sugar	
3	tomatoes, diced	
250ml olive oil		

Peel the eggplants lengthways in strips so that they are striped. Make a deep cut in each eggplant, leaving 2cm untouched at either end and without cutting through to the skin on the other side. Soak them in a large bowl of salted water for 20 minutes.

Saute the onions in oil for 5 minutes. Remove the onion with a slotted spoon, leaving the residue oil in the pan. Mix onions with garlic, tomatoes, parsley, salt, sugar and lemon juice.

Drain the eggplants and fry lightly on either side then arrange them in a large pan, with the split facing up. Fill the eggplants with the onion mixture, pouring whatever is left over the top. Add 500ml water, cover eggplants with foil or wax paper and then cover the pan with a lid. Cook on medium heat for about 45 minutes or until the eggplants are tender.

Let cool in the pan. Transfer to a platter to serve.

Karnıyarık is the same except minced beef is fried up with the onions, sliced tomato is placed on top of the stuffed eggplant and the whole lot is baked for about 30 minutes in a moderate oven, rather than cooked on the stove top. This dish is served hot.

A posse of chain-smoking men in Antalya – who insisted that science was on their side – suggested that patlıcan leaches nicotine from the body, thus countering many of the harmful effects of smoking. No wonder those puff-crazy Turks came up with so many patlıcan recipes. Their next revelation was that watermelon has nicotine in it (just a very little) and was thus a good snack for someone trying to give up cigarettes.

Eggplant stuffed with rice

Meze (Hors d'oeuvre)

Meze is an event rather than a type of dish. It's an evening gathering of family and friends for drinking, chatting and leisurely grazing on nibbles and tidbits. The defining feature of meze is that people are there to partake: there's no prescription for what must appear on the table. A spread could be as simple as bread, white cheese and melon. It could be as bar-snacky as nuts and olives. A more substantial meze will often constitute the whole meal and last for hours. This is the one course that Turks don't mind lingering over: as long as there's still a smattering of food and something in the rakı bottle, the meze will continue.

Typical meze dishes include **zeytinyağlı** (cooked in olive oil) accompanied by **sarmısaklı yoğurt** (garlic yoghurt), **kısır** (bulgur salad), **pastırma** (pastrami), **lakerda** (sliced and salted tunny fish), **havuç salatası** (carrot salad) and **fava** (mashed broad bean salad). Meze dishes are usually served cold, and many can be prepared a day in advance.

Most Turks find meze unthinkable without **rakı** (anise alcohol). Indeed, much meze lore relates to what tastes best with a tipple and what guards the body against the ill effects of alcohol. Purists insist that fruit, especially melon, is the only authentic and healthy meze. Others put olives and white cheese on the essentials list. In summer, many invite **erik** (plum), often dipped in salt, to their meze table.

ORIGIN OF THE MEZE

Apparently, times were tough in ancient Persia, because a successful ruler had to employ personal food tasters if he wanted to stay alive past the midnight snack. When Sultan Süleyman the Magnificent's Ottoman forces conquered the Persian Safavids in 1538, the Sultan took the idea of tasters home with him. Thereafter, Süleyman's staff of **çesnici** (taste) slaves were given small plates of food samples, known by the Persian word, **meze**, meaning pleasant, enjoyable taste.

As news of the Sultan's safety practice reached public ears, it became the fashion of the rich and famous to exercise a variation of it. Before long, replicas of the revered meze plates of Süleyman's **çesnici-başi** (chief food taster) were seen at posh dinner parties throughout İstanbul. The meze craze caught on in upper-class haunts as **gedikli meyhaneler** (all night bars) and, not to be outdone, the working men's clubs also adopted the idea. And so it was that meze passed into Turkish culinary culture, dutifully accompanied by glasses of Turkish rakı.

Jim & Perihan Masters

Salata (Salad)

Just about anything that could be called a salad is primarily served as a meze. Some simple salads, though, are served as an accompaniment to a main meat dish and wouldn't normally get a look-in on the meze table. These salads will normally be combinations of crudités, offering no distraction to the main event, but adding a little bit of crispy cut and thrust.

On a menu, you'll often see **mevsim salatası** (seasonal salad), a good bet for getting whatever's freshest and best. The dressing is just olive oil and vinegar or lemon juice, often on the table for you to administer as you please. **Çoban salatası** (shepherd's salad), a summer stalwart, is made from chopped tomato, cucumber, onion and peppers.

Cacık is a salad of yoghurt, cucumber and dried mint and is served in individual bowls as a kind of 'side soup'. It's eaten with a spoon, either interspersed between mouthfuls of kebab or as a stomach settler after the last meaty bite. Also favoured as an adjunct to meat (especially tandır kebabı) is **piyaz**, a gooey salad made with white beans, egg, tomato, onion and parsley. Sometimes tahini is added, making it extra squelchy.

Rus salatası (Russian salad) has become a bit of a standard. It's best described as mayonnaise studded

Cucumber, tomato, sweet chilli salad

with unidentifiable cubes and spheres which taste as though they might once have been something. Shockingly, canned peas are routinely used even in top restaurants.

OLIVES

In Hittite times, the **zeytin** (olive) was sacred, used to anoint the dead and grease their path to the gods. Since the 18th century, it has been western Turkey's cooking oil of choice. One large class of meze, **zeytinyağlı**, simply means 'cooked in olive oil'. Today, olives are also eaten whole for breakfast and as a meze, yet whole olives are hardly used at all in cooking.

Aegean Turkey is infatuated with the olive, but as olive trees are stoic creatures, able to thrive in bad soil and with little water, their fruit is a popular cash crop throughout Turkey. Even in eastern Anatolia, where olives are not a favourite food and lard has prevailed as a cooking fat, the fields are dotted with these dusty-looking scraggly trees.

Market stalls will often display a dizzying variety of olives. Your primary choice is between green and black: green olives are firmer, having been picked before they are mature, while black olives are sun-ripened and more tender. Other considerations include how salty you want them: **tuzsuz** means 'no salt' and **aztuz** means 'little salt'. If you like tasty, fleshy olives with small seeds, look for **tirilye**.

Olives, south Aegean

Meyve (Fruit)

The variety and quality of fresh fruit in Turkey is enough to give any observer a vitamin surge. The markets dazzle with their bounty, restaurants offer choice morsels, home chefs offer overwhelming parades of fresh fruit and every second street stall seems to specialise in strawberries or oranges or plums.

As well as being an essential meze and a common snack, a platter of fresh fruit will grace the table at the end of most meals. Enthusiastic domestic trade means you can find Aegean tangerines, Mediterranean melons, Anatolian apples and Black Sea cherries all over the country. Rural dwellers also collect wild fruit such as **dut** (mulberry).

For the grape harvest, timing is everything. Farmers watch the late summer weather keenly, looking for the picking interstice which will allow the grapes to ripen for as long as possible on the vines without being caught in the autumn rains. Once the grapes are picked, they're spread out on a sunny sandbank to dry. If it rains, everyone rushes out to cover or collect the grapes. If the rain sets in, the grapes can be dried in attics but this increases the risk of mould.

Once the grapes have been dried, the women embark on the laborious sorting process. They sit in a circle, talking and working, from morning to night until the grapes are piled in their various baskets and sacks. Smaller grapes are used for pilav and for stuffings. Larger grapes are often preserved. In many villages it's the women who keep track of the grapes, selling some at market and keeping the money aside. Many villagers sell grapes to wineries or rakı producers, even if they're teetotallers themselves.

Just about everything you see will be bursting with just-picked exuberance. The obsession with freshness also means that when it's cherry, plum and watermelon season, the *only* fruit you'll see is cherries, plums and watermelons.

If you're not keen on the seasonal fruit, ask around for the **turfandacı**, who sells out-of-season fruits and vegetables. This is the man who'll have the first of the apples or the last of the cucumbers or the only oranges in town. His goods are more expensive and largely disparaged by Turkish shoppers who would rather eat fresh fruit in season.

Konserve Meyveler (Preserved Fruit)

Preserving fruit is a big deal – it's dried, bottled, jarred and jammed. Drying fruit might be as simple as bunging some figs on the roof and letting the sun do its work or it could be a bit more involved. Before apricots are dried, they are split, the stone cracked and the sweet almond-shaped kernel is removed and tucked back inside the fruit.

Drying fruit could also mean pounding it into submissive strips of **pestil** (fruit leather). You'll see sheets of pestil, most often made from grapes, figs or apricots, hanging up in delicatessen windows all over Turkey. When pestil is rolled up with nuts inside, it becomes the succulent, flavourful, energy-rich **kume**.

Reçel (jam) is eaten with the breakfast loaf and also when breaking the fast during Ramazan. Fruit at all different stages of ripeness, flowers and even vegetables are made into jam. Alanya is a noted jam-producing town and you can find some of the stranger flavours there (see Mediterranean Coast in the Regional Variations chapter). **Composto** (compote or fruit stew) makes a good dessert as it's syrupy without being too sweet. Apricots, plums and pears make nice composto but just about any fruit can be used.

Pekmez (Fruit Syrup)

Pekmez is boiled, thickened fruit pulp and it's a core food in Turkey. It is most commonly made from grapes but pomegranate, apples, quince and even rosehip can be enlisted to make this gorgeous glop. It's traditionally made by piling grapes in a stone trough and stamping on them with bare feet. The juice is drained, sieved through muslin and poured into a huge tin-lined copper pot. A pit is dug, a fire lit and the juice is boiled up. Thickener is added which in some villages means carefully chosen greyish soil. Once the mixture is viscous as high-grade oil, it's sealed into jars.

Though pekmez looks and acts a bit like molasses, it's much more versatile. It's eaten with bread as a sort of jammy dip, poured over composto, baklava or ice cream and is extremely popular with kids.

Until the arrival of sugar in the late 19th century, pekmez was an all purpose sweetener and many village desserts still use pekmez in preference to sugar or honey. **Öksüz helvası** (orphan helva) is made by making a dough of pekmez and flour then shaping it into a squat volcano on a serving tray. Melted butter is poured into the central crater, adding to the geology experiment flavour. But before anyone gets too scientific, the helva is broken off with hungry fingers from the perimeter and the morsels dipped into the butter for eating. The name, orphan helva, supposedly means that no one who eats this helva will be hungry like an orphan. There are many other unlikely sounding pekmez desserts, including **zile pekmezi** (pekmez whipped with egg white), a speciality of Tokat.

Another dish, made by cooking pestil, raisins or dried apricots in pekmez, is called **hoşaf**. Composto or hoşaf can be mixed with fresh fruit, making for pleasant textural contrast between juicy and crispy. Both are popular during Ramazan because they're gentle to the stomach.

Fruit preserves in an İstanbul restaurant

STAPLES

Pirinç (Rice)

Rice is used in soups, stuffings, puddings and in pilav. It's one of the few intrinsic Turkish foods which isn't grown abundantly here. Rice rises to its full potential in a good pilav, coaxed lovingly by an expert hand into a juicy cloud suspended flirtingly between firmness and flounce.

The reputation of a housewife and the career of a chef can stand or fall on their pilav. The essential quality is fluffiness: each grain of rice should stand alone, proud and independent, moist and glistening without being wet or oily. Producing a clumpy or gluggy pilav is a cause for great shame. The importance of the perfect pilav is nowhere better symbolised than by the Janissaries' custom of signalling their discontent by overturning the pilav cauldron and generally causing a scene. If they weren't happy with the pilav, well, they just weren't happy.

Most of the traditional pilav repertoire was handed down from the palace during Ottoman times, when rice was served as the last course before dessert. Today, there is an upstart suite of regional recipes just as delicious as the old stayers. Rice has the advantage of being a prestige food (stationed above the humble bulgur) but at the same time it can stretch a small quantity of expensive meat into a substantial platter.

As usual in the Turkish kitchen, making the best pilav isn't about following a recipe. It's about responding to the ingredients, experience and instinct. Older rice will absorb more water than perky, young rice; a rich mutton stock will act differently from a watery chicken one – you've just got to get in there and try it. Long-grain rice is preferred for the pilav; short-grain varieties are reserved for stuffings and soups.

Turkish celebrations would be unthinkable without rice dishes. **Zerde,** a sweet, gelatinous dessert made with rice, almonds, pistachio and pomegranate that has been coloured and flavoured with saffron, is at the top of the invitation list for every wedding and circumcision. The elegant **perdeli pilav** (veiled pilav), cooked with a pastry crust, is one of those dishes which guarantees a chorus of 'aahhh's from assembled diners. At the other end of the spectrum, every run-of-the-mill restaurant offers a pilav, sometimes modestly augmented with onions or currants, often served with a ladle of juice from another dish.

You will encounter rice in restaurants all over Turkey, but the fact that it's often an imported product means that rural people tend to make pilav with locally grown bulgur. Even the most isolated rural folk often use small quantities of rice in soup and other dishes and will endeavour to serve rice dishes on special occasions. But, broadly speaking, the further you travel from İstanbul, the less likely it is that rice will feature in typical family meals.

Sade Pilav (Plain Pilav)

Ingredients
2   cups long-grain rice
¼   cup **şehriye** (vermicelli)
4   tablespoons butter or ½ cup olive oil
    stock or water to cover

Heat butter or olive oil in a saucepan, throw in the şehriye and stir until it goes brown. Add the rice and mix until each grain is coated in oil. Cover the rice with water or stock, put a lid on the saucepan and cook till most of the liquid has been absorbed (little steam holes in the rice are a sign that you're there). Turn off the heat and wrap the whole saucepan in a cloth for 15 minutes. The steaming pilav which emerges should comprise robust, individual grains happy to separate from the pack.

Note: some authorities (ie grandmothers) say rice must be soaked in water (some say cold, some say hot) before cooking; others assert that giving it a good rinse is quite sufficient.

STAPLES

STAPLES

Bulgur (Cracked Wheat)

Bulgur may not have the palace-bequeathed prestige of rice, but it has the rural we-grow-it-we-eat-it seal of approval. Most villages harvest their own supplies in late summer and rely on it through the winter. To make bulgur, wheat is briefly boiled, drained and then dried on the roofs of houses. Once dry, it's gathered up and taken to the nearest mill for crushing; in many villages this means a donkey-drawn, stone-grinding operation.

Bulgur is a versatile food, eaten with salça or mixed with meat, lentils or other pulses to make a substantial protein-rich pilav. It can also be used for stuffing vine leaves, peppers and other vegetables. Anatolian villagers even make a bulgur sweet by mushing it up with **zeldeli** (wild apricots) and the ubiquitous pekmez.

Bulgur is most entrenched in rural areas and cityfolk prefer it as a meze rather than a main dish. **Kısır** (bulgur salad) can be pressed into little köfte which cry out to be eaten with rakı. Kısır varies from region to region in the coarseness of the bulgur, the ingredients and the shapes.

Yarma is another version of crushed wheat. The wheat is not cooked before it is milled and the grains are not ground as finely as for bulgur. It is most popular in central Anatolia where it's used in soups in place of rice.

Bulgur, İstanbul street market

Baklagiller (Pulses)

Pulses are the heartland of Turkish cooking, part of the essential daily intake of most Turks. They've always been loved as a filling food, easy to grow in unpromising climates and simple to store. These days they're also lauded by the nutritionally aware for being protein and energy rich and relatively inexpensive. Haricot, borlotto, broad beans, lentils and chickpeas are the most common pulses; lentils tend to be more popular in the Mediterranean, while beans dominate in Marmara and along the Black Sea. Chickpeas can be found throughout Turkey though the plantations around Samsun are said to produce the country's finest.

Winter is the party season for the pulses, when they find their way into just about every meal, usually as the substance of a hearty soup. In summer, keep your finger on the pulse with meze: **fava** (mashed broad bean salad) is extremely popular. **Fasuliye turşusu** (pickled beans) is a favourite with rakı all along the Black Sea. The usual chaperone for a pulse meze is garlic yoghurt, especially in central Anatolia and along the Aegean.

Pulses are sometimes regarded as 'poor man's meat'. In the dish **yuvar-lama**, a southeastern Anatolian soup consisting of dumplings made from chickpeas, flour and mince, only a very small quantity of meat is used to enhance the dish's meat dumpling-ness.

STAPLES

Legumes & pulses, İstanbul street market

Makarna (Pasta)

We confess to a sinking feeling the first time we were served pasta in Turkey. It was the same tummy plummet which attended our discovery of pizza in Moscow and banana pancakes in Shanghai. But food purism is rarely less than silly, and in this case it was simply ignorant: the Turks have been noodling since they were long-haired nomads in Central Asia. Just to confuse things, **pasta** here means pastry. **Makarna** is the generic word for what English (and Italian) speakers know as 'pasta'. The most common forms you'll strike are curly macaroni, **şehriye** (vermicelli) and **mantı** (little pasta packages). A simple yet popular dinner dish is makarna topped with **çökelek** (cheese made of skim milk or yoghurt curds). Other common toppings such as **salça** (tomato puree) and ground beef are reminiscent of Italian bistro fare. **Fesleğen makarna** is a basil-based pasta with onion, garlic, tomato, fresh green chilli and (just so you know you're in Turkey) eggplant. Şehriye can also be added to soup and pilav.

Mantı have their origins in Central Asia, a heritage shared with other noble pasta packages such as the Uzbeki dumpling and the Chinese won ton. In Turkey today they're often filled with ground beef, onions, hot pepper, cumin, mint and parsley. A plate of mantı is most often doused with a garlic yoghurt sauce, though you will sometimes find them languishing under a buttery tomato topping. Kayseri, in central Anatolia, is famous for its dolls' house mantı, so small that 30 will nestle comfortably in one spoon. **Sosyete** (society) mantı is a modern version of this old favourite in which a long pasta tube is filled, coiled up, stood on its end and baked. It looks fancy shmancy but is easy enough to construct, even if you're *sans* engineering degree.

Women tending sugar beet near Kayseri, Central Anatolia

Çorba (Soup)

Soup is for breakfast, soup is for lunch, soup is for dinner. Soup starts the meal and soup is a meal in itself. Soup is carefully planned and soup is a slapdash sopping up of leftovers. Soup sets you up for a day in the fields and brings you down after a night on the town. Soup is for life, Turkey's silent call to prayer and all its prayers answered.

The classic Turkish soup is based on a meat stock, though water can be substituted. Head, trotters, innards and bones are common stock fodder. There are then three basic ways of proceeding: thickening the soup with flour, **terbiye** (a mixture of egg yolk and lemon juice) or yoghurt; adding some sort of grain, pasta, dumpling or meat to the soup; or adding a vegetable or pulse and pureeing it. Soups are generally served lukewarm, though in eastern Turkey it's not unusual to have your soup arrive stone cold. Squeezing lemon, dashing vinegar or sprinkling hot pepper into your soup is par for the course. Soup without bread is unthinkable – it's the happiest marriage in the land.

Tarhana is a soup base made from curds and flour (or yarma), often with the addition of tomato and parsley or other herbs. The dough is made in large batches, dried in the sun, then crumbled and stored. To make **tarhana çorbası** (tarhana soup), tarhana is soaked in water for a couple of hours, then stirred into a broth. As well as providing body and bounce, tarhana gives a sharp, nutty taste to the soup.

Vegetable soup usually means no nonsense tomato or potato soup, made from grated vegetables, stock and a handful of rice or pasta. Thick pumpkin soup is a Marmara staple while cabbage soup is found along the Black Sea. Winter versions use dried vegetables (especially okra), beans and lentils.

Ezo gelin çorbası (bride soup) is named for Ezo, a new bride whose mother-in-law demanded soup. A flustered Ezo concocted a soup from what she had at hand: red lentils, bulgur, rice, tomato paste, hot pepper and mint. Luckily, the chaotic combination made a yummy, hearty soup.

Dumpling soups make much of little: **oğmaç çorbası**, native to the eastern Black Sea region, is a milk soup, bobbing with flour and water dumplings. In the Aegean, it's tarted up with yoghurt, parsley and tomato.

Tirit is a variation on soup. It's bread soaked in broth, topped with whatever's in the cupboard: onions, yoghurt, cheese, meat (minced or skewered) or vegetables. As well as being an economical pantry clearer, tirit is perfect for lazybones who don't fancy the aerobics of dipping bread into soup themselves.

İşkembe çorbası (tripe soup) is, perhaps, Turkey's most famous soup and a national hangover cure (see the boxed text İşkembe Çorbası in the Where to Eat & Drink chapter).

Süt Ürünler (Dairy)

Cows, sheep, goats and the occasional buffalo are all conscripted into Turkey's dairy army. It's hard to imagine a meal, let alone a day, that doesn't include some sort of dairy item. Most milk is dedicated to the higher callings of cream, yoghurt or cheese, which can make it difficult to get fresh drinking milk. The milk available commercially is usually in long-life cartons.

Yoğurt (Yoghurt)

When a country writes love songs to yoghurt, you know you're looking at a nation of dairy queens. One eastern Mediterranean town produces yoghurt so alluring, that its praises have been immortalised in a folk song which roughly translates as 'Oh, Silifke yoghurt, who gave birth to you? The mother who gave birth to you will be my mother-in-law'.

Yoghurt is made from sheep, goat or cow's milk and is drunk as **ayran** (yoghurt drink), spooned up as **cacık** (yoghurt salad), dolloped in soup, sauces and desserts or simply eaten as a snack. Kanlıca, a Bosphorus suburb on İstanbul's Asian side, is famous for its yoghurt, delicious with a sprinkling of **podra** (icing sugar).

At the markets, you'll encounter two main sorts of yoghurt: **sıvı tas** (the runny first pressing) is used to make ayran and cacık; and **süzme** (a thicker yoghurt that has been sieved to extract moisture) is used in cooking and to make herby spreads.

Peynir (Cheese)

If it's got an udder, Turks have milked it and made cheese. Early nomadic herders discovered cheese was the most practical dairy food, being transportable, storable and nourishing. It could even be matured on the go, drained in skins hung from saddlebags on the march and slung over branches at the nightly camps. Cheese's fitness for travel also made it a good candidate for domestic trade, enabling generations of İstanbullers to develop addictions to the far-flung curd of eastern Anatolia.

Shopping for cheese in the markets is overwhelming – the bigger stalls are veritable expos, displaying all shades of white, yellow, round, square, stringy, plaited and smoked. When you're looking for the cheese to please, you need to consider its age, saltiness, shape and origin. Home pastures make a big difference to the taste: the opiated output of Afyon's cows is quite different from the wot-you-lookin-at ruggedness of Erzurum's goats. The flagship Turkish cheese is **beyaz peynir** (white cheese), usually made from sheep's or goat's milk and, during production, left in brine for at least six months. This cheese is served at the slightest provocation for breakfast, lunch, sit-down snacks and meze and is the standard offering at hotels and restaurants. If you find this or any other cheese too salty, you can de-salt it by soaking it in tepid water for half an hour, changing the water every five minutes or so.

Diyarbakır örgü is a mild white cheese livened up aesthetically by being woven into a plait. **Erzurum gegil**, also quite mild, is stringy and shreddable. **Dil** is soft, moist and pull-apart, a little like mozzarella, while **füme** (smoked) cheese is drier and more pungent. **Van otlu** is famous throughout Turkey: it's sharp, juicy and intermingled with grassy herb stalks. **Lor** is a fresh cheese which resembles ricotta and is made from the water residue of other cheeses. It's a common **börek** (pastry dish) filling. Also good in pastries is **kaşar**, a firm yellow cheese

Tulum cheese, Afyon

which turns gloriously gooey when it melts. The weirdest sight is **tulum**, a sharp, crumbly cheese cured in skin and often displayed still wrapped in hairy leather. The impression is that a goat was sliced open and, by some divine blessing, was found to be filled with cheese. Erzincan is known for the quality of its tulum.

If your arteries aren't coming to the party, look for **az tuzlu** (low salt) or **tuzsuz** (no salt) cheeses. Urfa is famous for the quality of its tuzsuz cheese. **Tatlı sepet** (sweet basket) cheese is salt free too. Unsalted cheese is popular with villagers who salt it to their own taste, crumble it and pack it into clay pots which are buried in the garden while the cheese matures.

Kaymak (Clotted Cream)
Kaymak is cream so thick it can be sliced, rolled and no doubt used as a doorstop. It's served with desserts as a topping to top them all; it also comprises the filling in some kinds of baklava. Afyon is famous for its extraordinarily rich kaymak, attributed by some to the opium poppy straw with which the local farmers supplement their groovy cows' grassy diet. Kaymak is also produced from buffalo milk.

Hamur Işleri (Pastries)

Turks must be genetically bound to love pastries by now – they've been eating them since the nomads of Central Asia called a prototype **börek** (pastry dish) 'buğra', after Buğra Khan of Turkestan. Böreks are distinguished by their filling, cooking method and shape: they are square and cheesy, cigar-shaped and meaty, plain and moist, pointy and potato chunky. Most people buy börek by the slice from their local **pastane** (pastry shop) and eat in with an **ayran** (yoghurt drink) for a quick breakfast, or grab a box to augment the perfect picnic platter.

Kol böreği is long and shaped like an arm, filled with cheese, potatoes or meat. For the juicy **su böreği** (water börek) **yufka** (filo pastry) is boiled first, making it very soft. Then the yufka and the filling are layered into a

Peynirli Börek (Cheese Börek)

Ingredients

400g	beyaz peynir (or use a mixture of cream cheese and fetta)
15	sheets of filo pastry
1	cup parsley or dill, coarsely chopped
3	eggs
½	cup milk
300g	butter
	salt

Mash cheese, eggs, salt, half the butter, half the milk and the parsley together. Mix well. Melt the remaining butter and mix it with remaining milk. Lay a sheet of pastry into a greased 30 sq cm baking tray and brush it with the butter and milk mix. Lay down four more sheets of pastry in the same fashion, brushing each as you go. Spread half of the filling over the fifth sheet of pastry. Lay down another five sheets of pastry in the same way then spread the rest of the filling on top. Lay down the last five sheets of pastry, slather butter over the top and cut the börek into 16 squares. Bake in a moderate oven for 30 minutes or until golden brown and crispy on top.

Börek & gözleme seller, Olympus, west Mediterranean coast

round metal tray which revolves over a flame. As the börek cooks, it's flipped until golden brown. Su böreği are a cross between a pastry and a lasagna – the good ones are succulent, not too oily and full of punch-packing flavour. Homemade börek is no two-minute noodle affair. If someone bakes you a börek, it's a labour-intensive act of love.

During Ramazan little gifts, trinkets and coins are hidden in children's evening fast-breaking böreks, though the kids probably need no incentive to eat after fasting all day.

Gözleme (filled filo pastry) is common all over Turkey, though different regions tend to make it in different shapes and with different fillings. The classic is stuffed with spring onions, parsley and cheese. **Çökelek** (similar to cottage cheese, though drier) or any other white crumbly cheese will do fine. Mincemeat, spinach or mashed potato are also possible fillers. A mix of yoghurt, milk and oil is brushed on the yufka to seal it, and also to give it a bit of sizzle when it's dry fried on a wok. In markets women in traditional dress sell gözleme, making the dough, then doing the filling, folding and grilling on the spot.

Poğaça is the name given to a variety of buns, substantial or small, sweet or savoury, plain or stuffed. **Pişmiş** and **çörek** are also buns, often combined with nuts. All three are often eaten for an afternoon snack with tea.

Making gözleme, with mantı in foreground, Taksim, İstanbul

Baharat (Herbs & Spices)

Turkish cooking stands and falls on its core ingredients so herbs and spices are used to augment, highlight and complement dishes, never to mask or dominate. This isn't to say that they're of little importance – on the contrary, most dishes have a couple of herbs or spices which are integral to their identity. It's just that if you come across a dish in which the main flavour is that of its seasoning, it's probably the result of an overenthusiastic flick of the wrist rather than a recipe.

The top rung seasonings are mint, parsley, garlic and pepper – a savoury dish is scarcely imaginable without one or more of these additions. Salt is a national passion, and when it's not mentioned, it should be assumed. Other kitchen favourites include basil, dill, sumac, tarragon, allspice, cumin, thyme and cloves. Some foods are seen as natural partners to a particular herb: dill is always mashed with broad beans and thyme partners grilled lamb. Saffron and cinnamon are the most common spices used to spark up sweet dishes. Generally, fresh herbs are preferred but there are exceptions. Dried mint is used in **cacık** (yoghurt salad) and soups, even if the herb patch is sodden with the fresh stuff.

It's fair to say that Marmaran cooks use a wider range of herbs and spices and employ them with greater subtlety than those further from the influence of İstanbul's palace cuisine. The Mediterranean soil seems to throw up basil, oregano, thyme and sage as fast as it can be picked, giving many salads and seafood dishes in the area a distinctly Italian tinge. The further east you travel, the more spicy the food tends to be, though some eastern towns (such as Urfa) are more noted for their plain food.

Special mention should be made of **biber** (chilli pepper) as it brings tears to the eyes in more ways than one. Not only can they be squinchingly spicy, inducing eye droplets of exquisite anguish, but they're also a much-missed taste of home for many a roaming Turk. Red, green, black, fresh or dried – the chillies Turks grow up with are the chillies they cry for. Victims of homesickness yearn for the full-bodied chillies grown in Maraş or slobber at the thought of the nasty-but-nice Erzurum variety and end up calling mum to have her send supplies on the next express bus.

Turkish cooks often leave the exact degree of spiciness to the diner. If you're eating kebabs or köfte, you'll probably find red **pul biber** (chilli flakes), **kara biber** (black pepper) and **sumak** (sumac) on the table. Chilli flakes are made by frying dried red peppers in oil – the longer they're fried, the hotter they get. Sumac powder, made from dried red berries, has a lip-shrinking lemony flavour and is a popular accompaniment to grilled meat dishes. Black pepper is often ground fresh for each meal and put on the table in a little dish to be pinched or spooned onto each plate as desired.

Herb shop, Spice Bazaar, İstanbul

Herbs and spices are also popular for their health properties. Though ginger is not a traditional Turkish seasoning, it's been adopted not only to add a little zing but also because it's thought to stimulate the digestive system. Coriander is used in meat dishes in eastern Anatolia where it's thought to help with gastric complaints. Another application for coriander is to cover the seeds in sugar to make **kişniş şekeri**.

Tatlı (Dessert)

Sweet eats are more than a delicious assault on the tastebuds; they are equated with a kind heart and a sugary tongue. Any special occasion *must* include sweets; even a funeral may be 'sweetened' with sugary confections. Guests will routinely bring a box of goodies for their hosts (accounting for the slew of confectionery stalls at any roadhouse or bus station).

Turks tend to round off an ordinary meal with fruit, either fresh or preserved. Sugar hits are saved for social afternoon teas and celebrations. But sometimes, for no particular reason, it will be decided to follow up a normal meal with tatlı, and when this does happen, everyone finishes up sugar coated and dripping in syrup. Don't expect to get away with picking daintily at one square of baklava. Restaurants sometimes have a small selection of sweets, perhaps just **sütlaç** (rice pudding) and **telkadayıfı** (shredded pastry squares), but many are content to leave desserts to the specialist **pastane**, **baklavacı** or **muhallebici** (see Tatlıcı in the Where to Eat & Drink chapter and Pastane & Baklavacı in the Shopping chapter). Home cooks will often whip up some sort of helva or pudding, but they too are likely to head to the pastry shop for complicated desserts such as baklava.

During Ottoman times, **cevirme** (a fondant flavoured with vanilla, bergamot, mastic and cream) was the most popular confection, and was served in a ceremonial show of respect. The cevirme was served and each guest was given a glass of water with a spoon balanced on top. Diners took a spoonful of cevirme, then would be compelled to glug down a whole glass of water because the fondant was so rich. Coffee followed to wake everyone up and the cycle began again. Today cevirme is very rare.

SWEET SONG

As you're moving onto dessert, ask a Turkish 'sweet tooth' to sing this folk song for you:

Haydi güzelim tatlı yiyelim
Tatlı Tatlı yiyelim
Tatlı anlaşalım, şeker ezelim, Hadi güzelim
Tatlı Tatlı Tatlı

Let's go eat sweets, my lovely
Let's eat sweets, eat sweets, Let's understand each other well
Let's go, my lovely
Sweets, sweets, sweets

Lokum (Turkish Delight)

Until the arrival of refined sugar in the late 18th century, lokum meant an amalgam of honey or pekmez and wheat flour. In fact, it was more deserving of the name Turkish Glop than anything more alluring. But when confectioner Hacı Bekir got his hands on white sugar and cornflour, he began to have delightful dreams of a new lokum. His smooth, translucent, jellied dreams turned into what we know today as Turkish Delight.

Such was Hacı's fame and acclaim that he was soon appointed chief confectioner at Topkapı Palace. The sweet came to international fame after a delighted British traveller took a sample back to Blighty, wowing his mates.

The quaint shop Hacı Bekir opened in 1777 has been restored and is still doing a roaring trade in

Hacı Bekir, Turkish Delight Shop, İstanbul

sugary lovelies, now overseen by the fifth generation of the family. The original shop is at Hamidiye Caddesi (near Şeyhülislam Hayri Efendi Caddesi), Bahcekapi, İstanbul. There's another branch at İstliklal Caddesi 127, Beyoğlu.

Sade lokum (plain Turkish delight) is just the beginning. You'll see it mixed with all sorts of different nuts, dried fruits, **kaymak** (clotted cream) and coconut. **Sakız** (mastic) can be added to make a chewier delight; this addition also makes it easier to make lokum rolls. Some towns are known for their particular lokum invention: Safranbolu, a town north of Ankara, is known for its colourful roll ups, often coated with desiccated coconut.

Akide (hard candy) was discovered after glucose-crazed experiments with boiling, kneading and flavouring of refined sugar. It was Hacı Bekir who managed to work the flavoured sugar water into long malleable ropes which could then be cut into individual lozenges, avoiding the painstaking need to individually pour each candy. Akide flavours include just about every fruit, herbs such as mint, spices such as cinnamon, as well as rosewater, nuts and seeds.

Turkish delights, Spice bazaar, İstanbul

STAPLES

Lokum (Turkish Delight)

Ingredients:
500g sugar
600ml water
1   teaspoon lemon juice
2   tablespoons rose-water
60g   cornflour
      icing sugar

Lay a piece of muslin in a tin (about 20 sq cm) and dust it with cornflour.
Boil the sugar, water and lemon juice in a saucepan, stirring constantly.
Stir the rose-water in with the flour in a separate bowl then slowly pour
the flour into the saucepan, stirring all the while over medium heat.
When the mixture thickens to jelly, pour it into the tin and let it cool.
Once cool, turn it onto a bench dusted with icing sugar. Cut into squares
and cover generously with more icing sugar.

If you want to work those jaws, add ground mastic towards the end
of the cooking process. If you want to add nuts or fruit, mix them in once
you've removed the lokum from the stove.

Lokma

Lokma are soft, deep-fried, syrup-drenched yeast fritter delights often wrought into sensual and seductively named shapes. **Dilber dudağı** (beauty's lips) and **kadın göbeği** (ladies' navels) – Turkish soft porn or downright saucy desserts? Standard lokma comes in ping-pong ball piles while **tulumba**, a piped lokma in a hook or ring shape, is the no-nonsense street version.

Helva

Helva is the collective name for a family of simple-sounding desserts. Any cooked combination of a grain or nut (like flour or semolina) combined with something sweet (like honey or pekmez) can be called helva. Just to prove that just about anything can be called helva, a popular 19th century dessert served in wealthy İstanbul homes was **kar helvası**, snow mixed with sugar. These days, shop-bought helva is made with **tahin** (sesame puree), mixed with honey and often plugged with whole pistachios. Homemade helva could still be anything though. It changes between villages and from one occasion to the next. Whatever the ingredients are, they're always simple, but the skill involved in making helva which doesn't hit the stomach like a boulder shouldn't be underestimated.

Pistachio helva, Afyon

Hoşmerim is a classic Anatolian helva, made with milk, flour, butter, sugar, walnuts and pistachios. The story of the name is so good that it doesn't matter that it's probably not true. A man returns home after a long absence and asks his wife to make him a meal which encapsulates their village: the smell, the taste and mood. She makes a sweet fried pudding of flour, nuts and cream and tops it with **pekmez** (a thick syrup commonly made from boiled grape juice). While her husband eats the pudding, the wife nervously sits before him asking '**Hoş mu erim? Hoş mu erim?**' (Is it good, my brave man?), which eventually became shortened to 'hoşmerim'. By the way, he loved it.

Helva is an essential guest at any feast, celebration or funeral. It's also traditional to seal peace between two quarrelling friends with the sharing of helva.

LOLLY LOYALTY

Akide (hard candy), which also means 'faith', was used as a symbol of loyalty at feasts held for the sultan's Janissary soldiers. As the empire faltered, the Janissaries slumped from merely decadent to downright brattish. They held palace officials on tenterhooks until the end of the ceremonial meal when they either presented akide, thus expressing satisfaction with their conditions, or withheld it, causing a flurry of dismay, alarm and panicked reparation.

Baklava

The prince of pastries, the swooniest sweet thang – our own ode to baklava would be passionate and unreserved. It doesn't feel right to pull the stuff apart unless it's with tooth and tongue, but let's dive in, strictly in the interests of science. Baklava is layers of **yufka** (filo pastry), folded over, rolled around or otherwise fondling a filling of nuts, **şöbiyet** (a butter and sugar cousin of sherbet) or kaymak. The whole lot is drowned in syrup. Baklava is most often eaten as a snack with coffee during the day, but Turks also save a corner of the tummy for after dinner visits to the baklavacı.

It's not easy to make good baklava: it ranks with pilav as a test of a chef's skill. For a start, the yufka has to be thinner than a soprano's skin while still being resilient enough to withstand being twisted and rolled and laden with nuts and syrup. The nuts must be fresh and succulent – we're after melt-in-the-mouth, not rearrange-the-dentures. And, to balance crunch with collapse, the syrup must be poured on at the exact right moment only perceptible to the practised performer. The result is a messy heaven which is sweet without being cloying, and resistant without wanting a fight.

Classic baklava should be made with 40 layers of yufka, though baklava geniuses have been known to cram 100 layers of membrane-thin pastry into a baking dish. The secret to making dough which can handle such exertions is to start with hard-grain durum wheat flour, but if you ever have the privilege to watch yufka making in progress, you'll soon see that the ingredients are but the beginning of the beginning. The rolling, the flouring and the rhythm is what really makes yufka. The maestro will roll out a dozen layers at once, rolling them right round the pin with enough flour between each sheet to stop them sticking but not so much that they dry out. They're peeled, shuffled and rolled again … and again … and again.

Baklava comes in many shapes and sizes and goes by many names, some almost as delightful as the confection itself. **Bülbül yuvası** is a very syrupy, rather abstract 'bird's nest'. **Havuç** (literally, carrot) is a large

Buying a slice of baklava

round tray sliced into cartoon 'carrot' shaped slices. Screamingly good **sarma baklava** is yufka rolled up with crushed pistachios, scrunched together, then arranged in circles or in rows for baking. Different towns lay claim to different incarnations: Antalya's **kuş gözu** (literally, bird's eye) and the **gelin bohça** (literally, bridal clothes packet) of Kahramanmaraş are but two of the myriad regional specials. If it's all a bit overwhelming, you can have your baklava **sade** (plain) – a neat square without any nuts.

Kadayıf with kaymak (clotted cream)

There are a few desserts which modify more than size, shape and moniker but are still welcomed into the baklava pantheon. The most common is **telkadayıfı**, tangled pastry shreds welded together with nuts and syrup, and the closest most **lokantas** (basic restaurants) get to baklava. **Kadayıf** is made by pouring dough through a pierced ladle onto a hot metal plate – it comes out slightly crunchy and very messy. **Ekmekkadayıfı** is a further refinement, consisting of a bread rusk topped with pastry squiggles and drenched in kaymak and syrup. **Ezme** forgoes the pastry: it's just a little green pellet of finely ground pistachios and sugar, an energy pill if ever there was one (at least, that's how you can justify it). Antep, in southeastern Anatolia, is famous for baklava made with its equally famous **fıstık** (pistachios; see Eastern & Southeastern Anatolia in the Regional Variations chapter).

SPOOKY DESSERTS

As well as making desserts with just about everything conceivable, Turks make some inconceivable sweets. The weirdest is **tavuk göğsü** (chicken breast pudding; see the recipe in the Turkish Banquet chapter). Hard to find and harder to stomach is the Black Sea's **hamsi tatlısı**, a milk pudding with the unlikely addition of anchovy. Back in the vegetable kingdom, there's **kabak tatlısı** (dessert made with pumpkin, sweet syrup and crushed walnuts) and the Anatolian **mantar tatlısı** (mushrooms combined with sugar, grated apple, orange, lemon, figs and carnation petals).

Muhallebi (Pudding)

A typical lokanta dessert is **sütlaç** (rice pudding) baked to have a brown skin. A slightly fancier pudding is the gummy milk-based **sakızkı muhallebi**, usually found quivering under some sort of fruit syrup topping. **Gül suyu** (rose-water), a delicate distillation of rose petals, is used to flavour puddings.

Dondurma vendor, Turkish ice cream, Taksim, İstanbul

STAPLES

Dondurma (Ice Cream)

Traditional Turkish dondurma is made from goats' milk, sugar and **salep**, an allegedly aphrodisiac powder made from pounded tapioca roots (see Salep in the Drinks chapter). Dondurma is beaten into submission with a metal rod by a specialist who produces a confection so thick and substantial that it's served in fist-sized blocks which can be eaten with a knife and fork. It's powerful stuff and long, hard (but entirely rewarding) work to eat, requiring plenty of wrist action and a dollop of elbow grease. The salep makes the ice cream melt slowly so it doesn't so much liquefy as sneak down your throat in a 'who, me?' show of understated seduction. Of all the ice-cream loving towns in Turkey, Kahramanmaraş is the best known (see Eastern Anatolia in the Regional Variations chapter).

Other qualities of dondurma are rather bizarre. It's so strong that great chunks of it can be hung from a hook. It can also be twisted and tugged into ropes resilient enough to be used for skipping and even to lift a car from the ground. So if you're ever stuck on the highway without a towrope, you'll be glad to have some dondurma in the ice box.

Turks tend to stick to the natural flavour but there are lots of others to choose from. Some common flavours include **limonlu** (lemon), **fındıklı** (hazelnut), **kaymak** (clotted cream), **vişneli** (cherry), **muzlu** (banana), **karamelalı** (caramel), **bademli** (almond), **çilekli** (strawberry), **karadutlu** (mulberry), **portakallı** (orange), **cevizli** (walnut), **hindistan cevizli** (coconut), **çikolatlı** (chocolate), **böğürtenli** (blackberry) and **frambuazlı** (raspberry).

Fresh honey in the comb, Koycegiz, west Mediterranean

Bal (Honey)

Bal is a common guest at the breakfast or lunch table. In hotels and restaurants it will usually appear in disappointing plastic sachets but at people's homes honey might be served still in the honeycomb. In this case, you can scrape some honey out to spread on bread or pick up a segment with your fork or spoon and suck the honey from it. Honey is also used in helva and occasionally as a sweetener for tea.

Çam (pine) or çiçek (flower) honey are the most common. Çam balı is dark brown, intensely flavoured and mostly comes from around Marmaris. Siyah çam balı (black pine honey) is even richer, thicker and darker. Eastern Turkey is well known for its çiçek balı, especially around Malatya, Kars, Erzincan and Siirt.

If you see seçme çiçek in the market, it means 'chosen flowers', that is, the bees are sent to particular blossoms known for their deliciousness. Portakal (orange) honey is light, sweet and runny while akasya (acacia) is glowing and ruddy. Kara kovanbal means that the honeycomb was made by the bees themselves, not prefabricated for them by landlord humans. Expect to pay about three times more for this premium gear.

Arısütü (literally, bee's milk – royal jelly) and arıpoleni (bee's pollen) are much-prized for their many health properties. They're available wherever honey is sold.

drinks

The culinary landscape of Turkey is dotted with tulip-shaped glasses of tannin tea. Drinking here is a truly social activity, a way of meeting people or having an excuse to sit down and watch the world pass by. As well as omnipresent tea, there's the famed aromatic coffee or, for a different buzz, the Turks make tasty beer and reasonable wine. And then there's the flagship firewater, rakı.

Alcoholic Drinks

Though most Turks consider themselves Muslims (and therefore banned from intoxicating liquor), many have a special understanding with God which entitles them to a drink every now and then. Consequently there's no need to scurry back to your hotel room with a bottle of grog. Other than in devout households, most adult social evenings will include alcohol. Family occasions will often pass without any alcohol but it's by no means scandalous for parents to drink in front of their kids.

Men are more likely to drink than women. In fact, women, even younger women, often don't drink at all. Frequently, men talk about drinking in a 'hush, don't tell my wife' kind of way and then go out on a bender with their mates. In the east, but also in conservative cities such as Konya, booze is largely a housebound affair.

Driving under the influence is a big problem – it's mostly middle-aged men who are the culprits. Getting smashed isn't trendy among young people; students can easily spend a night out on soft drinks or just one or two quiet beers. The legal drinking age is 18 but it's very rare for an alcohol vendor to question the age of someone wanting to do business.

Rakı (Anise Alcohol)

Turkey's national drink is a clear, strong spirit made of grapes infused with aniseed. An evening with rakı is much more than liquid refreshment: it's an insight into a whole lifestyle. Most of Turkey's rakı comes from grapes distilled in government distilleries. Yeni brand is the table plonk you'll see everywhere. Kulüp, from Marmara, is a bit stronger while the Cappadocian Altınbaş is the strongest and most aniseedy.

When the sun goes down, the rakı comes out, usually with meze hot on its aniseedy heels. So intertwined are meze and rakı that the meze spread is often called the 'rakı table'. People go wild over combinations of food and rakı: seafood and rakı, çiğ köfte and rakı, kısır and rakı, white cheese and melon and rakı, işkembe çorbası following rakı. Sometimes it can seem that food is only an excuse for rakı. The founder of modern Turkey, Mustafa Kemal Atatürk, served his guests **leblebi** (roasted chickpeas) with rakı. If you do the same, a Turk is likely to remark upon (and approve of) your statesman-like behaviour.

Rakı is potent gear. The average person will feel a little merry after just one glass. Given that rakı sessions can extend for hours, it's not hard to understand how evenings can turn a bit rowdy. Sedate co-workers may end up singing with their arms around each other, conversation routinely moves from chatter to gossip to scandal, the slightest wisp of music will inspire full-scale dancing and there's a not uncommon segue into tears and fighting.

If you're out drinking with Turks, be prepared for constant pressure to drink up and drink on. Hospitality demands this encouragement but no one is going to mind if you sip modestly and refuse their liquid advances. If you are aiming to keep up with your companions, make sure you stand up every now and again, just to make sure you still can.

Many people enjoy drinking their rakı neat. They will top a couple of fingers of liquor with cold water, turning it into chalky white **aslan sütü** (lion's milk), so called because it makes the drinker feel like roaring. If you want to add ice to your rakı, put it in after adding the water – dropping ice straight into rakı will kill the flavour. A glass of plain water will accompany the rakı glass in front of you. Rakı has a high alcohol content and it can really knock you out. Sip slowly, swig liberally on your glass of water and keep nibbling.

Bira (Beer)

Though it's nowhere near as loved as rakı, beer has a firm foothold in the Turkish grog parade. It's often drunk in the afternoon, when people don't want to get too gaga. In tourist areas you'll get a choice of Turkish and imported brews but most shops and restaurants only sell one brand. Bars are the only place you'll find beer on tap.

They don't do a bad beer here. The most widely available is Efes, a perky pilsener, which comes in bottles, cans and on tap. Efes also brew light (low alcohol), dark and extra strong beers. The Efes company (named after the classical Roman city) has done well from its tasty beers, expanding to four breweries within Turkey as well as one in Romania. The two other local beers you'll see are Troy pilsener, which has a lighter taste and more bubbles, and Tuborg, a Danish beer made in Turkey under licence. Tuborg is available **beyaz** (pale, pilsener style) or **siyah** (dark, throaty style).

DRINKS

CHEERS, ME DEARS

When drinking, the standard toast is **şerefe** (to your honour) but you can also say **sağlığınıza** (to your health). In the annals of drinking etiquette clinking your glass lower than your companion's shows them respect; conversely, high-clinking is a wee bit arrogant. Touching your glass to the table after clinking and before drinking shows even more respect. This kind of rigmarole isn't a big deal in modern Turkey, but you might want to casually aim for a low clink.

RAKI: THE LION'S MILK OF TURKEY

What is Rakı?

It's said that you never forget where, when, and with whom you sipped your first glass of rakı – Turkey's alcoholic beverage of tradition and choice. Its anise aroma and flavour are reminiscent of French cafes along the Champs Élysées where Pernod, Ricard and Pastis still flow – but rakı history is a good deal older. The Turkish name for it derives from the Arabic 'arak' which means 'sweat' or 'sweating'. But according to knowledgeable sources, it first came from East India where they'd produce it by distilling sugarcane sap mixed with rice yeast. The same sources say that dried grapes and dates were used to produce it in Iran. In Turkey it was originally made from barley and corn. There, the name evolved over time from 'arak' to aroka, ariki, araki, arakı, and ırakı – until it was finally shortened to rakı.

How is Rakı Produced?

These days, rakı is produced from fresh summer grapes or from rich, well preserved dried grapes. These are fed through an automatic chopping machine where they are diced, mashed, shredded, then mixed with water. The resulting mixture, called **mayşe**, is sterilised with steam, after which begins the fermentation process. The anise flavouring is added and the mixture is heated again, then cooled. This launches a very slow distillation process. The first 35 hours of distilled product goes unused – rakı is obtained only from the product obtained during 35-40 hours of distillation (when the rakı, at that stage, has an alcohol strength of 78-80%). Later, during a process called **sondurme**, water is added to reduce the alcohol level. Sugar is also added, 4-6g per litre. The end product, which has an alcohol strength of 45-50%, is left in oak barrels for 60-75 days, then bottled and sold.

Şarap (Wine) & Alkol (Spirits)

In the eastern region of Mt Ararat, there is archaeological evidence of wine production dating back to 4000 BC. The prohibition days of Ottoman rule put a serious dent in local wine production, but Kemal Atatürk's drive for 'westernisation' in the 1920s brought a renaissance in viticulture. Atatürk established the first winery Turkey had seen for seven centuries.

Turkey makes a lot of perfectly drinkable table wine. It's not exceptional stuff but it's here and it's very, very cheap. Most of the nationally distributed wine comes from Cappadocia, where vineyards are subject to snap-freeze winters and scorching summers. The two big wine companies are Doluca and Kavaklıdere. Doluca's Nevşah is a sweetish light white.

Rakı Etiquette

For 'true' rakı drinkers, there is something ritualistic in the way they take their drink. Firstly, it should be cooled in its bottle to 8-10°C before it's served. It must be sipped from a straight cylindrical drinking glass, never knocked back from a shot glass. According to preference, it may be taken with or without ice, and with mineral or soda water (either added or on the side). When mixed with any of these, the normally pure clear rakı turns a milky white colour. Once true rakı drinkers have established the preferred formulaic way to drink their poison, don't ask them to change. You may as well ask them to change the way they write their signature, as many a chastened apprentice waiter has learned.

Rakı (anise alcohol) drunk with meze and served with water

What Goes with Rakı?

To soften the effect of this strong drink, it is most often consumed (between main meals) together with cold meze such as cacık, sheep's brain, shrimp, mussels or pilaki. It also goes extremely well with fruits, melon and white cheese, and a main course of fish.

Jim & Perihan Masters

Kavaklıdere's premium white is Çankaya, its best red is Dikmen and it also does a rosé called Lal. In early June there's a wine festival with tastings and tours at Ürgüp, near Kayseri.

There are dozens of small wineries in Cappadocia, along the Aegean and in Thrace, where the warm coastal climate helps produce grapes such as semillon, pinot noir and some indigenous varieties. Cappadocian wineries open for wine tasting include Turasan, Duyurgan and Mustafapaşa.

Cin (gin), **votka** (vodka), **vermut** (vermouth) and **kanyak** (cognac) are made by Tekel, the government alcohol authority. The standard bottles are real headache inducers – make sure you ask for **kaliteli** (quality) stuff, or you'll pay for it the next day.

Non-Alcoholic Drinks
Çay (Tea)

The day starts with tea, the day happens in between tea, and drinking tea only stops because no one has worked out how to drink it while they're sleeping. Turks so love to share their tea passion that the visitor can sometimes feel like a tea-vessel on legs, sloshing from stop to stop, loaded on tannin and caffeine.

Tea was imported from Europe, via China, during early Ottoman days. A cuppa was enjoyed by small pockets of society but import levels stayed low. Then about 200 years ago, enough people developed the taste and it turned from an elite beverage into the nation's brew of choice. These days Turkey grows much of the tea it consumes, most of it on the steep, steamy hills east of Rize, near the Black Sea coast. Keen tea-heads eulogise the rich Rize crop but there are a lot of other varieties of tea if you fancy a change. **Elma çayı** (apple tea) is a relatively new creation. Invented mostly for the benefit of tea-sodden travellers, it's now quite popular with Turks, though the further you get from the tourist hot spots, the less it's about. Don't drink it for health: the vague fruity tang has nothing to do with apples.

You should never say no to a cup of freshly brewed tea – it's flavoursome and aromatic without the deep-set tannin of a brew that's been topped up a few times. Tea is served in a delicate tulip-shaped glass on a saucer holding two cubes of sugar. Most Turks will stir both cubes into the tea – some even ask for a third. Strong Turkish tea mellows out with a bit of sugar, but apple or herbal tea is lovely unsweetened. Once you've added sugar, stir your cup vigorously, and then put the spoon on the saucer. As soon as you finish your cup (and often before), you'll be offered more tea.

Flower and herb teas are drunk mostly for their health properties. **Adı çayı** (sage tea), also called **ata çayı** (island tea), is especially common along the Mediterranean coast. **Kekik çayı** (thyme tea), called **zahter** in eastern Turkey, is good for indigestion; **ıhlamur çayı** (linden flower tea), **tarçın çayı** (cinnamon tea) and **kuru nane çayı** (dried mint tea) are good for stomach complaints. **Portakal çayı** (orange tea) and **limon çayı** (lemon tea) are mostly drunk for their flavour. **Oralet çayı** is a lurid lemon tea – you might want to wear sunglasses while drinking it.

If you like milk with your tea, forget it. In tourist areas, milk will occasionally be offered but lemon is more common. Powdered creamer is part of the deal on long haul buses. If you can't face black tea without milk, stick to herbal brews.

Reflections in a tea maker, Eminönü, İstanbul

Tea time, semaver in foreground, Emirgan Park, İstanbul

Preparation

Turkish tea is brewed on a **demli** (double boiler). To make a pot, boil water in the bottom section, with the top section acting as a lid. When the water boils, add one heaped teaspoon of leaves for each person. Add water to the top section too, put the demli back on a low heat and brew for at least 20 minutes, taking care the pot doesn't boil dry. To serve the tea, pour the brew from the bottom section into tulip-shaped glasses and top it up with hot water from the top section to the desired strength. You can keep adding water to both pots until the tea is stale.

A **semaver** (urn) is used for making tea at a picnic or in any other away-from-the-stove situation. These decorative vessels have a central, tubular water chamber, drained with a simple tap. This chamber is surrounded by hot coals which rest in the body of the semaver. The tea is brewed in a separate pot which sits on top of the semaver, heated by the coals.

Tea Etiquette

The most important thing to remember is that there is *always* time for a cup. Everything else is mere detail. You'll be offered tea just about every time you stop moving: waiting for a bus, visiting a friend, shopping. It's hard to refuse – and an initial 'hayır, teşekkürler' (no, thank you) won't register.

It's hard not to get caught up in the national tea craze. Soon you'll be looking forward to wake-up tea sessions in the mornings, calculating bus trips in tea-stops, taking time out in tea gardens. There's something extremely soothing about sitting in a shaded courtyard, having your tea supply constantly replenished, chatting, writing letters or simply sipping, among scores of others doing exactly the same.

Every business has a **çaycı**, often a boy, who spends the day delivering tea around the neighbourhood, catering to a never-ending demand. Even restaurants may get their tea (and coffee) delivered. The tea is made in a little shop nearby and rushed to its destination on a tray or in a wire basket. At home, it's the job of the **gelin** (oldest daughter or daughter-in-law) to serve the tea. She won't sit down with everyone else but will concentrate on keeping everyone's cup full.

DRINKS

TEA TOUTERS

Many invitations to tea have a commercial basis and if you sat down with every single carpet dealer, jeweller or tour organiser, you'd never get anywhere. Most vendors are friendly people and won't be upset if you sit down and have a cuppa without buying anything. Even so, sometimes all these requests 'just to look, just to talk' can feel like harassment and the temptation is to ignore or sharply rebuff insistent salesmen. Our advice is to keep taking those deep breaths: you'll have a better time if you respond with a friendly but firm refusal rather than succumbing to snappy exasperation.

Kahve (Coffee)

The regard given to coffee as social cement is expressed in the saying 'bir fincan kahvenin kırk yıllık hatırı vardır' (One cup of coffee assures – and is worth – 40 years of friendship). Coffee isn't drunk as frequently as tea so it can feel more like a special occasion. Coffee hit Turkey around the 10th century, brought from Ethiopia and Syria, but it didn't gain popularity for 500 years or so. Certainly after the conquest of Egypt in the 15th century, coffee importation began in earnest. By the mid-16th century, coffee houses were well established in İstanbul and no party or banquet was complete without the vicious, delicious brew. Various party-poopers tried to ban coffee and its

Pouring Turkish coffee

brother-in-arms, tobacco, but both became such an entrenched part of Turkish life that prohibition attempts were abandoned. It was via the Ottoman empire that coffee climbed north through Europe, arriving in London in the late 19th century.

Kıraathane (reading rooms) were very popular in İstanbul in the 19th century, providing both coffee and newspapers for their all-male customers. Each kıraathane had a distinct clientele: one was for actors, another for mechanics, another for lawyers. They were gathering places, meeting halls, dens of gossip and networking.

While the men were out getting their coffee fix, the women were brewing coffee in the house – their sessions were just as social and significant. The assessment of prospective brides was one 'business' aspect of the women's gatherings. All would gather at the single girl's house and see how she performed as a hostess. To ascertain whether she had a sweet voice (an important quality), each woman would ask for her coffee a different sweetness. When the bride-to-be came back, she would announce the sweetness of each cup so they could hear if she purred or screeched. If they approved, they might say 'ağzından bal akıyor' (her voice is like honey).

Coffee was drunk in the evenings too, as it was thought to aid digestion. In family settings, men and women drank coffee together. In recent years,

Turks have fallen for **neskafe**, the generic term for any instant coffee. Sadly, many restaurants and hotels don't even make Turkish coffee anymore, just tea and instant. Though traditional coffee is always taken black, Turks drink their instant coffee with diluted sweetened condensed milk. At kiosks and on buses and planes, you get powdered creamer. You can usually count on traditional coffee being available at a **kahve** (coffee house) and in sweet shops. Lokantas won't usually make their own coffee but they may be able to order it in from their çaycı. In the home, traditional coffee is often saved for special occasions.

However you wrangle it, when you get a good, strong Turkish coffee brewed with fresh grounds, it's like imbibing energy and indulgence all at once. The caffeinated sorcery begins with the aroma, hitting your nostrils and cranking your heartbeat up a notch or two. The first sip hits the back of your throat in a rush of steam, the rich flavour lingers, the beans do their work and your eyes shine brightly. It comes over like a vitamin boost but it's better because it's slightly naughty.

GET GROUNDED

Apart from tasting awful, a good reason for not swallowing the coffee grounds lurking at the bottom of your cup is that they hold the key to your future! Here's how to become a coffee fortune teller.

When you've finished your coffee, swirl the grounds around and turn the cup upside down on the saucer. Wet your finger with your tongue and place it on the bottom of the cup. Make a wish. Take your finger off and wait 10 minutes or so for the grounds to cool and settle. When the cup is cool, turn it back over and examine the grounds first in the cup, and then, for extra illumination, on the saucer. Once you've gleaned all you can, dip your finger in the grounds and suck it to seal your fate.

These are the shapes to look for and their meanings:

fish	–	good fortune
snake	–	enemies a'coming
bird	–	kismet, omen
water/river	–	money
road	–	travel
bed	–	sickness
a big lump	–	heavy heart

Sure, a river and a road might look pretty similar when they're built out of coffee, but if you're any kind of seer, you'll know what's what.

DRINKS

Preparation

Turkish coffee is made in a small pot with a handle known as a **cezve**; choose one which corresponds to the number of cups you're making. Measure one cup of cold water per person into the cezve. Add one heaped teaspoon of coffee per cup and sugar to taste. Stir and set over a flame. Watch the coffee come to the boil, pour the froth into the cups then hold the cezve over the flame and bring it just to the boil once more. Pour out the rest of the coffee between the cups.

If the coffee is a long time coming, someone may call out '**kahve Yemen 'den gelir**' (coffee comes from Yemen). This is a sarcastic way of saying 'well, I know that coffee comes from a long way away, but really! How long do we have to wait?' It recalls the days when Turkey's coffee came from the Middle East and Africa. Today Brazil and Colombia are the sources.

Coffee is cooked up with sugar so you need to specify how sweet you want it before it is made. There are four levels of sweetness: **çok** (very), **orta** (middling), **az** (slightly) and for the hardcore, **sade** (no sugar at all). People may drink their coffee çok for weddings (because it's a sweet celebration) and sade for funerals.

Etiquette

Coffee is served in dinky little cups, often with a small glass of water. The idea is that you swig the water before drinking the coffee to clean your palate. The actual coffee isn't lingered over – it's best when hot. Many will slurp the first few sips, then throw back the rest. Don't swallow the grounds.

In the eastern Anatolian town of Urfa, a different kind of coffee, **mirra kahve**, is served. You get a tiny dose of groundless coffee – two sips and it's gone. It's served in a cup without a handle and without a saucer. But don't knock it back and slam your cup down! If you do so, tradition has it that you have to pay the bride of the waiter his weight in gold. Avoid paying such a heavy tip by returning your cup directly to the waiter.

Su (Water)

Though tap water is theoretically fine to drink, many travellers and a fair proportion of Turks drink **memba su** (spring water), **maden suyu** (mineral water) and **soda** (soda water). Şişe su is a general term for bottled water.

At a restaurant, bottles of water will be placed on your table and replenished as you finish them. Note that you haven't bought the water because a bottle is placed on your table. You 'buy' it when you open it.

Turks may be puzzled if you only want to drink water – they don't think you're accepting enough of their hospitality. It's like being offered cake but taking crackers.

BLESSED SOGGY TURBAN

April rainwater was thought by many to be sacred and full of healing properties. In the 13th century, the Mevlâna would dip his turban in a special **nisan tası** (April bowl) and believers would take turns in soaking up its blessings. You can see the bowl – indoors and bone dry now – at the Mevlâna Museum in Konya (see the boxed text Mevlâna and the Whirling Dervishes in the Culture of Turkish Food chapter).

Ayran (Yoghurt Drink)

Ayran is a yoghurt drink, made by whipping up yoghurt with water and salt to the consistency of pouring cream. It's refreshing, healthy and goes well with meat and pastry dishes or just as a thirst quencher. Every little kebabcı, börekçi and büfe sells ayran, either in individual rip-top tubs or drained from a churn-'n'-turner. People also make ayran at home. The traditional vessel for making ayran (and butter) is a **yayık**, a big cigar-shaped wooden tub suspended on strings so that it

Gözleme with ayran (yoghurt drink), İstanbul

can be swung back and forth. The yayık is still used in villages, especially for occasions when a large quantity is needed, but these days a blender or whisk is more common. Ayran can also be made with soda water.

Meyva Suyu (Fruit Juice)

Before there were soft drinks, cold drinks meant one thing: **meyva suyu** (fruit juice). For straight up meyva suyu, apricot, grape and citrus fruits are favoured. For **şurup** (syrup), just about anything that grows on trees can be used. Cherry, grape, pomegranate, lemon, flower petals and quince can all be enlisted in the quest to quench. To make şurup, whole fruits are stabbed with a skewer, then packed into a clay jar with a plug at the base. Water is poured in and left to soak up the fruit flavour for a month or so before being drained. Şurup can also be made by boiling and straining fruit, such as oranges. Whatever the strategy, the juice is sweetened with **pekmez** (fruit syrup) or sugar and served with ice.

Fruit juice is available commercially in cans, bottles and cardboard packages. Freshly squeezed orange juice is widely available from any kebabcı or büfe.

COLD AS ICE ... NOT NICE

Many older Turks consider very cold drinks unhealthy, a cause of stomach cramps and general metabolic unease. You may even see parents warming up chilled cans of soft drink before handing them to their kids. The flip side is the gusto with which steaming hot tea is consumed in the hottest part of the day.

Salep

Salep is a hot drink made from crushed tapioca root extract. It has a mild, slightly nutty taste but is drunk more for its health and aphrodisiac qualities than for its flavour. Such is its power, a Turkish salep seller lamented the priapic prospects of a male salep drinker with a long bus ride ahead, 'you will make like minaret! Oh dear!'

It's magical stuff. Salep's aphrodisiac effects were first noted by the Greek doctor Dioscorides in the 1st century. Medics from Belgium to Pakistan went on to prescribe it for unsexy maladies like dysentery, catarrh, colic, tuberculosis, cystitis and typhoid. Salep has also been used to conceal the salty taste of seawater so that it may be drunk, as a 'fattener by sultans and women of the east' and as an adulterant of opium. It's been consumed in many different ways: in Greece, it was flavoured with honey and eaten for breakfast; in India it was mixed with milk and spices and given to invalids. It even appears in the early editions of France's foodie bible, *Larousse Gastronomique*, in recipes for salep soup and jelly.

Turkey's salep comes from central and eastern Anatolia around Kahramanmaraş, Erzurum and Sivas. Villagers collect the tubers during summer and hang them in strings to dry. Salep is also used to make gluey ice cream (see Dondurma in the Staples & Specialities chapter). You can buy the drink in winter from street vendors and the occasional restaurant or **pastanesi** (pastry shop). In summer, you can sometimes find salep powder but no one will be selling the drink itself.

home cooking
& traditions

Town or country, the domestic kitchen relies on seasonal ingredients selected and prepared carefully but without fuss. The difference between urban and rural households is in the origin of the food and in the amount of food preparation done in the home. The country cook is much more likely to grow produce, bake bread, dry and preserve fruit and even grind flour. There's one thing, however, which almost every Turkish household excels in: hospitality.

Village dwellers usually have a vegetable garden, some fruit trees, grape vines and probably some chickens or a couple of goats. Flat roofs are the norm for village houses, not because mama's up there having a terrace party but because she's drying, storing and fermenting all sorts of produce. Summer grass goes up there to be crisped into winter hay, grain is spread out to be baked golden, fruit and vegetables are laid out or strung up from beam to balcony. And there's probably also a woodpile to fuel a barbecue or outdoor **ocak** (oven). Families tend to eat up top during summer, getting into the evening cool, sparking up the grill, laying down carpets and cushions and kicking back among the peppers and the apricots and the grapes and the grass.

In the cities, apartment dwellers often use their balconies to dry and store vegetables, fruits and grains. Some apartment buildings come with an ocak installed on the balcony. If not, people are likely to set up a portable grill to satisfy the Turkish passion for cooking and eating outdoors.

In most Turkish families the kitchen is a female domain, a social space for women as important as coffee houses are for men. As many households are multi-generational, especially in the countryside, there are usually at least two women sharing the baking. Some food preparation is communal: for tasks like making bread for winter, pitting a harvest of apricots or sorting grapes, local women will gather in one kitchen or yard to tackle the task at hand.

Woman and child preparing beans, Milas, south Aegean

Chillies and peppers drying, Black Sea Coast

Don't get the idea that all the chatter at these gatherings is about the weather. Scarved and skirted these women may be but they can also get quite risque. We came upon a group of grape sorters telling dirty jokes about a zucchini and shocking a young bride-to-be with what she could expect in the bedroom. When any men turn up, the demure screen clunks back down.

In summer, women make a batch of pide every week or so but in winter they tend to prepare a large quantity communally and store it for use throughout the colder months. This involved operation takes place over two days. On the first day, a salty dough is made from brown flour and laid out on a cloth sheet. Another sheet is laid over the top and the dough is kneaded by people walking over it (this is especially popular with kids). The trampled dough is left overnight and the next morning it's wrenched into baseball-sized spheres. Each women sits with her legs under a **tahta** (wooden slab table) to roll the dough balls into big, flat circles. The pide is cooked quickly on a wok over a grape-wood fire, then piled up and stored for winter. Just before meals, a batch of dry pide is sprinkled with water and heated, making it pliable again.

The household kitchen is more of a food factory than a place to eat. There might be a small breakfast table somewhere in the room but most meals are eaten in a separate living area or outside. The typical kitchen has a refrigerator/freezer, pantry and oven with a stovetop – one burner will be smaller than the others to accommodate a **cezve** (coffee pot). Microwave ovens, pressure cookers and food processors are fairly common these days, especially in towns.

FAMILY DINNER AT THE MANAV'S ANKAR APARTMENT

Despite pleading that I *want* to help, I'm not even allowed to hover while Aylin and Ayşe, her elderly mother, prepare our dinner and lay the table. My sister Amy and I are banished to the living room where we talk with Huseyin, Aylin's husband, Burcu, their 15-year-old daughter, and Bulent, their 12-year-old son. We met Burcu and Bulent at the bus station, where they wait after school for travellers they can practise their English with. After leading us to a pleasant guesthouse, they rang to check with mum before inviting us back home for a meal.

As more and more delicious smells emanate from the kitchen, we talk in a mixture of English and Turkish with half an eye on the television, tuned to a soap opera with the sound turned down. Burcu is soon summoned to carry dishes to the dining room table and a few minutes later, we are all called to eat.

We start with **yayla çorbası** (plateau soup) served with mountains of bread, and as soon as we empty our bowls, Aylin and Ayşe campaign for us to have more. When it's clear – after the third helping – that everyone's had enough, the main course is brought in. We serve ourselves from a spread of **cacık** (yoghurt salad), noodles sprinkled with **çökelek** (cheese made of skim milk or yoghurt curds), **çoban salatası** (shepherd's salad) and eggplant cooked with tomato, onion and chilli. It isn't a fancy meal but it's delicious and satisfying and all vegetarian, as is quite normal for a low-key family meal. We are all encouraged to refill our plates as soon as they're even slightly visible under the food. The nice thing about Turkish food being served cold or lukewarm is that there's no need for the host to keep dashing out to the kitchen to finesse the next course. In most cases, all dishes are made ready for the

Fried eggplant, tomato and chilli salad

beginning of the meal and it's just a matter of ploughing through them.

Before we're finished picking at the food on the table, Ayşe fetches dessert, a fruit platter with watermelon and strawberries. When everyone is adamant that they can't eat another thing, we are ushered back to the living room for tea. Bulent comes around with a cologne bottle and shakes some into our hands. I splash some on to freshen up and spend the rest of the evening happily smelling like clean laundry.

The Turkish pantry is very often split between the kitchen and an outdoor area like the porch or balcony. Indoors, a sneak peek might reveal spices, pasta, tea, Turkish coffee and neskafe. Outdoors, in bags or a grill-front cupboard, dried staples such as rice, grains, pulses, nuts and seeds are stored to see the family through winter. A Turkish fridge is likely to be stocked with white and yellow cheese, **salça** (tomato puree), olives, **sucuk** (spicy

Farm fresh eggs, Black Sea Coast

sausage), mince, eggs, butter, margarine, soft drinks, soda and perhaps beer and rakı. When it's hot, the essentials – onions, tomatoes, cucumber, parsley and mint – may also find their way into the icebox. The freezer will have lots of ice and perhaps some sheets of **yufka** (filo pastry).

Nothing if not resourceful, old style country cooking employed charcoal as a gentle rising and crisping agent in pastries and desserts. Cherry kernels were ground into a powder known as **mahlep** for use in biscuits and cakes.

Meals usually take place around a regular table and chairs but some households still use a traditional village **sofra** (low round dining table). When eating at a sofra, diners sit on the floor, on carpets or cushions. The traditional posture is to sit with one foot tucked under your bottom and the other one bent so your foot is flat on the floor. It's also acceptable to sit cross-legged. People may look aghast if you put your palms on the ground for support – it's thought the devil can enter through them! A **masa örtüsü** (tablecloth) extends far beyond the sofra's perimeter, acting as a communal napkin – you drape it over your lap and it's gathered up at the end.

Whether you're sitting at the table or on the floor, most meals will be casual, chatty affairs and you will be encouraged to help yourself again and again. Families eat together unless there's a lack of room. In this case, the men eat first followed by the women (or the women will eat in the kitchen). Foreign women are often treated as 'honorary men' and thus entitled to eat with the fellas at first sitting. Children are treated in a relaxed fashion – the Politeness Police aren't regular callers – and once they've finished eating, they're outta there. Unless you're drinking rakı, dinner can be over pretty quickly. Sometimes it can seem like the meal is considered an obstruction of the real business – tea drinking. Once you've eaten your fill, you may be invited to leave the dinner debris where it is and move to a more comfortable sitting area for tea.

Hospitality & the Art of Being a Guest

Hospitality is more than a Turkish tradition, it's a duty. It runs in the blood of Turkish people and is enshrined in religion, folklore and countless songs and sayings. Formal hospitality dates at least to Selcuk times when religious communities would provide travellers with basic sustenance. To this day, simple but ample meals are offered to thousands of people every day.

As you travel in Turkey, you'll encounter disarming hospitality wherever you turn. Visitors are often welcomed into locals' homes – if you can accept graciously and extricate yourself before you become a burden, you'll have a wonderful time. When you arrive at someone's home they will welcome you by saying **hoş geldiniz** (welcome). You should reply with **hoş bulduk** (thank you for your welcome). Guests are thought to confer blessings on a household: **misafir on kısmetle gelir; birini yer dokuzunu bırakır** (a guest comes with 10 blessings; he eats one and leaves nine). But on the other hand **balıkla misafir üç günlük oluncaya kadar** (fish and guests are good for three days). Even so you'll never be told that you're a bit on the nose: even if your hosts are good and sick of you, they'll still be devastated when you leave. It's nice to carry small gifts with you so that you can go some way to repaying the generosity of the people you meet.

The vast majority of invitations are genuinely friendly, though women will want to keep their sleaze detector charged up. Be alert but don't let paranoia isolate you from the great Turkish tradition of hospitality.

FIERCE HOSPITALITY

Waiting for a connecting bus in a nowhere town, I went to linger over a tea in a grimy lokanta. Some of the regulars came over and insisted that I miss my bus and stay longer. They promised a tour, and a family to stay with, inspected my ticket and assured me they could change it. Someone ran out to buy celebratory baklava. Someone else dashed off and came back 10 minutes later with a massive muddy watermelon. I explained that I couldn't possibly stay, that I had friends waiting for me at the other end, a schedule to keep. A cell phone was offered to me. "Call your friends! Tell them you will come in two days". The friendliness was fierce. The host instinct seemed to explode out of these people as soon as they knew I was a visitor. They had hospitality, and by golly, they weren't afraid to wield it. After a couple of hours of me insisting I would catch my bus, it eventually arrived and they waved me off sadly. My watermelon rolled up and down the aisle for the entire journey.

Adding filling to gözleme, Taksim, İstanbul

NASRETTIN HOCA

The saying '**pilavı paylaşan kaşığını yanında taşır**' effectively means 'be prepared', but literally it means 'if you love pilaf, you carry the spoon with you'. The importance of carrying the right spoon is illustrated in a tale by the well-loved 13th century mystic, Nasrettin Hoca (the Hoca), whose tales hold a strong sense of the absurd.

Food to Die for

On a stinking hot day, iced fruit in syrup was brought for the Hoca and other guests at a feast. Unfortunately, the Hoca couldn't pick anything up with the tiny spoon he had brought. The host, on the other hand, had a serving ladle and was feeding himself by the faceful, all the while declaring "Oh, how heavenly, oh, I am dead". Finally, the Hoca couldn't take it anymore and implored "Please lend me your ladle so I may die a little too".

Kazan Sham

Nasrettin Hoca borrowed a large pot from his neighbour and returned it the next day with a smaller pot inside. When questioned, the Hoca said "Oh, I forgot to mention that your pot gave birth to that small one". The amazed neighbour gladly accepted the extra pot. A week later, the Hoca borrowed the large pot again. A few days went by before the neighbour visited to ask its whereabouts. The Hoca said "Oh, didn't you hear the terrible news? Your pot has died".

The neighbour was outraged and said "come on, you don't expect me to believe that, do you?"

The Hoca responded, "well, you are indeed a funny fellow – you had no trouble believing your pot gave birth but now you won't believe that it has died".

Kazans, Turkish cooking pots

Salça (Tomato Puree)

You won't need a blender to make salça, but you will need a roof and a month or two. To make traditional salça the last crop of tomatoes is tied up in plastic sacks and fermented on the roof. It's then rubbed through a sieve, mixed with garlic and salt, poured in big plastic tubs then put back on the roof where it's stirred every now and again until the liquid thickens and the water evaporates. A spoonful of salça is added to just about every savoury dish. For those without tomato crops, plastic sacks and a month or two, ready-made salça is available in all markets.

Special Utensils

Until the 20th century, eating utensils were a spoon and a piece of bread. Now the standard table setting is a fork and spoon. Knives aren't rare but they are often unnecessary as most cooked food comes in bite-size portions.

KITCHEN SOUVENIRS

While utensil-spotting, you may encounter some of the following unfamiliar items:

demlik	(double boiler) for brewing tea
semaver	(urn) used for making tea at a picnic or in any other away-from-the-stove situation. These decorative vessels have a central water chamber, drained with a simple tap.
cezve	small pot with a handle for making Turkish coffee
biber değirmeni	brass pepper grinder
şişkabı	metal canister for transporting prepared şiş kebab to a picnic
mangal	grill, brazier
güveç	clay stewing pot
oklava	wooden or metal rolling pin for making yufka and lahmacun. The oklava is thinner and longer than a western rolling pin
dolma taşı	thick clay disc with holes in it used for weighing down dolmas while they've cooking or vegetables while they're being pickled
aşurelik	a porcelain jug for transporting aşure (40 ingredient pudding; see the recipe in the Celebrating with Food chapter)

During Ottoman times it was the custom for travellers to carry their own spoons about with them, lessening the burden on their hosts. Spoons became a prestige item, carved from wood or wrought from metal, embellished with elaborate designs. The most precious spoons were carried in embroidered cases. All other traditional vessels and utensils – copper pans, clay storing and baking containers and wooden bowls and cutlery – are still available, but stainless steel, glass, enamel and plastic have made significant inroads. If you want to buy cooking implements and kitchen gear, ask for a **nalburiye** or **tenekeci**.

celebrating
with food

The stomach is a reliable meter for registering a special event. Not only can it sense the gravity of an occasion simply by how full it gets, it can appreciate subtleties – whether the occasion is solemn or joyous, momentous or raucous, religious or secular. All cultures use food as a signifier, but the Turks are among those who like to experience special occasions by attributing meaning to food. Food's sacred identity is a gift from God and a gift back to God.

Every special occasion in Turkey has concomitant food rituals. In many cases, **düğün** (feast) traditions were quite specific: dish A is served by Person B to Person C at Time X. These days, many of the more onerous, prescriptive traditions have lapsed. Celebrating with food can be as simple as having a lot of food, a lot of people and a lot of fun. But many traditions persist, especially in rural areas, and the most difficult and dramatic tradition, **Kurban Bayramı** (Feast of the Sacrifice, see later in this chapter) is the most widely adhered to of all.

Weddings

Marriage celebrations are the most extravagant of all. At the height of the Ottoman empire, royal wedding feasts could last for three weeks. A shopping list for the wedding spread of the daughter of Mehmet IV called for 50,000 chickens and 80,000 dishes among other necessities.

Mere mortals celebrated on a much smaller but by no means scanty scale, and these days even modest weddings may take a few days. The bride's family hosts an evening wedding feast (usually on a Saturday night) during which the bride sneaks off, gets married, but then returns to the fold. The next day, the groom's family holds a feast, welcoming the bride into their household. Wedding foods generally include a meat, vegetable and bulgur soup, a chickpea stew, macaroni or **mantı** (little pasta packages) with a garlicky meat sauce, **köfte** (mincemeat or bulgur balls), okra; chicken on a bed of rice and, as with circumcision, **zerde** (rice and nut dessert). The food may well be served in staggered sittings and it's likely that the whole village will be invited.

After two days of feasting and dancing, the bride and groom are finally allowed to bed down together. Before consummating the marriage, they nibble on some unsalted chicken, which is thought to bring blessings. It's also believed that the first nuptial food remains in the stomach for digestion in the afterlife, so it's obviously of quite some importance what is eaten. Meanwhile, baklava is distributed to the gathering of guests outside who stand around eating until the bloodied sheet – proof that the bride was a virgin – is displayed.

This basic structure of the wedding is amended, appended, truncated and elongated, according to wealth and regional traditions. In some parts, the groom (and perhaps his friends and family) must go to the bride's house on the second day, beseeching her family to give her up. The bride's family expresses ritualised misgivings but eventually gives their daughter to her new husband. Upscale weddings incorporate **paça günü** (trotters day) – the lucky bride is sent a dish of delectable sheep's feet by her husband on the day after the wedding.

In central Turkey, a traditional wedding feast has seven courses, with two of them sensibly consisting of a dessert. Naturally, soup kicks it off, followed by meat and pilav, the dolma, then zerde (the first dessert). After a suitable interval, börek is brought in, followed by helva (the second dessert). The shebang finishes up, perhaps a little strangely, with okra. The next morning, the groom's family presents baklava to the bride's family and their married life begins. In southeastern Anatolia, a plateful of **katmer** (sweet breakfast gözleme made with pistachio and clotted cream) is what the bride's family receives the day after. Bursa is one of the few urban bastions of the bridal **hamam** (public bath) picnic. Before her wedding the bride goes to the hamam, accompanied by her female relatives and friends who take a picnic of börek, sarma and olives to be enjoyed after a good steam and scrub. Along the Black Sea, the bride's family has to give another feast 10 days after the wedding. The first dish is fried eggs, brought to the table with the lid still on the pan. To have the lid removed, the groom must give money. After he does so, the feasting begins. Again.

TUZ TÖRESI (THE SALT CUSTOM)

When the issue of marriage rose among the nomads of Anatolia. The suitor's suitability would have to be put to the test. In those days lineage, charm and income weren't the gauges of a good son-in-law, the answer was in the salt box. If a daughter received a marriage proposal, her father would take the salt box from the kitchen, fill it to the brim, string it to a post and pierce a hole in its base. Now the test began. If, in the time it took for the salt to trickle out, there was no interruption or mishap, the proposal would be accepted by the family. However if there was any disturbance whatsoever, the wedding would be off. It may have been the suitors of Anatolia who discovered that salt caused high blood pressure.

Birth

The birth of a child is naturally a cause for warm celebration, and in Turkey the whole community makes sure the arrival of a new neighbour doesn't go unnoticed.

The traditional tipple for celebrating the birth of a baby is **lahusa şerbeti**, a boiled sugar drink with red chilli pepper, cinnamon, rose-water and sometimes lemon juice. The drink is dyed red, these days with artificial colouring, but traditionally with crushed cochineal, a Central American insect brought to Europe by the Spanish. The sherbet is served to guests who visit the house and also sent in decanters wrapped with red tulle to relatives and neighbours. If the baby is a girl, the lid of the decanter is also wrapped in tulle; if it's a boy, the lid is left unwrapped. If lahusa şerbeti is left to cool, it will crystallise and can be cut into a diamond-shaped candy.

One tradition enthusiastically carried out by local children involves heading to the newborn's house and throwing stones at the front door, demanding either 'the son or sweets'. The father, unwilling to release his child into the custody of the neighbourhood rabble, gives each of the children some **akide** (hard candy). A sweet ransom.

Circumcision

In Ottoman times the circumcision of a high-ranking son was cause for a massive celebration. The snip was scheduled when the boy was between five and seven years old. For a sultan's son, the feast included whole cows roasted in massive pits with horns still intact. The revellers tore the beast apart with their bare hands. Just to keep things interesting, the cows were stuffed with whole wild animals such as wolves and rabbits, often inserted while still alive. Those who made it through the meat course were treated to an astonishing array of sweets and puddings, always including **zerde** (rice and nut dessert). The feasting could go on for days.

These days, the pruning party is less extravagant though still significant. The boy is dressed in a spangly hat and a white satin suit bound with a red sash (you'll see these suits on sale in İstanbul's Egyptian Market). After a pre-snip parade around his neighbourhood, the boy is accompanied to the doc for the docking and then brought home to rest and enjoy the congratulations of his friends and relatives.

Today's celebratory feasts still include the likes of zerde, but the rabbit-stuffed cows don't feature.

Death

Funeral ceremonies occur as soon as practical after death, the next day if possible. The body is brought to the mosque where it is wrapped in white cloth, placed in a casket and laid on a special stone slab in the mosque grounds for prayers. The mourners take turns carrying the casket to the burial ground, where further prayers are said before the body is lowered into the grave.

İrmik helvası (semolina helva) is delivered by the bereaved to neighbours and friends the day after a death and again 40 days later. The helva may be made communally by women gathering to lament the passing of the deceased. In this case, the stirring spoon will be passed around the circle of mourners and whoever has it will lead the reminiscing.

Ramazan

The ninth month of the Muslim calendar is one of daylight fasting and darkness feasting. Keeping Ramazan is one of the five pillars (basic duties) of the Muslim faith, a worthy sacrifice which confers blessings on the faster and all Muslims. Pregnant women, the sick, the aged and travellers are not expected to fast.

Those who are keeping the fast don't eat, drink or smoke between dawn and dusk, but they still manage to fit in two substantial meals each day. The first is **imsak** or **sahur**, a breakfast to beat the earliest of birds. The main emphasis is on foods which will give energy for the long, hungry day ahead such as soup, bread, dates, olives and pastries. Naturally, lots of tea is drunk. Some may also have coffee or lemon sherbet; smokers suck on their cigarettes with gusto. You don't have to worry about sleeping through imsak – drum-banging boys walk through the streets a couple of hours before dawn to ensure that everyone has the opportunity to eat before the sun comes up.

Some people have a two-tier imsak, which starts with a snacky bread, olive and cheese spread, and then moves on to a more substantial meal of rice, macaroni and salad. Ramazan shifts 10 days back each year so many of the actual foods change with the season. Whatever the season, **reçel** (jam) and **hoşaf** (stewed pestil) are Ramazan mainstays because they are gentle on the stomach and full of energy.

Sunset, Pamukkale

The day of fasting is over at sunset. The exact minute that it's okay to eat is signalled by mosques, drumming boys and radio announcements. Hungry people may start the evening with **iftariyelik**, a light snack of dates and olives to accustom the body to food. Men may then go to evening prayers while the women prepare **iftar**, often a long, relaxed, social meal.

Special care is taken over iftar because fasters deserve a good feed – not only must it be plentiful and tasty, it must also look beautiful. A palace-style iftar would begin with soup perhaps followed by **pastırma** (pastrami) fried with eggs, then meat, vegetables, börek and pilav. Lighter spreads could include beans, okra, chickpeas, vine leaves, yoghurt and sesame seeds mixed with pekmez. Traditional Ramazan **pide** (flat bread) is sprinkled with **çörekotu** (black cumin seeds). **Güllaç** (wafers soaked in sweetened milk flavoured with rose-water then layered with walnuts) is a typical Ramazan dessert.

If you're in Turkey in Ramazan look out for restaurants that serve iftar meals, often at a central table. In the cities, the government sponsors Ramazan dinners for the poor. Though men and women have to queue up separately, these dinners are open to all.

The last iftar meal before Şeker Bayramı, which celebrates the end of Ramazan, begins with **tarhana çorbası** (soup of dried curds). If in season, a whole **ayçiçeği** (sunflower; literally, moonflower) is pulled apart for the seeds.

Ramazan Etiquette

Even though many Turks don't fast for Ramazan, they are sensitive to those who are fasting around them. As a visitor, it's best to be considerate by not eating in public during daylight, especially in rural areas or the more traditional cities. It's also worth being extra-patient with the hungry Turks you encounter – fasters can be a bit on the grumpy side.

HAIR TRIGGER

Before clocks, the **muezzin** (mosque crier) would go outside with a hair, and stretch it out in front of him. When it became daylight and he could see the hair, the fast was on – and he'd shout it from the minaret. At the moment it became dark and he couldn't see the hair, the fast was off – and he'd shout that out to the ravenous below.

Jim & Perihan Masters

Blue Mosque courtyard, İstanbul

Aşure (40-Ingredient Pudding, or Bowl of Stuff)

Tradition has it that aşure (see last page in this chapter) should only be cooked by women who have a daughter. If you qualify, go ahead.

Ingredients

¾	cup whole wheat	½	cup dried apricots
⅓	cup broad beans	1	cup milk
⅓	cup chickpeas	1	tablespoon rose-water
⅓	cup rice	⅓	cup walnuts
⅓	cup raisins	⅓	cup pistachios
⅓	cup figs	¼	cup pomegranate seeds

Soak the wheat and beans separately overnight. Drain all and set the wheat aside. Boil the broad beans and chickpeas separately until tender. Remove from the heat and drain, conserving the water. Boil currants, chopped apricots and figs for 10 minutes, then drain and set aside. Cook the wheat and rice over low heat in two litres of the water you conserved earlier, stirring frequently. When the wheat is tender, add the dried fruit and cook for five minutes. Stir in the broad beans and chickpeas. After another five minutes, stir in the sugar and bring to the boil, stirring all the while. Add the milk and stir until smooth. The consistency should be like a thinnish porridge; add more milk if it is too thick. Finally, remove from heat and – you guessed it – *stir* in the rose-water. Pour into individual bowls or a serving dish and refrigerate. When cool, garnish with the nuts and seeds to serve.

Note: Feel free to fiddle with the ingredients and quantities – whatever you've got on the ark will work.

Şeker Bayramı (or Ramazan Bayramı)

The end of Ramazan is celebrated with three days of feasting. It's a time of renewal: the house is cleaned from top to bottom and people don their best clothes or even buy new ones. It's an important time for families to be together – the roads are full of people doing the rounds of parents and cousins, aunts and in-laws. It's also a time of reflection, with many families visiting the graves of those no longer around to share in the feasting.

The emphasis on the first day is on sweet food. Baklava and **şerbet** (sherbet) are ever-present; **muhallebi** (rice pudding) and **şeker pare** (sweet biscuit) are commonly served. As well as the parade of desserts, there are endless savoury nibbles such as nuts, seeds and pulses. One Şeker Bayramı tradition has the host peeling pieces of fruit for her guests and practically standing over them while they eat. If you're around for Şeker Bayramı, don't have a snack before you leave home! **Yuvarlama** (chickpea and dumpling soup) is an essential part of Şeker Bayramı feasting in the southeastern Anatolian town of Antep.

Kurban Bayramı (Feast of the Sacrifice)

Kurban Bayramı, which occurs 70 days after the end of Ramazan, is a spectacular day of slaughter and feasting throughout the Muslim world. In commemoration of God's mercy in allowing Abraham to sacrifice a ram instead of his son, 2.5 million animals are killed in Turkey each year. The story (which appears in both the Koran and the Bible) finds Abraham obeying the order of God to take his son, Isaac, to Mt Moriah in order to sacrifice him. Once Abraham has laid his son on the chopping block, God sees his faith and spares the boy. Abraham is ordered to sacrifice a ram instead. Today, every family or business kills a sheep (or goat or cow) in remembrance. Even unreligious families tend to take part in Kurban Bayramı – it's probably the most important festival of the year.

Male, healthy, robust animals are preferred, not only because they're bigger but also because it's considered a great misfortune to kill a pregnant beast. Parks and plazas are set aside for the slaughter. In villages, families use their own gardens or the street in front of their houses. The atmosphere is solemn and respectful rather than bloodthirsty. Sons, especially, have a sense that if not for the grace of God, there go them etc.

Anyone who knows the special Kurban prayers and the halal technique may wield the knife and, every year, hundreds of inexperienced butchers are injured. Wisely, most famillies leave the killing to roving butchers.

Once the animal is killed, blood is daubed on children's foreheads for good luck and the animal is butchered. The slaughtering family or business only keeps one third of the meat; the bulk goes to the poor. This is one of the most important aspects of Kurban Bayramı, and many poor families rely on Kurban charity to see them through the year. Nothing goes to waste: the wool is donated to the civil air force for fund-raising, the intestines are made into sausages, the stomach is cleaned and boiled for soup and the lungs are thrown to the dogs, for whom this is the happiest day of the year.

The first meal with the Kurban meat is cooked quickly and simply, perhaps on a wok with tomatoes and peppers, and eaten reverently. The leftover meat is hung in necklaces outside houses to dry or preserved in clay jars to be eaten over the following months.

Aşure Bayramı

The 10th day of Muharrem (the Muslim month) is the biggest day of the year for eating **aşure**, a sloppy, protein-rich dessert. The story goes that the flood waters were subsiding when Noah asked his wife to cook up all the food left on the ark. She formulated a bizarre 40-ingredient pudding which included beans, barley, chickpeas, cinnamon, sultanas and bulgur. It's a real pantry-emptying, stomach-filling confusion of profusion.

As well as its associations with Noah and the ark, this day is the anniversary of the martyrdom of Imam Hüseyin, grandson of Mohammed. The cooking and distribution of aşure was an especially important ritual for the Bektaşi order of dervishes, based in Hacıbektaş. The aşure was cooked over two days with everyone taking a turn in the stirring, symbolically 'cooking the soul'. Once ready, villagers would come and have their bowls filled and messengers would deliver the pudding to friends farther afield in a special **aşurelik** (pitcher). Once the pitcher had been emptied and cleaned, it would be returned to the Bektaşi filled with sweets.

OILED WRESTLING

Wrestling is one of Turkey's biggest sports and olives are one of its favourite foods – it makes perfect sense to combine these two passions in olive oil wrestling. Every summer big tough men squeeze into leather pedal pushers and get down, dirty and downright sloppy on the slipperiest seasonal produce around. The most serious competition, near Edirne in early June, culminates in the crowning of a national champion. There are other smaller events near Alanya and other olive growing areas – ask tourist offices for details.

regional
variations

At its widest, Turkey stretches 1700km west to east and a strapping 1000km from the Black Sea south to the shores of the Mediterranean. This provides plenty of room for markets, menus and what-mother-knows-best to shift and change. Different parts of the country are known – and loved – for their specialities. No one just wants **fıstık** (pistachios), they want **Antep fıstığı** (pistachios from Antep). **Karpuz** (watermelon) is one thing but **Adana karpuzu** (watermelons from Adana), now you're talking.

REGIONS

BULGARIA

RUSSIA

Karadeniz
(Black Sea)

İSTANBUL

GEORGIA

Sea of
Marmara

ARMENIA

★ ANKARA

IRAN

TURKEY

GREECE

IRAQ

Ege Denizi
(Aegean Sea)

CYPRUS

SYRIA

Akdeniz
(Mediterranean Sea)

Marmara
Aegean
Mediterranean
Central Anatolia
Black Sea
Eastern Anatolia
Southeastern Anatolia

Though dairy, meat, grain and vegetable staples are found all over Turkey, diverse cultural heritage and geographical conditions mean that dinner can taste pretty different from one part of the country to the next. Generally, the further south and east you travel, the spicier the food gets. In the west, olive oil is the dominant cooking agent; the further east you go, the more lard is used. Seafood is more popular along the coasts, though this isn't as foregone a conclusion as you might assume.

Even when staple crops are grown in various regions, they are often harvested for different purposes. For example, central Anatolian wheat is used mostly in bread and for bulgur, eastern Anatolian and Mediterranean wheat is made into **makarna** (pasta) and northern Anatolian and Black Sea wheat is ground to make yarma. Often the same basic dishes are adapted to local ingredients. For example, **tarator** (a garlic and nut sauce commonly paired with fish) is made with **badem** (almond) on the Aegean Coast, **ceviz** (walnut) in central Anatolia and **fındık** (hazelnut) along the Black Sea.

Turks are mobile people, with many living far from their birthplace. As a result, regional specialities are transported and adapted. Much to the distress of many older people, some regional dishes are simply forgotten in the move to a more urbanised society. You'll hear it said that all types of

Turkish food are available in İstanbul but this isn't true, not really. You *can* get food from just about anywhere, but you can't get all of it and you can't get it as good.

Even transplanted Turks are enthusiastic about their hometown food, going all misty-eyed at the memory of food from home. Muammer in Antalya sings (literally) the praises of the wild mushrooms he used to find in Samsun. Adnan in İstanbul has his mum in Erzurum send spices four times a year. Mehmet in Trabzon gets pomegranate pekmez sent up from Antakya. This is still a country that takes its regional specialities seriously.

COOKING COMPETITIONS

Cooking contests are held annually in many Turkish towns. Some of them are fancy affairs with chefs getting serious in hotel kitchens but others are bake & cake style, with foods prepared at home and brought in for judging by chefs, dignitaries and other lucky folk. The joy of these amateur competitions is that they tend to feature regional specialities, keeping the old dishes alive as well as being a darn good nosh up.

Vegetarian salads at Nah'un Ambari Health Food Restaurant, Taksim, İstanbul

Marmara

The Marmara region is a mishmash of diverse cultures and geography in a small swathe of land. It includes Thrace, the European portion of Turkey bordering Bulgaria and Greece, and stretches through İstanbul on its way southeast as far as Bursa. As both a historical and physical crossroads, Marmara has entrenched traditions of trade: this is the part of Turkey most receptive to foreign ingredients, recipes and habits. The land borders are relatively recent, Bulgaria and Greece both having been part of the Ottoman Empire. The physical conditions – rich soil blessed by mild weather – are perfect for fruits, vegetables and livestock.

Due to the presence of İstanbul plus Bursa and Edirne (both early Ottoman capitals), Marmara is the heartland of Ottoman cuisine. This is where the spice trade routes terminated, where all those eggplant recipes were invented and where **lokum** (Turkish delight) was concocted.

The proximity to Greece is reflected in the similarity with many Greek foods – particularly in the form of eggplant dishes, stuffed foods, olive oil and cheese – though any patriotic Turk will be happy to tell you that the Greeks borrowed from the Turks rather than the other way round. Similarities with Bulgarian cuisine are manifold: sibling salads, grills, coffee, boza and liquor are all testament to shared eating habits which predate today's border.

The people here are the most urbanised, liberal and, along with Ankarans, the most cosmopolitan in Turkey. They're the most amenable to new foods and flavours and are also the most explicitly health-conscious folk in the nation.

İstanbul is a massive octopus of a city, sucking in produce and recipes from all over and spitting them back out on plates, wrapped in pide or speared on a şiş. If you can only eat in one place in Turkey, this should be it. As well as being the best place to find authentic Ottoman food, İstanbul has the best concentration of regional variations, though as we've said, *not* everything. İstanbul is also the best bet for satisfying your international cuisine dreams of sushi, dim sum, taco or *canard à l'orange*.

REGIONAL VARIATIONS

DON'T MISS

- Fish sandwiches prepared on Bosphorus shores
- Yoghurt from Kanlıca
- Bursa kebabs in Bursa
- Multi-purpose Marmaran olives

A squeeze of lemon on a stuffed mussel, Eminönü, İstanbul

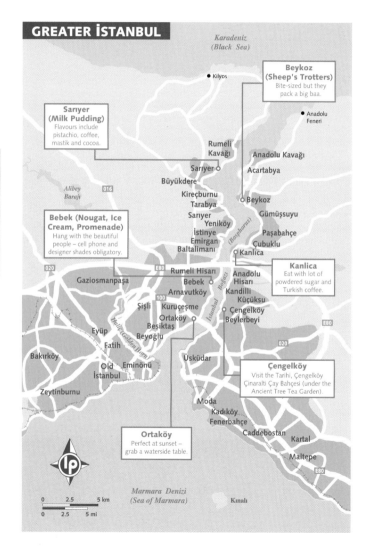

GREATER İSTANBUL

Karadeniz
(Black Sea)

**Beykoz
(Sheep's Trotters)**
Bite-sized but they
pack a big baa.

• Kilyos

• Anadolu
Feneri

**Sarıyer
(Milk Pudding)**
Flavours include
pistachio, coffee,
mastik and cocoa.

Rumeli
Kavağı

Anadolu Kavağı

Sarıyer

Acartabya

Büyükdere

Alibey
Baraji

016

Kireçburnu
Tarabya
Sarıyer
Yeniköy
İstinye
Emirgan
Baltalimanı

Beykoz

Gümüşsuyu

**Bebek (Nougat, Ice
Cream, Promenade)**
Hang with the beautiful
people – cell phone and
designer shades obligatory.

Paşabahçe
Çubuklu
Kanlıca

020

Rumeli Hisarı

E80

Anadolu
Hisarı

Kanlica
Eat with lot of
powdered sugar and
Turkish coffee.

Gaziosmanpaşa

Arnavutköy
Şişli
Kuruçeşme
Ortaköy
Beşiktaş
Beyoğlu

100

Bebek

Kandilli
Küçüksu
Çengelköy
Beylerbeyi

E80

Eyüp

Fatih

020

Bakırköy

Old
İstanbul

Eminönü

Üsküdar

Çengelköy
Visit the Tarihi, Çengelköy
Çinaralti Çay Bahçesi (under the
Ancient Tree Tea Garden).

Zeytinburnu

Moda
Kadıköy
Fenerbahçe

Caddebostan

Kartal

Ortaköy
Perfect at sunset –
grab a waterside table.

Maltepe

E80

Marmara Denizi
(Sea of Marmara)

Kınalı

0 2.5 5 km
0 2.5 5 mi

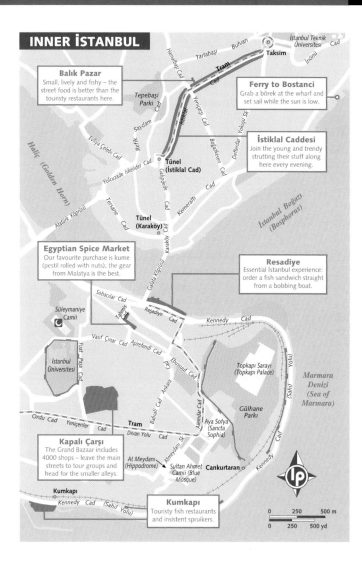

INNER İSTANBUL

Balık Pazar
Small, lively and fishy – the street food is better than the touristy restaurants here.

Ferry to Bostanci
Grab a börek at the wharf and set sail while the sun is low.

İstiklal Caddesi
Join the young and trendy strutting their stuff along here every evening.

Egyptian Spice Market
Our favourite purchase is kume (pestil rolled with nuts); the gear from Malatya is the best.

Resadiye
Essential İstanbul experience: order a fish sandwich straight from a bobbing boat.

Kapalı Çarşı
The Grand Bazaar includes 4000 shops – leave the main streets to tour groups and head for the smaller alleys.

Kumkapı
Touristy fish restaurants and insistent spruikers.

İstanbul Teknik Üniversitesi Cad
İnönü
Taksim
Hamalbaşı Cad
Tarlabaşı Bulvarı
Tram
İstiklal Cad
Tepebaşı Parki
Yeniçarşı Cad
Defterdar Yokuşu Sk
Saydam
Refik Cad
Boğazkesen Cad
Euliya Çelebi Cad
Halic (Golden Horn)
Yolcuzäde İskender Cad
Tünel (İstiklal Cad)
Galipdede
Kemeralti Cad
İstanbul Boğazı (Bosphorus)
Atatürk Köprüsü
Tersane Cad
Tünel (Karaköy)
Galata Köprüsü
Karaköy Cad
Sobacılar Cad
Süleymaniye Camii
Tahmis
Resadiye Cad
Kennedy Cad
Vasif Çınar Cad
Aşirefendi Cad
Firat Paşa Cad
İstanbul Üniversitesi
Ankara Cad
Babıali Cad
Ebussud Cad
Topkapı Sarayı (Topkapı Palace)
Marmara Denizi (Sea of Marmara)
Ordu Cad
Yeniçeriler Cad
Tram
Divan Yolu Cad
Alemdar Cad
Gülhane Parkı
Aya Sofya (Sancta Sophia)
(Sahil Yolu)
At Meydanı (Hippodrome)
Atmeydanı Sk
Sultan Ahmet Camii (Blue Mosque)
Cankurtaran
Kennedy Cad
Kumkapı
Kennedy Cad (Sahil Yolu)

0   250   500 m
0   250   500 yd

REGIONAL VARIATIONS

Sunday lunch, Yeni Cami, İstanbul

The Bosphorus is İstanbul's silver seam. At first glance it looks like a thoroughfare for freighters and ferries but it's really a fast flowing fish highway, a channel for an astonishing variety of finned and gilled creatures swimming between the Black Sea and the Sea of Marmara. Even though it can seem to be a stinky repository of plastic bags, drink cans and cigarette butts, streaming currents in both directions keep the fish oxygenated and edible. Consequently seafood has a prominent place in the region's cuisine. Though the old fishing villages strung along the Bosphorus shores are now absorbed into the metropolis, they're still home to small-time commercial operators, netting fish and bagging mussels. Weekend fishermen cast off from Bosphorus boardwalks, their families waiting for them on the traffic islands on smog-snuggled picnic blankets. Small commercial operators grill their catches on the decks of their little boats and sell fillets wrapped in bread to promenaders (see the boxed text Bosphorus Fish Sandwiches in the Street Food chapter).

İstanbul's knack for absorbing what were once distinct villages has endowed it with some internal 'regional specialities'. Kanlıca, on the Asian side of the Bosphorus, is famous for its yoghurt, served on site with **podra** (icing sugar). Late afternoon is the perfect time to jump on a ferry and chug over to Kanlıca's waterfront teahouse, where you can sit with a tub of the mild, strangely alluring yoghurt and squint at the view. As well as being a place to observe the impressive Fatih Bridge, the pleasureboats, freighters and mussel-netters, this is a popular meeting spot for couples engaged in secret rendezvous.

Çengelköy is famous for its fat and crispy little cucumbers, sold by the roadside in summer; Sarıyer is known for **muhallebi** (pudding) and **börek** (pastry dishes) and Beykoz for its special garlicky preparation of sheep's trotters. Bebek's **badem ezmesi** (almond paste) is sought out by lovers of the sweet and nutty.

Bursa lies in the shadow of the 2500m-high Uludağ (previously known as Mt Olympus). Before refrigeration, ice was hacked from Uludağ and taken across the Sea of Marmara to İstanbul where it was used to cool the royal drinks. Bursa's residents are justly proud of their innovative role in the evolution of Turkish cuisine. Not only was the vertical döner grill invented here in the 1860s, it also led to the invention of the Bursa (or İskender) kebab, a jazzed up combination of pide, meat, yoghurt, browned butter and tomato sauce (see Kebab under Et (Meat) in the Staples & Specialties chapter).

Locals insist that the only place to eat this succulent kebab is right here, in its birthplace. Restaurateurs secure their customers – and drum up passing trade – by promising an authentic rendition of this homegrown classic. There are some good kebabçıs along Ünlü Caddesi, just east of Heykel, the main square. Bursa is also a great place to try **İnegöl köftesi** (a köfte of beef rib meat, lamb and onion) and **çiğ börek** (fried börek made with raw mince, onions and spices).

Anchoring the other end of the food pyramid are the region's peaches, considered the best in Turkey, and **kestane şekeri**, a syrup-soaked chestnut dessert. A portion is simply unfinishable but is easier to tackle when coupled with a sugar-free Turkish coffee. Olives grown here are eaten fresh or made into oil for cooking and wrestling (see the boxed text Oiled Wrestling in the Celebrating with Food chapter). Grapes grown in this region account for 40% of Turkey's wine production and are also used to make **rakı** (anise alcohol).

REGIONAL VARIATIONS

Aegean Region

This area includes the whole western chunk of Turkey, from the coast to about 200km inland. The region doesn't soak up quite as much rainfall as Marmara but the sun strikes a bit hotter – perfect conditions for stone fruit, citrus fruit and olives. It's pretty countryside for the most part, with gentle hills falling to merrily zigzagging rivers through a jaunty tapestry of fields.

Sea, sun and sand-worshipping Aegean dwellers are second only to the fish-crazy Black Sea folk in their love of seafood. The shellfish scooped up in the north Aegean are the best in Turkey as they're plump, tender and delicately flavoured, best eaten grilled with a squeeze of lemon. The squid caught around İzmir is the most scrumptious in the nation – it's typically served as **kalamar** (calamari), battered and fried with a crisp salad accompaniment. Eating a calamari ring is a mini-odyssey beginning at resistance and ending in rapturous release: the initially recalcitrant morsel gives in to the bite down, releasing its juices in a flood of mild fishy flavour. Look out

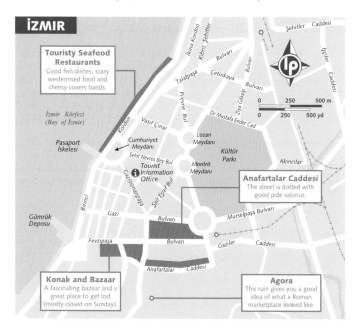

Opium seed Turkish delight, Afyon

for local markets or for fishermen selling their haul right on the beach, either raw or cooked on the spot over a wood or gas fire. Restaurants in large towns like İzmir serve a wide range of elaborate seafood dishes while simple eateries in small seaside hamlets may just have one or two things available. Wherever you're dining, ask for the freshest and best and have it cooked quickly and with minimum fuss.

CURED ... BY GUM!

Manisa, northeast of İzmir, holds a Spring Equinox festival to celebrate **Mesir macunu** (power gum). This remarkable gum was invented by a local pharmacist to cure the mother of Sultan Süleyman the Magnificent who caught a mysterious illness. After she was cured, the munificent mum supplied all Manisa's residents with the remarkable gum at her own expense. These days, the government picks up the tab for 10 tonnes of Mesir macunu, chucked ritually from the dome of a central Manisa mosque. Chomping down on some gum will make you healthy and potent beyond belief. Trust us.

İzmir Köfte

The recipe for this Aegean favourite comes from the kitchen of Turan Cevik, mother of five, in İzmit.

Ingredients

2	cups of crumbled stale bread
1	small onion, chopped
1	cup parsley, coarsely chopped
450g	of ground lamb
8	medium potatoes, sliced and fried
	salt, pepper, mint, cumin

For the sauce

2	tomatoes, peeled and finely chopped
	butter, salt

Put the stale bread into a bowl or flat pan. Add onion, parsley, the ground lamb, sprinkles of salt, black pepper, dried mint, cumin and a little water.

Mix by hand with strong clenching squeezes, grabbing from the perimeter and working to the middle. It's well-combined when the kneaded mound peels clean from the mixing surface. Roll the mix into flattened thumb shapes then fry them up in half an inch of oil. Flip when dark brown (less than five minutes) and fry the other side.

To make the sauce, heat the butter and salt in a pan and add the tomatoes. Stir, reduce, add a little water, let it bubble away. You can add **salça** (tomato puree) to make it richer, if desired.

Arrange the potatoes on the bottom of a deep pan, lay the köfte on top, then pour over the sauce. Cover and cook for 10 minutes, turn off and leave to settle. Serve warm with bread and cacık (yoghurt salad).

The coastal towns of Ayvalık and Kuşadası are famous for their olives. You'll see the stunted, dusty-looking trees dotted all over the hills rolling down to the coast. The majority of the region's olives are pressed into service as oil for sale all over Turkey. Oranges, mandarins and tangerines clog the trees in winter; in summer look out for artichokes and figs. Interestingly, and for no particular reason, black-eyed peas are only used in this part of Turkey, turning up in soups, salads, pilavs and stews.

İzmir prides itself on seafood, figs and its international savoir-faire, stemming from decades as a NATO base. This means you can expect cheeseburgers, schnitzels and 'spaghetti wonderful' to appear in restaurants along with cover bands singing American Pie. Just as an example of how things change town to town, 'gevrek' is the word for **simit** (bread ring) here and sunflower seeds, called **ayçekirdeği** all over Turkey, are called 'çiğdem' in İzmir.

Afyon is an inland town famous for its **kaymak** (clotted cream) and confectionery. Afyon also means opium, which is appropriate as the region is a big producer of poppies. They're grown both for pharmaceutical use and for the poppy seeds, which are employed in place of nuts in some local breads, pastries and confections. The poppies are harvested early, to discourage any poaching, and the cuttings are harvested in government factories. The only locals who get to enjoy the narcotic effects of the homegrown crop are the cows, who always look pretty mellow as they chow down.

The cream from these cows is churned into precious kaymak, much of which turns up in the town's unmissable desserts. There are more sweet shops on Millet Caddesi than is probably decent – it can seem as though the locals needs extend only to the syrupy and sugary. Though the browser is likely to get a glucose rush from mere minutes of window shopping, that's no subsitute for sampling the local lokum or kaymak-clogged **kadayıf** (dough-based dessert). Though not strictly narcotic, many visitors become swiftly addicted and the stores at the bus station do swift business in Afyon toothrot for travellers stocking up before they depart.

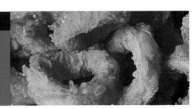

DON'T MISS

- İzmir's calamari
- The sweet shops of Afyon
- Aegean tangerines
- The fascinating Konak Bazaar

REGIONAL VARIATIONS

Mediterranean Coast

This long, rugged stretch runs from Bodrum east to Adana and south to Arab-influenced Antakya. Apart from a flat stretch between Antalya and Alanya, the coast is backed by the grizzled Taurus Mountains that push up to Anatolia. The Mediterranean coast is generally warmer than the Aegean, and the further east you go, the more humid it gets. In and around Antakya, Arab influences are much in evidence: Arabic is the first language in many families (though almost everyone speaks Turkish too) and the food has a distinctly Middle Eastern tinge.

It was a tradition until the mid-20th century for sea-level village dwellers to spend their summers on the plateaus. These seasonal migrations mostly took place on foot – only the elderly and infirm got a spot on a donkey – and were rich with ritual. For example, the journey could only begin after the mother had thrown cakes to her children from the back of a donkey. These days, many urban Turks have summer houses, sometimes

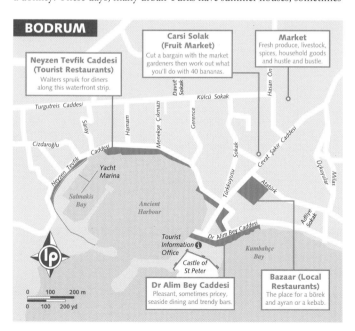

BODRUM

Neyzen Tevfik Caddesi (Tourist Restaurants)
Waiters spruik for diners along this waterfront strip.

Carsi Solak (Fruit Market)
Cut a bargain with the market gardeners then work out what you'll do with 40 bananas.

Market
Fresh produce, livestock, spices, household goods and hustle and bustle.

Dr Alim Bey Caddesi
Pleasant, sometimes pricey, seaside dining and trendy bars.

Bazaar (Local Restaurants)
The place for a börek and ayran or a kebab.

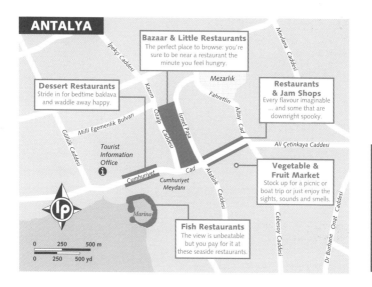

ANTALYA

Bazaar & Little Restaurants
The perfect place to browse: you're sure to be near a restaurant the minute you feel hungry.

Dessert Restaurants
Stride in for bedtime baklava and waddle away happy.

Restaurants & Jam Shops
Every flavour imaginable ... and some that are downright spooky.

Tourist Information Office

Vegetable & Fruit Market
Stock up for a picnic or boat trip or just enjoy the sights, sounds and smells.

Fish Restaurants
The view is unbeatable but you pay for it at these seaside restaurants.

Marina

İpekçi Caddesi
Mevlana Caddesi
Mezarlık
Fahrettin
Kazım Özalp Caddesi
İsmet Paşa
Allay Cad
Milli Egemenlik Bulvarı
Güllük Caddesi
Cumhuriyet
Cad
Cumhuriyet Meydanı
Atatürk Caddesi
Ali Çetinkaya Caddesi
Cebesoy Caddesi
Dr Burhane Onat Caddesi

0   250   500 m
0   250   500 yd

REGIONAL VARIATIONS

in the hills or in their family's old villages but also, in these air-conditioned days, by the seaside their forebears tried to avoid.

With a busy port and healthy tourism trade, Antalya is the commercial centre of the Med. Central Mediterranean fish, mostly enjoyed grilled, include **mercan** (red sea bream), **lüfer** (bluefish), **barbunya** (red mullet) and **palamut** (bonito). **Kefal balığı yumurtası** (grey mullet eggs) are farmed around Antalya. They're eaten fresh locally, but are also sealed in beeswax and sold across western Turkey. When the cadaverous wax package is sliced open, the soft pate-like eggs are scooped out and eaten with bread as a **meze** (hors d'oeuvre).

Antalya's favourite non-fish nosh is **tandır kebabı** (kebab cooked in a massive clay woodfire oven), usually made with sheep's head and served with **piyaz** (white bean salad) mixed with tahini. Further inland, the lake region around Isparta is known for its fragrant herbs and roses, mostly turned into rose oil and rose-water.

East of Antalya, Alanya lives with the pros and cons of being surrounded by some of the finest beaches in the country. You wouldn't think it to look at the multilingual restaurant menus lining the main drag, but Alanya is rich in local cuisine that is worth uncovering. Specialities include

Kısır (Bulgur Salad)

Ingredients

1	cup bulgur
³/₄	cup hot water
2	onions or 5 spring onions, finely chopped
2	tomatoes
3	tablespoons tomato salça
1	tablespoon red chilli salça
3	teaspoons red chilli flakes
150ml	olive oil
	juice of half a lemon
1	cup parsley, coarsely chopped
1	cup mint, coarsely chopped
	salt
	lettuce leaves

Put the bulgur in a bowl and pour in the water. Let stand for 20 minutes. Stir in the salça, chilli flakes, salt and onions (if using). Knead thoroughly. Add lemon juice and oil and knead again. Stir in peeled, chopped tomatoes, parsley, mint and spring onions (if using). Lay salad greens on a platter and arrange the kısır on top. Alternatively, spoon a little onto individual lettuce leaves for a DIY sarma.

Preparing kısır

Cinnamon sticks, Spice Bazaar, İstanbul

West Mediterranean coast near Kaş

hülüklü düğün çorbası (a thick, hearty soup of chopped tripe, meatballs, chickpeas and rice) and **laba** (a slab of ribs stuffed with mince, rice, nuts and vegetables). Laba is notorious for making you thirsty: it's a local joke to ask someone drinking a glass of water if they've been eating laba.

Alanya is also famous for its jam. Look in the shops along Cumhuriyet Caddesi for flavours you might expect – strawberry, apricot, cherry and orange – and some that might surprise – rose, watermelon, pumpkin, grapefruit, carrot and, of course, eggplant. Carrot also features in **cezeriye**, a lokum-style roll made with carrots and nuts.

Further east, Adana is where the Mediterranean spices up. Check out the chilli-heavy **Adana kebabı** (mincemeat worked into pellets and grilled on a skewer, served with onions, paprika, parsley and pide), often paired

A MYSTIC IN ALANYA

When the mystic, Nasrettin Hoca, came upon his son drinking water, he ridiculed him for wasting stomach space on water when he could be filling it with the magnificent Alanya food. Finishing his glass, the young upstart explained to his dad that he was drinking water to stretch his stomach so he could eat more delicious Alanya food than ever before. The Hoca, enlightened, immediately poured himself a drink. (See the boxed text Nasrettin Hoca in the Home Cooking & Traditions chapter.)

with **şalgam suyu** (turnip juice), which is itself often spritzed with chilli. Both the kebab and the juice are famously good with rakı. The steamy coastal orchards of this region are just right for growing citrus and tropical fruits. The region's melons are super, and Adana's watermelons are their premier product. This is the only part of Turkey which grows large quantities of mango, guava, kiwi, papaya, avocado and banana.

When the Mediterranean coast plunges south and makes a dash for Syria, the food gets distinctly Middle Eastern. The obvious sign is the sudden ubiquity of **humus** (chickpeas blended with sesame oil). Other hints include the move from rice to bulgur, grape pekmez to pomegranate pekmez and the fact that everything seems to pass through a chilli blizzard before it reaches your table. Specify 'acısız' (mild) if you don't fancy a spice session.

Muhammara (an oil-bound paste of bread crumbs, ground walnuts, pepper and cinnamon) is a common meze in this part of the country. You may also be served **kısır** (bulgur salad) patties as a welcoming dish, made here with pomegranate pekmez instead of lemon juice. Other signature dishes are **oruk köftesi** (boiled stuffed köfte) and **künefe** (sweet shredded pastry with cheese) made with walnuts instead of pistachios.

DON'T MISS

- Tasty tandır kebab
- Adana kebab with a turnip juice chaser
- Watermelon heaven
- A taste of the Arab world

Central Anatolia

Its position in the middle of Turkey makes central Anatolia a ripe candidate for culinary interpolation. The borders are therefore a little blurry – there are no lines on the ground showing where the centre gives way to the east or where the northern Black Sea strip begins. Nevertheless, there are some binding regional characteristics. The staple crop is wheat and yarma is used instead of bulgur in soups and stuffings.

Most of the countryside consists of plateaus and steppes, pushing up grass and greens and raising a mountainous fist here and there. Cappadocia, centred on Kayseri, has rich soil perfect for orchards and

KONYA

Mevlana Caddesi
Mevlana sekeri, a hard white candy, is the essential suckable souvenir.

Alaettin Bulvarı

Alaettin Tepesi

Şerafettin Caddesi

Alaettin Caddesi

Azizye Caddesi

Tourist Information Office ℹ️

Mevlâna Caddesi

Istanbul Caddesi

Teyfikiye Caddesi

Türbe Caddesi

Mevlana Muzesi 🏛️

Mimar   Muzaffer   Caddesi

Sircali Medrese Caddesi

Allaettin Tepesi (Teagardens)
All of Konya comes out for lazy evening tea drinking, cigarette smoking and gossiping sessions.

0   150   300 m
0   150   300 yd

Market Area
The old part of town has three mosques, a covered market, local lokantas and dozens of little shops.

DON'T MISS

- Kuşburnu pekmez for breakfast
- Amasya çorek
- Banquet fare of Konya
- Anatolian pizza

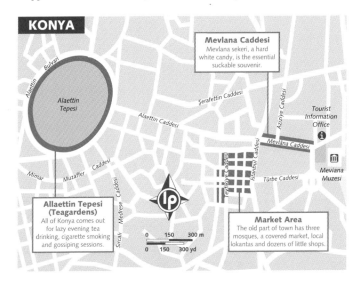

REGIONAL VARIATIONS

FOOD OF CLAY

Cappadocian man may not be made of clay but he sure likes eating food from it. The town of Avanos has been turning out red clay pots for centuries and they're still being snapped up for cooking and storing food. Squat clay pots are preferred for **güveç** (stew, cooked in a clay pot) while more elegant vessels are used for **testi kebabı** (pieces of lamb or chicken cooked in a mushroom and onion sauce). If you ask in advance, testi restaurants may be able to bake you up a private pot and smash it at the table in front of you.

---

vineyards, thanks to serious volcano action in time past. Throughout the region, winters are very cold, summers are very hot and the planting and picking shoulder seasons are delightfully mild. Rainfall tends to come in bucketing thunderstorms that flee as soon as they've dumped.

Villages are the staple community unit in central Anatolia, though the region also includes Ankara, the nation's capital, and the cities of Eskişehir, Konya, Kayseri and Sivas. Village dwellers tend to be conservative, kindly and heavily invested in the cycles of nature.

The town of Tokat has a revolving-door history, typical of Anatolia. No less than 14 states have left their mark on this town, including the Phrygians and the Mongol İlkhanids. Like its history, Tokat's **Tokat kebabı** is hard-core – lamb chunks, eggplant and potato slices and a head of garlic are impaled on a şiş and a gorb of lard is plonked on top. The skewers are then grilled vertically and as the fat melts, it dribbles over the charring kebab below. Tomato and chilli are cooked on separate skewers because they need less time to cook. When everything is ready, it's served on pide with a glass of **ayran** (yoghurt drink). If you decide to eat the garlic, it's quite acceptable to squeeze the flesh from each clove with your fingers. Tokat is also known for **zile pekmezi** (pekmez whipped with egg white).

Further south in Ürgüp, the über-kebab is **kiremit kebabı** (literally, tile kebab), a sizzle-up of finely chopped meat, onion, chilli and garlic on a flat clay tile. This is one of the few meat dishes that is served piping hot – the only time we burnt our mouths in Turkey was when tucking in here.

Böreks are extremely popular in this region, often baked in a tandır and filled with vegetables or meat. **Gözleme** (filled filo pastry) is a basic food throughout central Anatolia; the standard filling is gooey potato or cheese and parsley. Amasya does a very good **çörek** (ground walnuts baked in a fist-sized bun), much imitated but never bettered. This is also the town to look for wonderful concoctions that include **haşhaş** (poppy seeds), particularly **haşhaş sos** (poppy seed sauce) which is eaten with pasta and Ramazan baklava, and made only during Ramazan. Amasya is also known for its apples, pears and **kuşburnu** (rosehip) pekmez, delicious when eaten with bread for breakfast (or any time really).

Deep in Cappadocia, the town of Kayseri is known for its **mantı** (little pasta packages), served with a garlic yoghurt sauce. Nevşehir's stuffed quinces are a favourite winter dish and okra, both fresh and dried, is popular throughout the region.

As a Selcuk capital in the 13th century, Konya was the scene of banquets aplenty. The Mevlâna's emphasis on the spiritual aspects of cooking and eating contributed to the reverence in which food was widely held in Konya (see the boxed text Mevlâna and the Whirling Dervishes in the Culture of the Turkish Cuisine chapter). The combination of wealth and respect made this one of the best places in the world to get a good feed.

These days, there might not be a royal banquet everywhere you look, but there's definitely enough good stuff around to craft your own feast. Konya's specials include **fırın**

Mantı (little pasta packages)

kebabı (oven-cooked greasy lamb leg served on pide with onion), **etli ekmek** (long meat pizza), **saçböreği** (börek cooked on a griddle) and **Mevlâna şekeri** (white candy) also called **kavun şekerli** (melon sugar). In Konya there are stacks of sweet shops along Mevlâna Caddesi and at the bus station. Mevlâna şekeri makes a good gift as Turkish people generally hold Konya in some reverence.

Eastern & Southeastern Anatolia

Everything about this part of the country is extreme: the mountains, the heat, the cold, the hospitality and the generosity of its inhabitants. Most people live quiet rural lives on a small scale, procuring what they can from often parched fields and stock which get to nibble rather than graze. Many of the herders live semi-nomadic lives, staying on the plateaus all summer, tending to their sheep, goats and perhaps some bees, and moving down into a village for winter. Most of them will sell what surplus they have by the roadside rather than trek into market towns. Eastern Anatolia is home to the country's largest **Kürt** (Kurdish) population, who have maintained many of their traditions and recipes in the face of concerted assimilationist policies. One delicious Kurdish speciality is **Kürt köftesi**, a vegetarian dumpling made from bulgur, onions and mint.

Southeastern Anatolia is hot, rugged and proud, and so is its food. The local cuisine is imitated all over Turkey but it's worth making the effort to

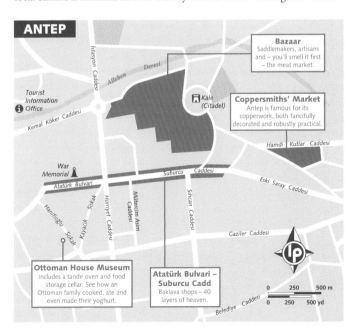

ANTEP

İstasyon Caddesi

Alleben   Deresi

Tourist Information Office

Kemal Köker Caddesi

Kale (Citadel)

Bazaar
Saddlemakers, artisans and – you'll smell it first – the meat market.

Coppersmiths' Market
Antep is famous for its copperwork, both fancifully decorated and robustly practical.

Hamdi   Kutlar   Caddesi

War Memorial

Atatürk Bulvarı

Hanifioğlu Sokak

Kayalık Sokak

Hürriyet Caddesi

Mü   Caddesi

Suburcu   Caddesi

Sihvan Caddesi

Eski Saray Caddesi

Gaziler Caddesi

Ottoman House Museum
Includes a tandır oven and food storage cellar. See how an Ottoman family cooked, ate and even made their yoghurt.

Atatürk Bulvarı – Suburcu Cadd
Baklava shops – 40 layers of heaven.

Belediye Caddesi

0   250   500 m
0   250   500 yd

try it here. Massive irrigation has turned what was a dicey region for crops into one of Turkey's richest agricultural zones. If it sprouts, ripens or grazes, chances are it's here: sheep, cows, wheat, lentils, chickpeas, onion, sugar, sesame, melons, peppers, spinach, nuts, olives, pomegranate and plums are all plentiful.

The fact that this region is at a cultural crossroads can be seen in its meze. **Soğuk** (cold) meze includes bitey Arab salads like **zeytin piyazı avrat salatası** (seedless green olives, parsley, onion, coarse ground walnuts, salt, red pepper, sour pomegranate and olive oil), humus, **abhkanuş** (baked eggplant chunks, garlic and yoghurt), **haydari** (yoghurt with roasted eggplant), **talatur** (parsley, tahini, garlic, yoghurt, oil) and the Mediterranean-style **bostana** (tomato and green chillies).

You don't need to make it as far east as Van and Kars to sample eastern produce. Van's **van otlu** (sharp, juicy cheese intermingled with grassy herb stalks) and Kars' **çiçek balı** (flower honey) are available as far away as İstanbul. You will have to go to Kars to sample an authentic **kete** (a Danish-style roll with spinach and nuts), though there are passable imitations elsewhere. Van is known for its love of egg dishes: **çılbır** (poached eggs and yoghurt) and eggy desserts crack up in many meals.

Erzurum, eastern Anatolia's biggest city, likes everything spicy. Meat is often marinated in chilli, as is the case with the fiery favourite, Erzurum kebab. Tortum, northeast of Erzurum, is credited with the **çatlak kebabı**, a horizontal döner which tends to come charred from all the sputtering.

Malatya, further south, is the apricot centre of Turkey. The fruit, dried and fresh, is rushed to every corner of Turkey where people ask for it by name. Malatya's **pestil** (fruit leather) and **küme** (pestil rolled up with nuts inside) are the best in Turkey – how so much flavour can be packed into such little strips is still a mystery to us.

Though **makarna** (pasta) is a big industry in this region, **fıstık** (pistachio) is the glaring star. Fıstık trees love hot weather and arid soil – just like the land around Antep and Siirt. The tasty nuts fetch a tidy sum, keeping these

HOME OF THE BRAVE

The reason we've got Antep fıstık from Gaziantep, Urfa kebabı from Şanlıurfa and Maraş dondurma from Kahramanmaraş is that these three towns were given resonant prefixes to their names in honour of their bravery in Turkey's War of Independence. Gazi means 'glorious', kahraman mean 'heroic' and şanlı means 'famous'.

Shepherd and flock, near Afyon

DON'T MISS

- Malatya, the apricot capital
- Van's grassy cheese
- Antep's baklava
- Kahramanmaraş' ice cream

communities housed and fed. The prized Antep fıstık are trucked to markets all over Turkey, but they're best fresh off the tree. People in Antep naturally use the nuts in a plethora of dishes, such as meze, meat and rice dishes and most of the region's killer desserts.

Urfa is notable for its zinging red chilli pepper. Called 'isot' in Kurdish, it's fried in oil then sun-dried to blackness. The town's coffee lore is also a lot of fun (see Coffee in the Drinks chapter). And your ayran often comes in a bowl to be supped with a spoon. If you've gone a few hours without eggplant and you're feeling a bit shaky, grab an **Ali Nazik kebabı**, where the heavenly vegetable is pureed with garlic and yoghurt, topped with minced beef or lamb and served with puffy **lavaş** (thin crispy bread). Otherwise, the straightforward **patlıcan kebabı** (kebab made with cubed meat or mince and eggplant discs), also known as **Urfa kebabı** should fix you for a while.

Çiğ köfte (spicy mince kneaded with bulgur for three or four hours, wrapped in a lettuce leaf and eaten raw with a squeeze of lemon) is one of those 'ya gotta try it if you're in the area' dishes. Be sure to choose a reputable, hygienic restaurant to eat your raw mince in, then do as the locals do and pair your köfte with a rakı chaser. Urfa is a good town to chow down.

Diyarbakır is so enamoured of its watermelons that it holds a festival in their honour in late September. The southeast also pumps out piles of grapes. Rather than being made into wine, they're largely eaten fresh or turned into pekmez or pestil, known as 'şire' around here. Pekmez made from **nar** (pomegranate) and **sumak** (sumac) is also popular, and is added to stewed meat dishes to give them a lemony kick. Olive groves are on the up, and here they're mostly harvested for cooking oil and soap. **Keme** (a local truffle) is collected in May if conditions are right. As well as being sauteed in butter, keme is lovely cooked up with meat chunks on a kebab.

Kahramanmaraş is famous for **Maraş biberi** (an aromatic chilli pepper which is crushed then rubbed with oil) and **dondurma** (ice cream). Why exactly Kahramanmaraş dondurma is so good is somewhat of a mystery. Some say it's because the local goats are so happy; indeed, we do think we saw a goaty grin on our drive into town. Some focus on the quality of the salep – most of Turkey's supply is grown in this part of Anatolia. Still others refer to the value of tradition: Kahramanmaraş has a long lineage of dondurma maestros. Whatever it is, it's ice cream worth screaming for. The best place to go for dondurma in Kahramanmaraş (and probably in all Turkey) is Yaşar Pastanesi, Kıbrıs Meydanı Trabzon Caddesi 2E. This place has been scooping since 1850; today it's a bit of a dondurma museum while remaining a favourite with the locals who turn up at any time of day for a cone or block. If you can't get over this way, look out for the Mado brand of ice cream, made in Kahramanmaraş and distributed all over Turkey.

Antep, what a great town for eating – after solid investigation we felt like overstuffed armchairs with extra cushions. The fresh produce is exceptional, most of it locally grown. In addition to the local specialities, Arab flavours and fads can make even the most ordinary lokanta a meal of discovery.

In Antep, pistachios turn up in **fıstıklı kebabı** (grilled köfte bound with ground pistachios). Antep's signature dish, however, is **içli köftesi** (fist-sized ground lamb and onion köfte with an outer covering of bulgur). **Simit kebabı** (mince mixed with bulgur and simit flour) is another stodgy staple.

Antep's sweets situation is very dangerous. The awesome **künefe** is an Antep speciality. This slow-baked, super-rich dessert consists of two rounds of kadayıf cemented together with cheese, swimming in syrup and dusted with pistachios. İmam Çağdaş, Eski Hal Civeri Uzun Çarşı 14, is the best place to overdose on baklava. The restaurant has been going since 1887, through three generations. You can sit down and scoff or take a box of baklava away with you. Unusually, it's also a grill house should you want a pre-baklava kebab.

Antep is also famous for its copper work, including kitchen gear. Pick up pots and pans, a semaver or cezve at the **Bakırcılar Çarşısı** (Coppersmiths' Market).

Künefe with cheese filling, insanely good

Black Sea Region

Lush and leafy, the Black Sea region sweeps west from İstanbul all the way to the steamy Pontic Mountains which push up to Georgia. Though the classic Black Sea resident is a fisherman and his fish-cooking wife, the Black Sea as a culinary zone incorporates the fin-free hinterland, which extends up to 200km inland, deep into feed-the-man-meat territory. Beef is at least as common as lamb here. The main crops are corn, apples, stone fruit, hazelnuts, poppy seeds and cabbage. The hills south of Rize are devoted to growing tea.

Legend has it that Ottoman nobles went hunting in the forests around the Black Sea town of Bolu and then had their kills prepared for them by the locals. So impressive were the meals that the cooks responsible were whisked off to the sultan's palace kitchens. These days, the white-hatted wooden-spooned tradition continues with a disproportionate number of Bolu-born chefs working in restaurants all over Turkey. In 1985, a cooking high school was inaugurated at Mengen, 45km from Bolu. The students mix regular classes with food theory and kitchen management and have

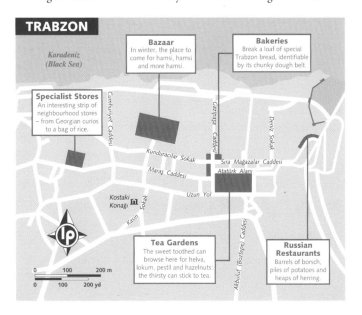

TRABZON

Karadeniz (Black Sea)

Bazaar
In winter, the place to come for hamsi, hamsi and more hamsi.

Bakeries
Break a loaf of special Trabzon bread, identifiable by its chunky dough belt.

Specialist Stores
An interesting strip of neighbourhood stores – from Georgian curios to a bag of rice.

Cumhuriyet Caddesi

Gazipaşa Caddesi

Deniz Sokak

Kunduracılar Sokak

Maraş Caddesi

Sıra Mağazalar Caddesi
Atatürk Alanı

Kostaki Konağı

Kaşın Sokak

Uzun Yol

Akbulut (Boztepe) Caddesi

0   100   200 m
0   100   200 yd

Tea Gardens
The sweet toothed can browse here for helva, lokum, pestil and hazelnuts; the thirsty can stick to tea.

Russian Restaurants
Barrels of borsch, piles of potatoes and heaps of herring.

Breads, Black Sea Coast

regular sessions whipping up wonky masterpieces in the kitchens.

Two of Turkey's tribal peoples are concentrated in the eastern Black Sea. The Laz are renowned fishers; **laz böreği** (a sweet custard börek) is available as far west as Trabzon. The Hemşin are great bakers. Many bakeries in the big Turkish cities are Hemşin businesses.

DON'T MISS

- Anchovy-a-rama
- Mountains of stone fruit
- Bread from Trabzon and simit from a stick
- Boat-shaped içli pide

It's a source of national amusement that Black Sea dwellers do everything with **hamsi** (anchovy). They sing songs, dance dances, pen poems about it – hell, they even *eat* the little tackers. You're liable to find hamsi in just about every dish that's baked, fried or fired – it's used in pilav, corn bread, it's stuffed, fried and stewed, portioned onto pide and stirred into omelettes. There's even **hamsi tatlısı**, a jellied sweet whose main ingredient is anchovy! Hamsi season is winter. In summer you won't get a real sense of how beloved they are, but salted hamsi will still be used in pilav and guveç. Other fish, most commonly **kefal** (grey mullet), **mezgit** (whiting) and **kalkan** (turbot) are available through the summer.

Much of the region's large corn crop is ground into **mısır unu** (cornflour) which is in turn made into corn bread. Wheat bread is still ubiquitous though. A Trabzon loaf is identifiable by being big and round, with a fat dough-ribbon plaited across the centre. The Trabzon **lahmacun** (Turkish pizza) is also round, with a thick crust. Black Sea **içli pide** is pinched shut like a covered dinghy. It can be made with vegetables and/or meat and onion and/or kaşar cheese. Gözleme here are folded into semicircles rather than thirds and are often filled with ingredients such as spinach, chilli and parsley. **Simit** (bread ring) sellers along the coast parade their wares on sticks rather than stacked up on a tray.

Stone fruit thrive along the Black Sea: cherries from Giresun are highly prized. Trabzon, Gumuşane and Erzincan are all known for their pestil and kume, mostly made with apricots. Black cabbage is a popular booster for soup and stews; cabbage leaves are also used for sarma instead of grape leaves. Due to an influx of Russian and Georgian immigrants to eastern Black Sea towns, it's not hard to find a bowl of borsch (cabbage-and-meat soup) or a plate of pelmini (meat dumplings in a pasta casing). **Tirmit**, a local wild mushroom, is found in autumn and eaten sauteed for breakfast. Locals swear by this mushroom's cure-all health properties. And in case you thought this was an eggplant-free zone, we've got to mention **Trabzon kızartması** (deep-fried eggplant with a garlic sauce).

shopping
& markets

Even if you have restaurant reservations for the rest of the week, you might find yourself coming back from the market with armfuls of produce. Not only is it hard to resist the colourful fresh fruit, the odoriferous herbs, the gleaming fish and the cheese (the cheese!), it's just about impossible to resist the merchants, many of whom are as enamoured of their goods as a Romeo at a Juliet convention.

Cheese vendor, Eminönü, İstanbul

Buying food in Turkey can be terrific fun. It's social and can be as leisurely as you like. The emphasis is on specialist vendors: if you go shopping with a Turk, she's likely to know each of the merchants – this is where she gets her cheese, this is her butcher and so on. This kind of continuity fosters lively discussions about the food and a genuine excitement about seasonal produce – everyone knows that the cucumbers are coming because they've been hearing of their progress for weeks.

Shopping is left largely to women, who buy fresh produce every couple of days or so. Dried foods are often bought in bulk and stored in the pantry, the cellar or on the balcony. In villages homegrown produce is augmented with goods bought at local markets or informally traded between households.

Most shops are open seven days a week from early morning until late evening. Wherever you end up shopping, prices are always marked and there's rarely any need to worry about being cheated. Most vendors are honest folk and will be much more likely to slip a few free apricots into your bag than to short-change you. However, to be on the safe side, it's best to familiarise yourself with the currency – and its bewildering strings of zeros – before you head out to market. It's easy to get confused when a bag of fruit and vegetables runs into the millions. Register receipts are not common but just about every vendor will happily show you the total amount on a calculator and, if you're still not sure, how much each item cost.

View from the Galata Tower, İstanbul

SHOPPING

MISIR ÇARŞISI (SPICE BAZAAR)

Nuts, fruit, sweets, Spice Bazaar, İstanbul

Mısır Çarşısı, also known as the Spice Bazaar, is situated in the heart of İstanbul. This beautiful building, its resonant history and its present-day fragrant bounty make this one of the world's breathtaking shopping experiences. The market was built in the 1660s to service the nearby Yeni Cami (New Mosque) – only 400 years old! Rent from the shops kept the mosque in paint and plumbing and contributed to its charities. At that time, the market lay at the end of many trade routes and was a magnet for weird and wonderful goods from all over the world.

The gunpowder (see the boxed text Folk Remedies in the Fit & Healthy chapter) and donkey's milk may not be there anymore but the spices are better than ever. They're laid out in the atmospheric arcades in big cane baskets, as colourful as a giant painter's palette. Alongside the spices, you'll find nuts, tea and a gasp-worthy confectionery selection. Specialist stores sell cheese, olives, meat and dried fruit. You can also find quail eggs (good for the throat) and **padişah kuvvet macunu** (sultan power paste), an aphrodisiac made from honey, bee pollen, royal jelly and 42 spices which enables the dosed up to make love five times a night (note that we weren't able to verify this).

As this is one of İstanbul's top tourist attractions, there's also a lot of knickknackery, week-old antiques and jewellery. Spruikers outside every stall have an uncanny ability to pick where you're from and shout out 'hello', 'bonjour', 'shalom' or 'gutentag' as appropriate. Unaccompanied women are likely to find browsing particularly draining. Insistent spruikers will stop you with ridiculous lines – prepare to be charmed or appalled. Among the sillier routines: the man calls after the woman: 'Wait! You dropped something!' and when she turns around, he clutches his hand to his chest and says breathlessly 'It was my heart'.

Mısır Çarşısı is open Monday to Saturday (8.30am-6.30pm). The streets around the covered markets are packed with little stores selling everything from ducklings to pot plants – you'll get more jostled but less hassled browsing around outside.

On the other side of the Golden Horn is the Balık Pazar, off İstiklal Caddesi, Beyoğlu. This is a much smaller market with an emphasis on fish but it also has an impressive selection of spices, confectionery and fresh produce.

At the Pazar (Market)

Markets are bustling, vibrant places with a lot of by-play and theatre as well as a profusion of wonderful food. The cheese seller solemnly offers you a morsel to try. The strawberry man presses glistening fruit into your hand with a secret agent smile. The watermelon vendor yells '**kesmek**' (I can cut it) implying that this melon is so good, he'll prove it by hacking it to bits on the spot.

There are two main types of market. The first is the purpose built market, with shop-like stalls. These are open between five and seven days a week, and are found in sizeable towns and cities. The second is the outdoor market, set up in a street or plaza once or twice a week, and found in just about every village or town. Big towns may have three or four such markets, each one in a different location. You are also likely to come across specialist markets, such as the must-experience fish market on the Bosphorus in İstanbul.

Some markets have no apparent logical layout: a T-shirt seller is set up next to a pile of potatoes which are next to a pots-and-pans vendor who is hard up against a fish van. Others are more ordered: the cheese, olive and salça sellers cluster together, the spice and nut sellers are in a row, the fish and meat sellers are set up in a line of refrigerated kiosks. A part of the scene may be devoted to livestock: goats stinking up a trailer, chickens clucking, lambs bleating, all available for inspection and sale. In larger markets, there may be a section set aside for market-gardener folk, peasants who have come to town with a bit of everything. These are great places to scout around for garden-fresh fruit & vegetables.

Stallholders are always more than happy for you to taste their wares. Ask '**tadına bakabilirmiyim?**' (can I taste it?) while pointing at what you want to try. If you show a particular interest in say, olives, it won't be long

SHOPPING

COME ON DOWN!

In villages, the **belediye** (council) places loudspeakers throughout the town to keep everyone abreast of municipal business and the arrival of merchants. If tempted by the opportunity to buy or sell, villagers come down to the town square with their wares or their cash and get straight into haggling. Tekel, the government body which controls the production and sale of alcohol, sends trucks to scores of villages, buying up grapes. It's not always that grand though: the belediye may also announce the arrival of an itinerant broom vendor, or a lost donkey.

before you've had about fifteen varieties offered to you by a delighted pur-
veyor. Sure, they want you to end up buying something, but Turks take a
genuine pleasure in sharing their culinary culture with interested visitors.

If you don't fill up on free samples, you can rely on ready-made food
vendors dotted between the produce stalls, who provide sustenance for the
hard work of shopping. The classic snack is **gözleme** (filled filo pastry),
made in front of you by bescarved women, but döner and **kokoreç** (grilled
intestines) are also market mainstays. Of course, you could always dip into
your own shopping bags to munch on a piece of fruit, or tuck into a bag
of nuts and raisins.

As well as the stallholders spruiking in front of their produce, there are
also roaming vendors trying to offload surplus goods. For example, you
might find a boy tagging alongside, imploring you to buy lemons. He'll
have a lemon between each finger, his hands splayed impossibly, insisting
on your serious need for citrus fruit while looking like he's about to do a
conjuring trick.

Fruit & nut seller, Balık Pazar, İstanbul

SHOPPING

This can get annoying. If you're really sure you don't want whatever it
is they're selling and you've said **hayır** (no) a hundred or so times, you can
bring in the gruffer **yok** (don't want it) and a sharp 'no' head jerk. Raising
your chin rapidly, rolling your eyes and clicking your tongue is the most
negative body language you can muster in Turkey – it's worth practising
before you head to market.

Bosphorus fish market, İstanbul

Food in markets is sold by the kilo and prices are usually marked. Though you'll find most food very reasonably priced to begin with, a bit of good-natured bargaining is possible if you're buying a reasonable quantity. Even so, bear in mind that the folk who've trucked their onions in from hand-hoed fields aren't exactly moguls.

Theft is rare in most markets but pickpockets do operate in the larger cities. Remain alert without getting paranoid.

Overall, hygiene is good and you shouldn't have any trouble finding fresh, clean food. If you're not used to Turkish tap water you might have short-term tummy troubles from washed fruit and vegetables – consider rinsing your purchases with bottled water. Be careful of poorly handled fish and meat: sometimes the only refrigeration is a bed of ice and the occasional hose-down.

Specialist Shops
Market (Grocer)

A **market** sells basic groceries, snacks and sometimes a small selection of fruit and vegetables. Core trade tends to be in soft drinks, cigarettes and biscuits but it's possible to scrape up a simple dinner from the various canned and packaged goods. Larger stores are likely to have a section with sacks of rice and beans and other dried goods which you can plunder for the exact quantity desired. You may also be able to purchase beer at these stores. A **bakkal** is another name for a market, though it's usually a smaller version.

Seyyar tüccar (mobile merchants) do neighbourhood rounds for those who can't get to the shops and markets. These can vary from a guy, a donkey and a cart full of strawberries to a mobile food store in the back of a refrigerated van.

Fırın (Bakery)

Also called an **ekmekçi**, the Turkish bakery provides the divine dough that fuels the human engine. It has an almost sacred air. Most bakeries churn out bread from before dawn to lunchtime, supplying corner stores and roving vendors, as well as selling direct to the public. The core item is springy crusty sourdough loaves that tumble from the ovens at regular intervals. As each batch is baked, gorgeous smells flood local nostrils, and the amount of happiness in the world is expanded. Such is the wonder of the Turkish bakery that you feel like either running in to salute the baker or sitting down in the gutter to weep at the sheer goodness of simple pleasures. Many bakeries also make **simit** (bread ring), **açma** (savoury bun), **poğaça** (flaky pastry) and biscuits.

Şarküteri (Delicatessen)

The name şarküteri is a patent transliteration of the French *charcuterie* and, though there's no *pâté*, the array is definitely ooh-la-la. As well as olives and pickles, this is the best place to come for **sucuk** (spicy beef sausage) and other cured meats. You may also come across **jambon**, a Muslim version of ham made from beef or chicken.

Sausage seller, İstanbul

Kasap (Butcher)

The local kasap will often be little more than a shopfront to a smallish abattoir. Animals are slaughtered out the back and their carcasses hung in the window, obviating the need for a sign. Some specialise in one type of meat; others will sell chicken, mutton and beef. If a whole beast isn't your bag, you can ask for the cut of meat you want and it will be cleaved expertly to order. Whether it's the head, the feet or a nice bit of rump, the cost is calculated by weight.

An **et pazarı** (meat market) is a larger butcher with supermarket-style trays of cut meat in glass cases. The whole set up is more removed from the kill; the butchering probably takes place in a back room or off site. The displayed meat is already cut, cubed, minced or marinated, and ready for cooking. There may be a şarküteri selection of cured meats too.

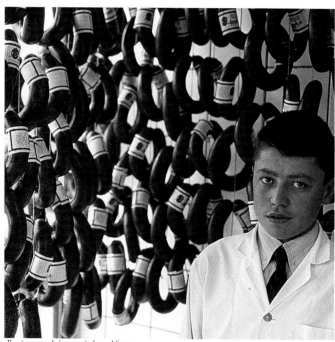

Boy in a sucuk (sausage) shop, Afyon

Round baklava, İstanbul

Pastane & Baklavacı (Pastry & Sweet Shops)

These delectable torture chambers draw in the unsuspecting by the skin of their sweet teeth. In a flash, the hapless victim has stocked up on calories from here to Friday but is still batting the eyelids at the gooey treats in the window. Basically, resistance is useless so you might as well enjoy.

A **Pastane** (pastry shop) sells **kuru pasta** (dry pastry) such as biscuits and cookies perfect for snacks, picnics and gifts, as well as **yaş pasta** (moist pastry), the cakes and syrup-soaked wonders which will have you swooning. Usually there will be tables where you can sit down and eat, and drinks (certainly tea and perhaps coffee) will be available. Some early openers also serve a simple cold breakfast. Though many pastanesi also sell baklava, true devotees get their layered lovelies from the specialist baklavacı.

Gıda Pazarı (Supermarket)

Well-stocked supermarkets can be found in all towns and cities. They are good for packaged food and bottled drinks but weak on fresh produce. This is about the only place in Turkey where you're liable to see a floppy carrot or a soggy tomato – stick to the produce markets.

The big national supermarket chains are Migros (look for the tuff kangaroo logo), Gima and Çetinkaya. The produce will be mostly Turkish, but if you are looking for a foreign brand, these are the stores to try. Many of them have serviced delicatessens and bakeries, variety sections and car parking so they can be a good bet if you want a one-stop shop.

SHOPPING

SPECIALIST STORES – WHERE THE GOOD EGGS GO

Some **özel mallar mağazası** (specialist stores) are almost surreal – imagine walking through a narrow doorway framed by egg cartons into a room piled floor to ceiling with teetering stacks of eggs. Any random traipse through an old shopping district will uncover such shops, some of them little bigger than cupboards: a man surrounded by halos of sausage, boys shimmering like apparitions in clouds of flour, or two blokes sitting in silence while cages of chickens chatter around them. You may not need three dozen eggs or a sack of flour on your visit to Turkey, but these stores offer a whole new world of window shopping.

Preserves, İstanbul

Things to Take Home

Though it would be brilliant to take a few bunches of cherries and a plate of iman bayıldı home, there are plenty of more logical culinary souvenirs which you can slip in your carry-on. Markets, especially İstanbul's **Mısır Çarşısı** (Spice Bazaar) are the best places to pick up jars of nut-embedded honey, apple tea, Turkish delight, nuts and **pestil** (fruit leather). Spices are a good choice too, as they don't take up much room in the bag and are often much cheaper than at home. Most packaged food can be taken across international borders but be sure to declare all food items to customs when arriving home.

Non-edibles also make great gifts or practical souvenirs. Şiş sticks, some of which have beautiful decorative handles, and coffee or tea pots are popular choices. If you've got a bit more money to spend and surplus room in the suitcase, you might consider engraved platters, copper saucepans and clay pots. Be warned though, many 'antique' items can be dated in weeks rather than years.

where to
eat & drink

You're faced with a plethora of choices when eating out in Turkey, from the most casual grill parlour with one thing on the menu, to the a la carte plenty of a five-star hotel. Wherever you end up, the food on offer and the prices you can expect tend to be obvious as soon as you walk in. The only surprise will be how consistently good the food is.

Where to Eat

Dining out in Turkey is a social affair. In particular, Turks have a long love affair with outdoor eating and drinking – Europe's open air restaurants and cafes have their origins in Ottoman Turkey. Whenever it's warm enough, restaurants and tea houses put extra tables on pavements and plazas, to be filled by sippers or diners. This is especially common in balmy seaside locations, where a string of seafood **meze** (hors d'oeuvre) and rakı will comprise a relaxed meal.

The concept of sitting down at a table for one is hardly normal in the urban centres, let alone in the country. For the average woman, especially in rural areas, eating out is restricted to special occasions or when travelling. Single women should look out for the **aile salonu** (family room) if the atmosphere in the main area is too oppressive. The aile salonu tends to be a sedate space, reserved for women and mixed groups. This is where young men bring their dates, where women eat alone or with their children and where families can sit down together.

One of the joys of eating out is that there's no need to order your whole meal at once. It's perfectly acceptable to order one or two small dishes, see how you go, and order more later if you're still hungry or tempted. Be careful of nibbles which appear on your table without you having ordered them; that innocent looking dish of nuts or olives may turn up on your bill at a ridiculous price. On the other hand, don't be paranoid about being ripped off – it is quite the Turkish thing to keep the food rolling until you say you've had enough. For example, if you order a plate of fruit to accompany your rakı, the fruit will usually be replenished for no extra charge. When in doubt ask '**bedava mı?**' (is it free?).

Lokanta

This is the basic Turkish restaurant, varying from starkly simple to homely and charming. The food on offer is mostly **hazır yemek** (ready food) laid out in dishes kept warm on hot ash or in a bain-marie. More often than not, the kitchen is open and visible, right behind the food.

Your table may be covered with butcher's paper or a tablecloth; water and bread will arrive and keep on coming as long as you sit there. Even if there is a menu (and usually there isn't), you should go up and choose whatever takes your fancy.

Most of the time the dishes won't be labelled so you can practise your Turkish or take pot luck. A normal spread will include a soup, an eggplant dish, a chickpea stew, maybe some beans and a few meat dishes (perhaps one chicken and a couple of lamb). Look out for seasonal vegetable dishes, which are delicious with garlic yoghurt. There will always be pilav available,

Roadhouse food: lamb stew, chickpeas and rice

either rice, bulgur or both. You might also get (or you can ask for) chilli peppers, lemon and raw onion with your hot dishes. These are good for refreshing your palate in between tastes. Although you can't count on getting dessert in your average lokanta, it's fairly common to find **kadayıf** (dough-based dessert) and rice pudding.

A city lokanta's core trade is lunch for workers and shoppers. Some lokantas close in the late afternoon or offer a smaller selection for dinner. In big cities, there are cafeteria-style lokantas complete with salad bar, open until late at night catering to students, and post-movie snackers.

On the highways, look out for **dinlenme yeri** (roadhouse eateries), open 24 hours in many cases, and serving surprisingly good ready-made dishes. Buckets of bread on every table belie the fill-'em-up-and-send-'em-on-their-way objective of such establishments.

Restoran

The line between a restoran and a lokanta can be blurry – a low end restoran is pretty much a lokanta under alias. But, as you move up the price scale, closed kitchens, menus and alcohol will appear. And where there is alcohol, there is meze. A cold meze display may be paraded on a trolley and you can select your desired morsels. There's a lot of crossover with main dishes at a lokanta and a restoran, but you're more likely to find **pirzola** (chops), **biftek** (steak) and 'international' meat dishes like schnitzel at a restoran.

WHAT'S YOUR PORSIYON?

Meat dishes are often sold by the **porsiyon** (portion). One portion is about 100 grams, enough to satisfy a moderate appetite. If you're hungry, ask for **bir buçuk** (one and a half); if you've been licking your lips at equine passers-by, ask for **iki porsiyon** (a double helping).

Typical büfe, İstanbul

Büfe

The büfe is a kiosk, a food stand, a store all rolled up into one. It's a place where you can certainly buy cigarettes, soft drinks, ice cream, crisps and confectionery, but perhaps also ayran, kebabs, fruit juice, sandwiches and even alcohol. You can not enter the büfe but you may be able to perch on a stool around its perimeter or you may be shooed away like a pesky puppy, kebab or no.

Kebabçı

These are low-key, cheap eateries focused on grilled or roasted meat, but usually offering soup, simple salads, cold drinks and ayran. Don't expect tablecloths or waiterly flourishes – these are quick-fire joints, specialising in high turnover and no-frills nourishment. A **köfteci** is similar in style, but the food staple is broiled meatballs rather than grilled kebabs. If you spot the word **ocakbaşı** in the menu or the eatery's signage, it means the food will be cooked in front of you.

Cooking kebabs, İstanbul

OI KOSHER B'GOSH

Though there are around 20,000 Jews in Turkey and a large community in İstanbul, there are no kosher shops or restaurants to be seen. The Orthodox Jewish shechita method of slaughter is similar to the Muslim **halal** method: the throat of the animal is cut and the blood is drained from the body. Even so, practising Jews in Turkey may prefer to eat purely vegetarian dishes. Those who continue to eat meat can at least be sure of not eating pork by accident. And meat is usually cooked in vegetable or animal fat rather than butter, but you will need to look out for meat cooked with yoghurt. Shellfish are never hidden in places you wouldn't expect, but **kalkan** (turbot) does turn up in a number of dishes.

Pideci

The Turkish version of the pizza parlour is a slice of heaven if you're after quick and tasty belly fuel. Choose your **lahmacun** (pizza) from cheese and various meat toppings and sit back with an ayran or a cola, or get a lahmacun **paket** (wrapped to go). Look for places using woodfire ovens – the pide always tastes better.

Pide with fillings

Börekçi

These places are a big favourite of ours. A börekçi is often a tiny window in the wall or a cupboard-sized kiosk with a few stools and benches. The only stuff on sale here is a few different types of **börek** (pastry dish)and a small selection of cold drinks, ayran always among them. They're a great place for a quick breakfast or lunch or a between meal carbo tweak. Börekçi stock is often sold out by mid afternoon.

Tourist Restaurants

In tourist towns, you'll come across strips of homogeneous restaurants supposedly catering to the tourist trade. Spruikers greet passers-by with a spray of 'good evening, guten abend, bonsoir' and wave multilingual menus under their noses. These places serve spaghetti, burgers, pizzas, steaks and chicken prepared 30 different ways. But even with bastardised food, the Turkish produce is good enough to elevate the meals. In some tourist areas, competition is so keen that you can score meal deals including a free beer or cocktail. Sometimes the hustling can be a bit much; saying '**şimdi yedik**' (we've just eaten) might be helpful in deflecting the attention of insistent greeters.

Tourist areas and big cities are the easiest places to find international cuisine. İstanbul, Ankara and many coastal resorts have a pretty good selection of foreign restaurants catering to cosmopolitan locals, expats and travellers who have overdosed on kebab. There's everything from Chinese, Japanese and Indian to Mexican and Italian. Boring McWhoppers and their ilk can be found, or avoided, on major highways and in most of the larger towns.

Hotel Restaurants

Overwhelming buffets are the norm in hotels. Expect a selection of soups, a vast array of cold dishes, a slew of warm meat dishes, too many desserts to deal with and substantial fruit platters. The cuisine will be slanted to the nationality of the bulk of the hotel's guests but will always include some Turkish favourites.

Hotel food can be exceptionally good as Turkey's most qualified chefs work almost exclusively in hotel restaurants. It's a shame that they're serving food to people who are often more interested in the beach or the bar scene than the food.

Elaborate and outlandish fruit, vegetable, butter and ice carvings are very big in Turkish hotel restaurants. Though most of them are floral or abstract, some are representative. The best one we saw was a formation of plucked uncooked chickens, positioned on tiny chairs in jazz band formation with tiny musical instruments carved from carrots and radishes.

Most two-star hotel rooms will have a minibar. Once you get up to three stars, you can even count on the fridge being plugged in and the drinks being cool. The bare minimum stock is still water, soda and cola. Some hotels make it a bit more exciting by adding fruit juice, beer, nuts and biscuits, both sweet and savoury. Refreshingly, most Turkish hotels desist from insane mark-ups on minibar goods. It's only the real marble-bathroom five-star hotels that can't resist. If there's a complimentary basket of fruit by your bedside, it's a fair sign that the price tags on the drinks in the fridge will be inflated.

View from Side Pension, Sultanahmet, İstanbul

Tatlıcı

It's normal for a main meal at a restaurant to lead onto the tatlıcı, a specialist dessert place. As well as the classic tatlıcı, where you can overdose on baklava, helva and lokum, look out for the **muhallebici** for milk-based puddings, and the **pastahane** (or **pastanesi** or **baklavacı**) for baklava, European-style cakes, ice cream and any local specialities.

Understanding the Menu

Sometimes the most difficult thing about the menu is finding it in the first place. Even if there is a menu, diners so rarely consult it that the waiters won't think to offer it to you. Ask '**menünüz var mı?**' (Is there a menu?) but keep in mind that a menu that emerges from a dusty drawer may not be the most accurate reflection of what's coming out of the kitchen.

Many restaurants specialise in one or two dishes so a menu would be as minimal as a haiku poem. In many cases, the restaurant's name will be all a menu requires. **Mutlu Çorba ve Lahmacun Salonu** (Mutlu's Soup and Pizza Place) is self-explanatory; this isn't the place to order a fish kebab.

The average lokanta may not bother with menus. The open kitchen tradition is much more descriptive anyway. It also bypasses most problems with translating from the Turkish – you can see, smell and probably even taste the food before ordering.

Eateries are obliged to display their tariffs, so if there isn't a menu there will be a price list on the wall. However, such a list will only tell you the types of dishes (soups, grilled meats, cold drinks, desserts) and their cost. But even this sketchy catalogue can help the uninitiated work out what kind of dishes are on offer, if not their exact composition.

Think of menus as a catalogue of possibilities rather than promises. For starters, seasonal variety lessens their efficacy: restaurateurs cook with the best produce available so if something is not in season then it's probably not in the kitchen.

The first section on menus will be meze, listed under either **mezeler** (the plural of meze), **soğuklar** (cold things), **ördövr** (hors d'oeuvre), **başlangıçlar** or **girişler** (starters). On more detailed menus, meze might be subdivided into **zeytinyağlı** (cooked in olive oil), **dolmalar** (stuffed vegetables), **sarmalar** (stuffed leaves) and **salatalar** (salads).

stew.ediamb.veretaite
Stuffed lamb.rice
Stuffed chickey
Egebplant.kebab
Egep ant.kebab
Roast.chicken
Hot.vegetable.d'shes
Ege.plant.vith.minle meat
Assoped vegetabees
Stuffed.marrov
Stuffed pepper.ordomato
Pure.sp nace .. Grefen peas
Cold.vegetables
String beans
Artihoke
Charcohal grill
Camb.shish.kebab
Lamb.chaps
Fillet.of.the.lamb
Fillet.steak
Veal.grill.chops.orentre.
Grilleb.steak

Strange Anglo-Turk menu board, İstanbul

WHERE TO EAT & DRINK

Main dishes may be called **ana yemekler** but more often they'll be divided into **ızgaralar** (from the grill) and **kazan yemekleri** (from the pot). **Tatlılar** are sweet dishes. **Meşrubatlar** or **soğuk içecekler** (cold drinks) and **sıcak içecekler** (hot drinks) will take up the back page or bottom section of the menu. If the restaurant serves **şarap** (wine), there will usually just be a choice of **kırmızı** (red) and **beyaz** (white). Restaurants tend to carry just one brand of beer, so the generic **bira** will be all that appears. The most expensive restaurants have extended wine lists with international selections.

Menus rarely describe a dish's ingredients, let alone whether it's vegetarian, low fat or spicy. Seasonality and chef's inspiration result in terms like **çeşitleri** (different things) and **ve diğerleri** (other things). You'll see these words a lot – they are an invitation to talk to the waiters or visit the kitchen to see what's cooking. You may also see **mutfağımızdan** (from our kitchen) and **şefin tavsiyeleri** (chef's specials). Some places have a cycle of daily specials (Tuesday is içli köfte day) that are always worth trying.

Multilingual menus are the norm in hotel restaurants and places that cater to foreign visitors. Some seaside resorts have menus in a huge variety of languages: as well as Swedish, German, Dutch, English, French and Spanish we even spotted a restaurant with a Sami menu.

There should never be an extra charge for tax on your bill as the law requires that it be included in any listed price. **KDV dahildir** (tax included) sometimes appears on a menu. In more upmarket restaurants, it's becoming common for service to be added to your bill. If **servis** (service) or **garsoniye** (service charge) isn't indicated, you can ask 'servis dahil?' (is service included?). If not, it's normal to leave a 10-15% tip at upmarket places.

Your bill will often be presented folded in half with the total written on the back – this is common practice all over Turkey and there's no problem with opening it back up and checking your waiter's sums. It's usual to get an itemised bill.

ONE COMPLICATED JUICE, PLEASE

Certainly, it's good business practice to advertise your products in a language most travellers are going to understand, but Turkish versions of English can raise a giggle. How about the fresh juice stand where you can choose from 'orange, apple, carrot or complicated juice' or the chicken döner available 'normal breed' or 'Turkish breed'. Fowl also features in chicken roulette. The cutest we've seen, though, is a menu describing **işkembe çorbası** (tripe soup) as 'paunch soup'.

Vegetarians & Vegans

Though it's normal for Turks to eat a vegetarian meal, the concept of vegetarianism is quite foreign. Veganism may as well mean a preference for eating peanut butter horseshoes for all it's understood. There is a sprinkling of vegetarian restaurants in the big cities and resorts, frequented almost entirely by foreigners and students, but the travelling vegetarian certainly can't rely on specialist restaurants.

Luckily, it's not too hard to avoid meat and fish in Turkey as the fauna is usually cooked separately from the flora. Meat free salads, soups, pastas, omelettes, pastries, and hearty vegetable dishes are all readily available. Ask 'etsiz yemekler var mı?' (is there something to eat which has no meat?) to see what's available.

People will often be curious about your eating habits and will ask you to explain the reasons for your abstinence. You'll also hear a lot of well-meaning comments like 'but it's only a little bit of meat'.

The main source of inadvertent meat eating is **et suyu** (meat stock) which is often used to make otherwise vegetarian pilavs, soups and vegetable dishes. Your hosts may not even consider et suyu to be meat, so they will reassure you that the dish is vegetarian. Ask 'et suyu var mı?' (is there meat stock in it?) to check. Other things to be wary

Tomatoes, İstanbul street market

of are flour dumplings which may be mixed with small quantities of mince and stray bits of meat dropped from a passing spoon into vegetable dishes. Chicken is the biggest hide-and-seeker in Turkish food, lurking in salads, meze and puddings. Be suspicious of anything yellow and unidentifiable, and steer well clear of **tavuk göğsü** (chiken breast pudding, see the boxed text Spooky Desserts in the Staples & Specialities chapter).

Most vegetable dishes are cooked in olive oil rather than butter so they should be fine for vegans, so long as meat stock isn't added (though the further east you go, the more you should suspect the use of butter). Vegans need to look out for yoghurt, usually served on the side of vegetable dishes but often mixed into soups. Cheese is rarely used in cooking, except in böreks and gözleme. Böreks and baklava should be made with butter, but they can be made with margarine, so you could investigate. Egg glazes are usual but not a foregone conclusion for pastries. Forget about soy products or tofu – they just aren't available.

Where to Drink

Drinking out is a national obsession – just about every urban Turk makes regular visits to a tea garden for a few social cups of tea and a bit of people watching. And if they don't go out for tea, the tea will come to them: waiters roving the tea garden often make excursions into the wider neighbourhood to deliver their brew to the office or shop-bound thirsty. Coffee and alcohol drinking establishments are generally reserved for he-who-wears-the-pants; the home delivery angle extends to coffee but not to booze.

Çayhane and Çay Bahçesi

The **çayhane** (tea house) and **çay bahçesi** (tea garden) are Turkey's shared lounge rooms and balconies; social spaces where people can meet, chat, play games and sip on endless cups of dark, sweet tea. Any place that people are likely to visit will have a tea house nearby – it's an unwritten law that any Turk must be able to get tea anywhere at any time.

Most tea houses will have normal tea, apple tea and some soft drinks. Some give you the choice of a **küçük bardak** (small cup) or **büyük bardak** (big cup). A büyük is sometimes called a **duble** (double). The **çaycı** (tea seller) will do the rounds periodically but there's no problem sipping from one drink for as long as you want. In summer, waiters may run around spraying water over the ground – not to drown ants, but to keep the dust down. Don't worry about getting peckish – simit and other snack sellers usually wander by, catering to those who want to snack and sip.

Tea gardens will sometimes have an **aile çay bahçesi**, an area set aside for families and ladies alone. When it's busy, women can sit at tables with women they don't know and men can join other men. Sitting down with someone of the other sex that you don't know is not really appropriate. **Koza** (cocoon) tea gardens are in enclosed squares and they can be very charming. If you're in Bursa, be sure to visit the koza near the covered market.

There's really no better way to get the flavour of Turkey than to slug back about ten cups of tea in such a setting. Breezy outdoor atmosphere melds with intellectual gravitas. Men sit down with their newspapers and their opinions, students bat ideas around, women share stories and strategies, soldiers write letters home, children pester their parents for ice cream, old men doze off chin to chest. It's purposeful relaxation at its very best.

Kahve

The **kahve** (coffee house) is usually a dingy place without a name or signage, furnished with cigarette-scarred tables and football posters. Inside you'll find blokes sitting around talking, reading the paper or playing okey or backgammon. Despite its name, the predominant beverage of the kahve is

Mystical water pipes & tea gardens, İstanbul

tea. Many men spend hours every day at the kahve, if not inside then out front watching the passing trade and traffic. An outsider entering will be a cause for great excitement; if the outsider is a woman, the locals will be struck dumb with surprise. But if you know the rules of okey (see the boxed text Okey-dokey, Let's Play later in this chapter), you'll probably end up having fun.

Meyhane

Also called **birahane** or **pub**, the meyhane is a drinking place that also does food. Almost entirely a

Tea drinker, Milas, South Aegean

male domain, women brave enough to enter are likely to be looked at so askance that it's sideways. You can also expect ratty posters of scantily-clad ladies on the walls and a TV tuned to a soccer match. The main point of being at the meyhane is to drink and talk – every man here will have half a bottle of rakı at hand and he'll serve himself generous nips, topped up with water or ice.

Even the scungiest bar will have a bowl of nuts for patrons to pick at while they're drinking. As you go upscale, the bowl of peanuts will include chickpeas, sunflower seeds, pistachios and hazelnuts. The coolest bars will have the standard nibbles, but you might also come across weird snacks like carrot sticks dipped in orangeade. Some bars have a wider range of food (such as grilled meat, meze and salad), which is eaten communally. Often individual diners don't have their own plates so eating is a simple matter of forking straight from the central platter. At some point in the evening, someone is sure to break out into drunken song.

There is another modern, city version of the meyhane, loosely equivalent to the European tavern, where mixed company is not so rare. You should be able to tell if you've struck one of these with a brief peek in the door.

Gazino

Also a drinking and eating place, the gazino may feature mixed company but in a super seedy setting. Particularly along the prostitute-prone eastern Black Sea, gazinos tend to suggest the possibility of arriving as a one and leaving as a two. Eating isn't the main thing at these places but meze and grills are available.

İŞKEMBE ÇORBASI (TRIPE SOUP)

Turkey's most famous soup is a pungent slurp fest made from chopped lamb's tummy. It's not to everyone's taste, but if you can stomach it, a visit to the **işkembeci** (tripe soup eatery) is an essential element of any carnivore's visit to Turkey.

İşkembe Çorbasi, tripe soup

Some say you might as well sup a bowl of sweaty wool boiled up with old boots sauteed in rancid butter. We suggest these infidels didn't have enough rakı before tucking in. Because, according to işkembe mythology, a bowl of post-bender tripe soup will ward off a hangover. This is why many işkembe eateries stay open past dawn, catering to pubbers evicted after last drinks, partygoers cooling down from the last dance and assorted bar-hoppers and tipplers hoping to round off the night with a sobering bowl of belly. Though the physiological benefits of tripe soup haven't been unravelled by science, cynics have suggested that it's a form of culinary shock therapy: once the tipsy taste it, they realise how bad their judgement must have been for them to order it and they're shocked into sobriety!

Garlic, vinegar and chilli are the soup's usual accomplices. Sometimes you'll be asked if you want them heated with the soup, otherwise, they'll be sitting on your table for you to administer yourself. When you've finished your soup, you'll be given some breath-freshening cloves to chew upon.

The fact that Turks visit tripe soup restaurants when they've had a few can make them pretty rowdy places. And as it's mostly men doing the drinking (and night-crawling), they can also be very male-dominated – unaccompanied women should stick to less divey restaurants with an **aile salonu** (family room). The upside is that işkembeci waiters are likely to know some amusing and amazing tricks with matches, forks, toothpicks, even the vinegar bottle. Ask **'Hile biliyor musun?** (Do you know any tricks?) to see if your waiter is a budding illusionist.

OKEY-DOKEY, LET'S PLAY

Okey is a rummy-style four person game played with tiles numbered 1-13, in black, red, blue and yellow. There are two of each piece plus two jokers, making a total of 106 tiles. Tiles are scored at face value.

Each player starts with 13 pieces; the aim is to be the first to get rid of all tiles.

One tile is taken each turn unless you can 'meld'.

Melding: a new group must be a suite of at least three consecutive tiles of the same colour or at least three tiles of different colour with the same number. Each player's first meld must add up to at least 25 points in new groups but after your first melding, you can add single pieces to existing groups.

You are allowed to rearrange tiles already on the table to help you get rid of more. For example, if you take a red 5 from a group of four 5s, then add it to a 6-7-8 red run, you will be able to put down your red 4. In rearranging, remember that every suite must always comprise at least three tiles.

A joker can act as any other tile (and scores the value of the tile it replaces), but it can only be moved if it is replaced with the tile it is posing as.

Runs can go from 13 to 1, but not further (ie. 12-13-1 is okay, but 13-1-2 is not).

The first player to get rid of their tiles wins all the points in the other player's hands. A joker in hand is worth 20 points.

Sometimes games are played for money, but more often the loser buys everyone playing, and all those watching, a glass of tea.

Playing okey, İstanbul

Tea drinkers, Old Bazaar, İstanbul

Children

Turkey is a family-oriented society and children are welcome in nearly all situations. Turkish children are usually the responsibility of their female relatives, so anywhere a woman would go, children can be found too. Patrons in an obviously male retreat, like a kahve or a meyhane, will look twice at a father bringing in his child, though there's no rule against it. Turks are tolerant of children and won't be outraged by a grizzly toddler, though it must be said that Turkish children are more used to sitting quietly in 'adult' situations than many of their western counterparts.

Restaurants never have special menus for children, but because ordering Turkish food is often a mix and match affair, it's easy to create child-sized portions from the different dishes mum and dad order. High chairs or booster seats are rarely available – kids too small to sit on regular chairs can generally be found on their parents' laps.

Typical foods given to Turkish babies include yoghurt, fruit (fresh, compotes and conserves), and semolina. Many parents swear by **pekmez** (fruit syrup) mixed with just about anything. Bread dipped in pekmez is a favourite breakfast or a never-fails-to-shut-'em-up snack. Mixing pekmez with yoghurt or semolina makes for an instant dessert. Hazelnut and chocolate spread is very popular for breakfast or snacks (and not just with kids). **Pestil** (fruit leather) is always good to have on hand – it's chewy, nutritious and doesn't look anything like fruit. The Turkish emphasis on fresh produce extends to baby foods. Larger supermarkets stock baby formulas and some jars of baby goo, but don't rely on finding this stuff outside major towns.

Children's sensitive tummies are more prone to reacting against local water. Even if you're drinking tap water yourself, you might consider keeping the kids on the bottled stuff. Having them eat yoghurt (or ayran) will provide some protection against bacteria.

street food

You'll never need to be out, about and hungry for long in Turkey. In fact, you can eat only from street vendors and maintain a delicious, healthy and wallet-friendly diet. Some of Turkey's most typical foods are almost exclusively available from kiosks and roving merchants. Also, as keen travellers themselves, the Turks have elevated eating-on-the-run to more than mere refuelling.

STREET FOOD

The ubiquitous vendor is the **simit** (bread ring) man, seen all over the country from busy city thoroughfares to freeway toll booths and sleepy village bus stations. He may display his chewy bread rings in a glass trolley, on a flat top pushcart, on a tray balanced on his head, in a basket tucked under an arm or strung from his limbs in great hoops. As well as the classic sesame seed topped simit, your choice may include **açma** (a soft O-shaped roll) and **çatal** (lip-shaped and seed-studded bread). The sweet version is **tulumba tatlı**, a fluted fried fritter served in sweet syrup.

Other common street offerings include corn on the cob (roasted or boiled), mussels (either in the shell or battered, fried and skewered), sandwiches (usually white cheese and tomato), fruit, ice cream, nuts (including roast chestnuts in season) and seeds. In larger towns, especially if there's a university or a military base around, you're likely to strike popcorn and baked potatoes with a slew of possible toppings.

Roving kebab and **dürüm** (kebab rolled in pide) sellers sometimes turn up at outdoor tea gardens. **Gözleme** (filled filo pastry) is the snack found at fruit & vegetable markets, and is perfect for rejuvenating tired shoppers. This is one of the few times you'll buy cooked food from a woman.

Drink vendors are a common sight in the streets, plazas and bus stations of Turkey. There are roving boys selling bottled water and sumptuously costumed cherry juice sellers with ornate dispensers strapped to their backs. In winter, vendors of cool drinks may switch to salep or **boza** (fermented millet drink, see the boxed text).

In summer, look for dondurma sellers attacking their tubs of ice cream with metal rods and (literally) drumming up trade. The best fairground purveyors of iced niceties make a real performance of it. Pre-packaged ice cream in familiar shapes and flavours is widely available from wheelie freezers outside eateries.

BOZA – PORRIDGE IN A CUP

Boza is a thick, nourishing winter drink made from fermented barley or millet. It's a little like drinking tangy liquid porridge. There's evidence that the Central Asian nomads of the 4th century enjoyed a version of boza, making it one of the oldest surviving Turkish foods.

These days it's mostly sold from special boza booths or on the street. The classic boza accompaniment is a handful of dried chickpeas; you can also sprinkle your boza with cinnamon. If this isn't enough incentive, boza is rich in vitamin B and, if you're forced to skip a meal, it's a good way to keep you going until dinner time.

Simit seller, Old Bazaar, İstanbul

BOSPHORUS FISH SANDWICHES

Eating fish sandwiches, Ferry Terminal, Eminönü, İstanbul

Şimdi İstanbul'da olmak vardı Boğazda balık ekmek yemek.
Now I wish I was in İstanbul eating a fish sandwich by the Bosphorus.

This song of love is dedicated to İstanbul's legendary fish sandwiches, which are sold from little fishing craft moored right by the ferry terminal on the Eminönü side of the Galata Bridge. Bosphorus fish fillets are woodfire-grilled on the deck of the boat, wrapped in a bread roll and handed up to the waiting, salivating commuter. It's a mysterious fact that fish bought direct from a Bosphorus boat tastes better than fish bought anywhere else.

If fish isn't your dish, at least buy a simit and play seagull trainer. This highly entertaining sport proceeds as follows: once the ferry has pushed off, you break beak-sized pieces from the simit and throw them to the seagulls. The seagulls are well apprised of their role, swooping from nowhere to catch every piece before it hits the water.

Eating on the Road

Turks are great travellers and they wouldn't dream of succumbing to thirst or hunger en route. There are three sources of road trip snackery: the picnic of simit or börek and nuts or fruit that the passenger packs; roadstop stock-ups of döner, lahmacun and simit; and (if on a bus) the stream of coffee, tea, soft drinks and packet sponge cakes offered by the conductor.

Every long bus journey will be punctuated with stops at a **dinlenme yeri** (roadhouse) where the minimum offering will be tea, lokanta-style food and confectionery. Most passengers just have a cup of tea (or three) and watch the entertaining bus washers wielding broomsticks with strap-on hoses, rapidly turning the dusty bus into a soaped up highway limousine.

You need only step into a Turkish bus station to see how commonly sweets are bought as gifts. Many towns are known for a particular sweet and the road stops will be stacked with whatever it is. In İzmit, it's **pişmaniye** (a hairball of stringy candy); at Bursa it's **kestane şekerli**, (sugar soaked chestnuts); at Konya it's **Mevlâna şekerli** (atrophied marshmallow lollies); and at Safranbolu, it's technicolour lokum roll-ups.

If you have your own transport, you're in the enviable position of being able to stop at the fresh produce stalls by the side of the road. Somehow it seems that the cherries are sweetest, the oranges juiciest and the honey most ambrosial when you buy direct from the person who grew the stuff.

Sandwich stand, Eminönü, İstanbul

A Turkish Picnic

Turks are enthusiastic, expert picnickers and there are thousands of **piknik yeri** (picnic grounds) dotted throughout the country. Some are as simple as a slab table slapped under a tree, some have fireplaces, running water, toilet facilities and shaded seating areas. Some riverside picnic areas even have tables and benches planted in the shallows so people can eat while dangling their feet in the water. There are also government owned pavilions, often in very picturesque locations, which can be rented by the day for bigger parties.

The usual plan of attack is for two or three families to decide who's going to bring what, then they'll drive in convoy to the picnic spot. Everyone brings some food, either prepared at home or ready for cooking on the fire.

Family picnic at Emirgan Park, İstanbul

Typical picnic foods include bread, cheese, nuts, stuffed vegetables and different meats, either cold cuts or pieces ready for grilling on a fireplace or a portable **mangal** (grill). **Kuru köfte** (dry meatballs) are very popular because they are firm enough to travel well in the hamper. The köfte are mixed and rolled at home then fried in olive oil on site. Fruit and sugar-coated nuts round off the meal. Everyone pitches in to make the picnic happen: the kids clear the picnic site of debris, the men spark up the barbecue and cook the meat, the women prepare the side dishes and the oldies sit back and direct traffic. Picnics can last from lunchtime until well into the evening. As it gets dark, someone will light a fire and inevitably the rakı will come out. Expect fireside singing, dancing, loud talk and laughter.

Edibles are just part of the deal. Sometimes it looks like a Turkish family could easily set up house with what they bring along for an afternoon in the park. As well as chairs, cushions, rugs and games (cards, maybe a volleyball net, definitely a soccer ball), there will be a tea **semaver** (urn), music (rarely live, sometimes portable, often blaring from the car) and even electric lights.

Unfortunately, many long and lingering picnics leave a residue of litter. If there isn't a bin on site, make sure you carry your rubbish out with you. Also, be careful of drivers who have had too much rakı.

To plan your own picnic, pick up supplies from a pazar, gıda pazarı or şarküteri. Your spread doesn't have to be elaborate: bread, cheese, olives, fruit and something to drink are about all you need. İstanbul's **Emirgan Parkı** is a wonderful place to head with your nosh and your blanket – as well as grassy, shady picnic spots there are tea gardens, a couple of stately restaurants and, on summer weekends, hundreds of Turkish families for you to befriend.

PICNICKING WITH NASRETTIN HOCA (Turkey's Famed Mystic)

One day the Hoca and his friends decided to go on a picnic. They discussed who would bring what: one said 'the meat is on me', another said 'the chickens are on me', another said 'fruit and vegetables are on me'. The Hoca broke in, 'friends, it seems we are well provisioned for our picnic now. So for my part, may I add that, should this feast last for years and I miss a single day of it, let the curse of Allah be on me'. (For more on the Hoca see the boxed text Nasrettin Hoca in the Home Cooking & Traditions chapter.)

Lowbrow Snacks

Soft drinks, potato crisps, corn chips, cheesy puffs, chocolate and chewing gum are widely available and consumed throughout Turkey, both in readily recognisable international packaging and in their Turkish incarnations. Young people are the main consumers of junk food, with the exception of sweet fizzy drinks which are sunk with a passion by just about everyone. In fact, such is the enthusiasm for lolly liquids that a request for water when there's cola at hand is regarded as the sign of a brain gone slightly soft. Diet drinks are freely available for those concerned about their sugar intake. Businesses sell either Pepsi or Coca Cola, so if you know you aren't part of the Pepsi Generation, suss out what's fizzing before you sit down.

THE PICNIC WARS OF KONYA

Just by wandering the streets of Konya, it was clear to us that we had left the seaside strip. This town was mighty pious. Gone were the beach fashions of the coastal towns, men of Konya wore skullcaps and many women dressed in long black robes. I put on my only long-sleeved shirt and Karen made use of her headscarf. We left our shorts in the hotel.

Konya has a long and rich history of Islamic teaching, and we were here to visit the Mevlâna Museum, the home of the Whirling Dervishes. Following the tour, we went off in search of lunch. It was a clear autumn day, perfect picnic weather, and deep in the cavernous Melik Hatun Market we found everything we needed. There were crates of obese tomatoes, piles of chubby cucumbers and slabs of salty, white cheese. While on the shop we received much attention, but could hardly complain. Shopkeepers greeted us with strapping smiles, bumped a purchase up with a gift of tender olives, and refused to let us pay for the bread. This was the famed Turkish hospitality in action. We left on a high from our heavenly grocery shop, and found ourselves a lush patch of grass to spread out the hamper.

For a cheap lunch in Turkey, picnics are just the ticket. Market fare is the freshest and every town seems to have a park set aside for family hordes to roll out a blanket and stuff themselves stupid. Here in Konya we had one such picnic spot. The grass was freshly cut and the dusty streets were far enough away. Everything was picnic perfect. Karen took to de-stoning the olives while I chopped the tomatoes. We made sandwiches of Ottoman proportions, but before we chomped down on our DIY lunch, a shadow came across us. We raised our gaze to a stern-looking fella whose expression was not one of cheeriness. Guessing we couldn't speak Turkish (he was right), he explained to us in English and

Though it's not hard to find Mars Bars, Snickers and their ilk, you should definitely not overlook Turkey's own Ülker brand of chocolate and biscuits. As well as paying tribute to the best bars from around the world – Metro resembles a Mars Bar, Balmond mimics Toblerone – they have concocted many original and wonderful meldings of cocoa, nuts and sweet goo. The nattily named Kat Kat Tat is a gorgeous agglutination of hazelnut and chocolate cream squooshed inside a pastry **milföy** (mille feuille) roll. Ooh yeah. Ülker's dark variety balances bitter and sweet with great poise while the pistachio-embedded block is simply genius – it's baffling that this combo isn't craved in other countries. Their biscuits are also hard to beat. The most addictive is Biskrem, a sweet chocolate shell filled with

body language that we were on the grounds of a mosque, and that organising a banquet here was not the done thing. We were aware that Konya was more traditional than the larger towns and tourist areas, and had tried to respect this, but even so we managed to put foot in it.

In our best phrasebook Turkish we apologised and started packing up the hamper. But before our bags were zipped another man had arrived. He exchanged words of controlled disagreement with the groundsman, then motioned to us to stay put and enjoy our lunch. We didn't know what to do. The old men sitting on nearby benches had stopped solving the world's problems and were watching the incident unfold. Then they broke into heated discussion. It seemed our attempted do-as-the-locals-do approach to lunch had gone seriously awry and was consequently dividing the community.

At this point we thought it best to make for the bus station and leave the pro and anti picnic factions to take up arms. But before we could get to our feet, a third person had ventured into the fray. She must have been in her 70s, and was covered in black robes with a gnarled, surly face poking out from her headscarf. The two men had kept their emotions in check, but she immediately let loose, giving the groundsman an audible biff to the arm. We sat quietly, not daring to move for fear of her wrath. In a flurry of cloth she turned to face us and we both cowered in horror. She dug into her pocket. "She's got a gun" murmured Karen. But from her robes she pulled out a bag of pistachio nuts and forced them into my hand. "Eat" she said, gave the groundsman a killer stare, and strode off. In her absence the two men seemed happy that the problem was solved. Even the groundsman gave us a grin as he sauntered away. Obediently we ate everything, down to the very last pistachio.

Patrick Witton

Kebab corner, Taksim, İstanbul

chocolate cream, which seems to enjoy a particular popularity with back-packers. After witnessing one young woman's rhapsodic confession of her Biskrem-based voyage through Turkey, it is perhaps advisable to warn you, dear reader, to buy only one packet at a time. Turkish junk food is available at every grocer, bus station and newspaper kiosk – it's never hard to get a fix.

a turkish
banquet

Throwing a Turkish-style dinner party can be as extravagant or as relaxed as you wish. You could go for meze mania or make it a five-course feast. You can sit on the floor with one napkin between the lot of you or perch at the table as posh as you please. The best way to create an authentic atmosphere is to gather good friends and to serve them quality food prepared with love in your heart.

To begin in true Turkish fashion, you'll want to consider what is freshest and best in the markets. There's no point getting hung up on stuffed peppers if they are way out of season. If you're entertaining people who aren't used to Turkish food, it's a good idea to serve up a mix of familiar tastes with Turkish twists but to also throw in one or two wacky dishes that will have the whole table exclaiming. **Tavuk göğsü** (chicken breast pudding) is the obvious choice, but if you don't fancy it yourself, how about **perdeli pilav** (veiled pilav).

Perdeli Pilav (Veiled Pilav)

Ingredients
1	Sade Pilav (see recipe in the Staples & Specialities chapter)
	add ½ cup crushed pistachios or almonds
250g	puff pastry
1	egg yolk
1	tablespoon olive oil

Roll ⅘ of the pastry into a large circle. Drape it into a round baking tin, with the edges overlapping the sides. Tip the pilav into the centre of the tin, then fold the pastry up and over the rice so it is completely covered. Pinch the pastry together to seal it then brush with egg yolk. Roll out the remainder of the pastry and stick it decoratively over the seams of your 'veil'. Brush again with egg yolk mixed with olive oil. Bake in a low oven for 40 minutes or until golden brown.

It's fun to recreate village-style sofra dining, where your guests sit in a circle on the floor and the food is placed on a low round table. If you don't have such a table, you can spread a round tablecloth on the floor and place trays of food on it. Scatter a few cushions around for your guests to sit (or collapse) on.

Starting with meze is just about obligatory. You can make as much or as little effort as you wish. Meze can be as easy as laying out some bread, olives and a slab of white cheese (often called feta in western delicatessens). It's fun to linger over meze though – you can prepare most dishes a day in advance and lay them out all at once or stagger their arrival. Meze can also be served as finger food while your guests are arriving and then everyone can move to the table for the main meal. Your Turkish guests are likely to be relatively punctual and may bring something sweet as a gift.

A TURKISH BANQUET

Sarımsaklı Yoğurtlu Havuç Sote
(Sauteed Carrot Salad with Garlic Yoghurt)

Ingredients

8	carrots
200ml	olive oil
200ml	yoghurt
3	garlic cloves
½	teaspoon of salt
½	cup parsley, coarsely chopped

Mash the garlic cloves and mix with the yoghurt. Grate the carrots and saute them in olive oil. Add the salt and garlic yoghurt to the carrots, mix thoroughly and serve cold, garnished with the parsley.

Recipe provided by Perihan Masters

Yayla Çorbası (Plateau Soup)

This peasant soup has found favour all over Turkey.

Ingredients

1	litre beef stock (use water or vegetable stock for a vegetarian version)
1/2	cup rice
500ml	yoghurt
5	tablespoons butter
4	tablespoons dried mint
	salt
	pepper

Boil the stock and add the rice. Cover and cook for 20 minutes over a medium heat. Reduce heat and mix in yoghurt, stirring constantly. Season with salt and pepper. Saute the mint in butter and add to the soup.

Sometimes this soup is thickened with flour or egg yolk. In central Anatolia (especially around Amasya), yayla çorbası becomes the slightly chunkier yarma çorbası, with yarma replacing rice.

Stuffed peppers

When you invite your guests to the table, you can start with soup or move straight onto the main dishes. If you finish cooking the mains just before you serve the soup, they'll be perfectly – Turkishly – lukewarm by the time everyone is ready for them. Put all the food on the table at once and let everyone help themselves. If you're really playing the Turkish host, you'll insist that one serve isn't nearly enough.

COLOURFUL FOOD NAMES

Some of the names of Turkish dishes are just as colourful and inviting as the food itself:

- **Kocakarı Gerdanı** (Old Woman's Neck) – a dessert pastry of yoghurt and hazelnuts topped with sweetened lemon syrup, rolled and wound in a spiral inside the cooking pan.

- **Papaz Yahnisi** (Priest's Stew) – a stew made of beef, onion, garlic, vinegar, salt, pepper, and cumin.

- **Dul Avrat Çorbası** (Widow Woman Soup) – a soup made from chickpeas, lamb and mint.

- **İmam Bayıldı** (The Priest Fainted) & **Karnıyarık** (Split Belly) – two eggplant dishes famous throughout Turkey (see the recipe in the Staples & Specialities chapter).

- **Hünkâr Beğendi** (The Sultan was Pleased) – a lamb stew served with an eggplant (see the recipe on next page).

- **Hoşmerim** (from 'Hoş mu erim?' meaning 'Is it good, my brave man?') – a classic Anatolian helva (see Helva in the Staples & Specialities chapter).

- **Kadınbudu** (Woman's Thigh) – an appropriately shaped ground meat köfte.

Jim & Perihan Masters

Hünkâr Beğendi (the Sultan was Pleased)

Ingredients

1kg cubed lamb (beef or veal can be substituted)
2 tablespoons butter
2 onions, finely chopped
2 garlic cloves, finely chopped
3 tomatoes, diced
salt
pepper
1/2 cup chopped parsley

For the eggplant puree

6 medium eggplants
125g butter
4 tablespoons flour
500ml warm milk
juice of half a lemon
100g grated **kaşar peyniri** (sheep's milk cheese), cheddar cheese can be substituted
salt
nutmeg

Soften the onions and garlic in butter then add the cubed lamb. Saute for about five minutes, until the meat turns brown. Add the tomatoes, salt and pepper and saute until mushy. Add a cup of hot water, cover and cook for 45-60 minutes until the meat is tender.

Char the eggplants over an open flame until the skin is black. Scrape off the skin, discard stalks and seeds and mash the flesh with the lemon juice. Set aside. Melt butter in a saucepan, add flour and stir constantly into a smooth yellow paste. Slowly add the milk, stirring all the while, until it forms a thick lumpless sauce. Add the eggplant mixture, cheese, salt and nutmeg. Cook the mixture for 15 minutes on a low heat.

Pour the hot eggplant puree into a serving dish, make a dip in the centre and pour in the meat. Garnish with parsley.

The Daruzziyaffe Restaurant near Süleymaniye Mosque, İstanbul

Tavuk Göğsü (Chicken Breast Pudding)

Ingredients
½   chicken breast
5   tablespoons rice flour
3   tablespoons cornflour
1½   litres milk
200g sugar
       salt

Wash the chicken thoroughly under cool running water. Boil two cups of water in a saucepan, add the chicken and cook for five minutes. Plunge it into cold water then cut it into small squares. Split the meat into fine strands with your fingers, discarding any portion which doesn't separate. Soak the strands in warm water and pick a handful of them out, rubbing them between your palms, squeezing the water out, soaking them again in a clean tub of warm water. Repeat this process until no chicken smell remains, then leave the chicken to soak in warm water.

Stir the two flours together in a bowl along with half a cup of cold water. Boil the milk with the sugar and salt then slowly stir in the flour mixture. Cook over medium heat, stirring constantly, for about 30 minutes until the mixture has thickened to pudding consistency.

Squeeze the chicken strands and add them slowly to the pudding, stirring well until the chicken blends in and the pudding starts to boil. Lower heat and let simmer for 15 minutes, stirring intermittently. Pour the pudding into individual bowls or a large dish and let cool overnight.

Kazan dibi (kettle bottom) is the same basic dessert, but it's poured into a tray and the bottom is burned. It was discovered by accident but was so delicious that it is now recreated on purpose.

Music

Turkish tunes are essential for your banquet. Traditional **tasavvuf** music is plinky plonky, instrumental and religious, but can be good for a mellow evening. **Arabesk** music has been the soundtrack to many a wrist slashing but it's because of the mournful lyrics, not the music. If you don't understand the Turkish words, the music isn't sad at all. If you want to get your guests dancing, giggling and grimacing, go for featherweight pop music. The carpet-chested Tarkan and Ajda 'Superstar' Pekkan (she does a ripping Turkish version of 'I Will Survive') are goers. Also look out for Sezen Aksu or Barış 'Mega' Manço who incorporate some traditional elements into their pop schlock. Those hoping their dinner party will end in raucousness and complaints from the neighbours need to get some **fasıl** music on the stereo. Fasıl is good-time music, famously paired with rakı. **Hadi bir fasıl yapalım** (let's go hear some fasıl) basically means 'let's go out on a bender'. Women shouldn't say this to Turkish men – it's probably implying more than you realise.

Meze restaurants, Taksim, İstanbul

PARTY TRICKS

Though it seems there'd be nothing more useless than an empty rakı bottle, it's at least good for a couple of party tricks. Take the lid, smear the last droplet of rakı on the top of the lid and rest it upside down on the neck of the bottle. Lo and behold, the lid spits and jumps as though an invisible devil resides in the bottle. The second trick only works if someone is smoking cigarettes (not too far-fetched at a Turkish dinner party). Have someone blow smoke into the empty bottle. The task is for someone to work out how to clear the smoke from the bottle. The answer is to drop a lit match into it but you, as host, can pretend you worked that out scientifically.

If the conversation flags and the party tricks bomb you could soberly ask your guests to ponder these Turkish proverbs: **zemheride yogurt isteyen cebinde bir inek taşır** (he who wants yoghurt in the bitter cold of winter must carry a cow in his pocket); and **süt içerken dili yanan yoğurdu üfleyerek yermiş** (if you burn your tongue with hot milk, you end up blowing on your yoghurt).

Tea and coffee should be offered with dessert but don't stop offering drinks just because everyone has stopped eating. Your guests will probably stay as long as you keep offering them tea. If you really want your guests to hang around, you can keep filling their rakı glasses and entice them with the sure-fire işkembe çorbası hangover cure in the middle of the night (see the boxed text İşkembe Çorbası in the Where to Eat & Drink chapter). If the drink refills stop, they'll soon get the hint that it's time to scoot.

fit & healthy

It's easy to stay healthy in Turkey – most food is fresh and the typical meal is well-balanced and nutritious. Where Turkish food falls down is in its use of fat and salt. Meat tends to be fatty and many dishes are cooked in slicks of oil, lard or butter. Salt is added to everything savoury and many desserts seem designed to contain as much sugar and fat as physically possible. Keep this in mind, and do some picking and choosing in between inevitable indulging.

If you're here for a while, your own willpower is going to be your biggest challenge in eating well. Turkish hospitality, delightful though it is, can mean you're talked into eating more than you normally would. All that baklava! That said, many Turks have become concerned about reducing their fat, salt and sugar consumption. Health nuts are eating less meat and buying low-fat cheese, milk and yoghurt, all available in supermarkets and city stores.

FOLK REMEDIES – WHAT'S SUCK DOC?

Modern health care is readily available in Turkey, but folk remedies are still very much alive in the countryside. Herb teas, infusions and poultices are the first solution for minor stomach complaints, rashes and fevers. Blood sucking **sülük** (leeches) are used as all-purpose purifiers in village medicine – you can see bottles full of the wriggling black nasties in provincial markets. An unlikely sounding haemorrhoid remedy has thankfully died out: gunpowder boiled up with lemon juice, then drained and swallowed. If the gunpowder was mixed with garlic, it was also supposed to get rid of pimples.

Many Turks swear by tripe soup as a preventive medicine against hangovers (see the boxed text İşkembe Çorbası in the Where to Eat & Drink chapter).

Fluid Balance

Plain water, lots of it, is the best antidote to dehydration. Always have a supply of drinking water with you and remind yourself to sip from it regularly while you're out.

Use how much urine you're passing as a rough guide to whether you're getting dehydrated. Small amounts of dark urine suggest you need to increase your fluid intake. Passing reasonable quantities of light yellow urine indicates that you've got the balance about right. As a rough guide, drink enough so you produce a reasonable quantity of light-coloured urine every three to four hours while you're awake.

Eating the Right Stuff

Eating well should be fun, but it's also about making sure you get enough of the right nutrients to enable you to function at your best, mentally and physically. When you're on the road, your diet will be different from normal; in addition, a different lifestyle, stress and new activities may mean your nutritional requirements are increased.

Simit seller, İstanbul

With the help of this book you'll be able to identify available foods for a diverse and nutritious diet. But when you eat can be as important as what you eat. If you're on the move, be careful not to miss meals as this will make you more easily fatigued and vulnerable to illness.

THE 6 BASICS

Everybody needs six basics for life: water, carbohydrates, protein, fat, vitamins and minerals. You shouldn't find this difficult here, where the diet consists of a carbohydrate staple (rice, bulgur) which is eaten with a protein source (meat, beans, fish) and vegetables. Fresh fruit is widely available.

As a guide, you need to eat a variety of foods from each of five core groups:

- **bread and other cereals** (rice, bulgur) – eat lots of these, they provide carbohydrate, fibre, some calcium and iron, and B vitamins
- **fruit & vegetables** – eat lots of these, they give you vitamin C, carotenes (vitamin A), foliate, fibre and some carbohydrate
- **milk and dairy products** – eat moderate amounts for calcium, zinc, protein, vitamin B12, vitamin B2, vitamin A and vitamin D
- **meat, fish, nuts, beans** – these provide iron, protein, B vitamins (especially B12; meat only), zinc and magnesium; eat in moderation
- **fat and sugary foods** (butter, oil, margarine, biscuits, sweets, etc) – eat sparingly from this group, which mainly provides fat, including essential fatty acids, some vitamins and salt

Bear in mind that if you're already sick, your requirements change and you may need to increase the amounts of some food groups to increase your intake of protein, vitamins and minerals, for example.

Diarrhoea

The Sultan's Revenge is a relatively familiar complaint among travellers in Turkey. Most cases are the result of eating something disagreeable rather than outright poisonous and only last a couple of days. You can minimise the risk of the runs by eating lots of tummy-toning yoghurt and drinking bottled mineral water rather than tap water. Though Turkey's running water is drinkable, bottled mineral water is reliably pure and tastes better anyway.

What to Eat

If you do fall victim, take it easy, drink plenty of bottled water to rehydrate and eat plain foods. Turks swear by **lapa** (plain mushy rice) for stomach complaints – you can ask a restaurant to cook some up for you. If you feel like eating, go ahead, especially starchy foods which are known to promote salt and water absorption. If you don't feel like eating, don't force yourself. Unless you're really roughing it, you're going to be basically well nourished and able to withstand a couple of days without food. Make sure you add a bit of sugar or honey to your drinks to keep your energy levels up.

Your overworked guts will appreciate small amounts of food at regular intervals rather than great big meals. This may help make you feel less nauseated too. You may find that eating brings on cramps and you have to dash to the toilet. We all have a natural reflex whereby eating increases the activity of the gut, but this can get exaggerated in a diarrhoeal illness. It doesn't make you a great dinner companion, but you'll probably find that once you've answered the call of nature you can return to finish your meal.

Go easy on fibre providers like fruit, vegetables and nuts. As you recover, gradually add in more foods until you're back to normal and can resume your culinary escapade.

> **Food on the Runs**
>
> When you have diarrhoea, it's good to eat:
> - plain rice or **lapa** (plain mushy rice)
> - plain bread
> - dry biscuits, salty or not too sweet
>
> If possible, it's best to avoid:
> - fruit & vegetables, except bananas
> - dairy products, including yoghurt
> - greasy foods
> - spicy foods

Allergies

If you can't eat yeast you can still eat delicious Turkish pide, made without any rising agent and available everywhere. Those who need to avoid wheat can look out for cornflour bread, though it's only common along the Black Sea. Lactose-intolerant people won't find any of the soy substitutes they're probably used to. Most food is cooked in vegetable oil or animal fat rather than butter, but you should ask. If it's only cow's milk that you're allergic to, you can eat white cheese as it's made with sheep or goat's milk. People allergic to seafood have a pretty easy time of it. Fish stock is only used in obviously fishy dishes and most Turks have an aversion to shellfish – it's not likely to be lurking where you can't see it.

If you're allergic to nuts, watch yourself in eastern Turkey, especially around Antep, where you can count on pistachios in just about everything.

Turks don't always distinguish between different types of nut, for example **fıstık** can mean both peanut and pistachio. So if you're allergic to peanuts, but fine with pistachios, don't dive mouth-first into that fıstıklı kebabı.

Diabetics

The unprocessed fibre-rich foods most common in Turkey are generally good for diabetics. Turkish food usually looks like exactly what it is; sugary foods are soaked in syrup and fatty foods are swimming in oil, making it easy to work out what you should avoid. Olive oil is the common cooking fat in the west of the country; animal fat is used in the east. It's safe to assume that anything savoury has a pretty high salt content. Jam is the only diabetic-specific product widely available in stores.

Turkish transport is relatively reliable but delays do occur. If you're dependent on meals or insulin at set intervals, plan accordingly. With bus travel, don't rely on stopping at a restaurant or toilets more than every four hours. Carry **akide** (hard candy) to boost your sugar levels if you need it.

You're not likely to have any trouble should Turkish officials come across your syringes or insulin, even if it's porcine. It is, nevertheless, a good idea to carry a card, in Turkish, explaining why you need them. If you're travelling alone, carry Turkish instructions explaining how someone can help you if you're having a hypoglycaemic attack.

Indigestion

A change in diet, stress, anxiety and spicy foods can all make indigestion (burning pains in your upper abdomen) and heartburn (burning in your gullet, often with an acid taste in your mouth) more likely when you're travelling. The discomfort is often worse when you're hungry or just after meals. Smoking and alcohol exacerbate it.

Simple measures you could try are to eat small, regular meals – don't eat a huge meal just before you go to bed. Milk and yoghurt can be soothing, as can eating plain, starchy foods like bread, rice and bulgur. You could consider trying antacids (there are many products available without prescription), although stomach acid has a protective effect against infective agents, so taking antacids may make you more vulnerable to gut infections.

Children's Health

Travelling with children in Turkey can be a lot of fun, as long as you come with the right attitudes, equipment and the usual parental patience. All the usual health tips regarding food, heat and diarrhoea mentioned earlier should be followed with extra care, as kids tend to jump into everything with both feet.

Dried fruit, nuts and sweets, Spice bazaar, İstanbul

Recommended Reading

The Art of Turkish Cooking by Neşet Eren (Hippocrene International Cookbook Classics)
This venerable Turkish lady leads us through her kitchen with recipes aimed at the western cook and a sprinkling of elucidatory tidbits to whet even the lagging appetite.

Timeless Tastes; Turkish Culinary Culture by Semahat Arsel (İstanbul)
A luscious doozy of a coffee-table book with recipes supplied by Turkey's leading foodies. The historical essays which front the tome are definitely worth reading while you're waiting for the onions to brown. Published in İstanbul, this book seems to be available locally only.

The Complete Middle East Cookbook by Tess mallos (Lansdowne)
Includes an extensive Turkey section, as well as culinary descriptions of neighbouring countries.

Turkish Cooking by Carol & David Robertson (Frog, Ltd. Berkeley, CA)
An intimate look at Turkey and her food, from the perspective of people who clearly love their subject matter. The book includes plenty of recipes, as well as background information, sketches and photos.

eat your words
language guide

Pronunciation

As transliterations give only an approximate guide to pronunciation, we've included this guide for those who want to try their hand at pronouncing Turkish more like a native speaker.

Vowels

a	as the 'a' in 'bar'
e	as the 'e' in 'fell'
i	as the 'ea' in 'flea'
ı	as in the 'a' in 'about'
o	either as the 'o' in 'hot' or the 'aw' in 'raw'
ö	as the 'e' in 'her'
u	as the 'oo' in 'too'
ü	pronounced by shaping the lips to say 'oo' but then saying 'ee'

Consonants

Many consonants in Turkish are pronounced as in English. However, there are several differences to watch out for.

c	as the 'j' in 'jigsaw'
ç	as the 'ch' in 'cheese'
g	as the 'g' in 'gone'
ğ	silent, but indicates the preceding vowel should be lengthened
h	as the 'h' in 'half'
j	as the 'z' in 'azure'
s	as the 's' in 'sun'
ş	as the 'sh' in 'show'
v	as the 'w' in 'wet'
y	as the 'y' in 'yellow'

Double Consonants

Double consonants like *kk* in 'dikkat' are pronounced for longer than their single counterparts. For instance, the word 'dikkat' sounds like *dik-khat* not 'dikat'.

Stress

Stress is much less pronounced in Turkish than in English, and Turkish spoken with little stress is considered the most standard variety.

Useful Phrases
Eating Out
restaurant
rehs-toh-rahn/loh-kahn-tah   *restoran/lokanta*

cheap restaurant
uu-juuz rehs-toh-rahn; loh-kahn-tah   *ucuz restoran; lokanta*

Do you speak English?
een-ghee-leez-jeh koh-nuu-shuu-yohr   *Ingilizce konuşuyor*
muu-suu-nuuz?   *musunuz?*

Table for ..., please.
... kee-shee-leek mah-sah luuut-fehn   *... kişilik masa lütfen.*

Do you have a highchair for the baby?
beh-behk ee-cheen yuuuk-sehk   *Bebek için yüksek*
ees-kehm-leh-neez vahr-mih?   *iskemleniz var mı?*

Just Try It
What's that?
oh neh-deer?   *O nedir?*

What's the speciality (of this region; here)?
(buu yer-reh-neen; buu-rah-nihn)   *(Bu yörenin; Buranın) speşili nedir?*
speh-see-lee neh-deer?

What do you recommend?
neh tav-see-yeh eh-dehr-see-neez?   *Ne tavsiye edersiniz?*

What are they eating?
ohn-lahr neh yee-yohr-lahr?   *Onlar ne yiyorlar?*

I'll try what she's having.
oh hah-nih-mihn   *O hanımın yediğinden deneyeceğim.*
yeh-deee-een-dehn
deh-neh-yeh-jehh-eem

The Menu
Can I see the menu please?
meh-nuuu-yuuu   *Menüyü görebilirmiyim, lütfen?*
ger-reh-bee-leer-mee-yeem,
luuut-fehn?

Do you have a menu in English?
een-ghee-leez-jeh   *Ingilizce menünüz var mı?*
meh-nuuu-nuuuz vahr-mih?

What are today's specials?
buu-guuu-nuuun   *Bugünün speşili nedir?*
speh-shee-lee neh-deer?

I'd like ...
   ... ees-tee-yoh-ruum   *... istiyorum.*

I'd like the set lunch, please.
   sih-tahn-dahrt er-leh   *Standart öğle*
   yeh-meh-ee ees-tee-yoh-ruum,   *yemeği istiyorum, lütfen.*
   luuut-fehn

What does it include?
   neh-lehr vahr ee-cheen-de?   *Neler var içinde?*

Is service included in the bill?
   sehr-vees heh-sah-bah   *Servis hesaba dahil mi?*
   dah-heel mee?

Does it come with salad?
   sah-lah-tah ee-leh beh-rah-behr   *Salata ile beraber*
   mee gheh-lee-yohr?   *mi geliyor?*

What's the soup of the day?
   buu-guuu-nuuun   *Bugünün çorbası nedir?*
   chohr-bah-sih neh-deer?

Throughout The Meal
What's in this dish?
   buu yeh-mehh-een ee-cheen-deh   *Bu yemeğin içinde ne var?*
   neh vahr?

Not too spicy please.
   fahz-lah bah-hah-raht-lih   *Fazla baharatlı*
   ohl-mah-sihn, luuut-fehn   *olmasın, lütfen.*

Is that dish spicy?
   oh yeh-mehk bah-hah-raht-lih mih?   *O yemek baharatlı mı?*

It's not hot. (temperature-wise)
   sih-jahk deh-yeel   *Sıcak değil.*

It's not hot.(spice-wise)
   ah-jih/bah-hah-raht-lih dey-eel   *Acı/baharatlı değil.*

I didn't order this.
   buu-nuu see-pah-reesh eht-meh-deem *Bunu sipariş etmedim.*

I'd like something to drink.
   ee-cheh-jehk beer shey   *İçecek bir şey istiyorum.*
   ees-tee-yoh-ruhm

Can I have a beer please?
   bee-rah ah-lah-bee-leer   *Bira alabilir miyim lütfen?*
   mee-yeem luuut-fehn?

Can you please bring me some/more ...?
   luuut-fehn bah-nah/dah-hah ...   *Lütfen bana/daha*
   gheh-tee-reer mee-see-neez?   *getirir misiniz?*

Thanks, that was delicious.
teh-shehk-kyuuur-lehr,
choke lehz-zeht-leey-dee
Teşekkürler, çok lezzetliydi.

Please pass on our compliments to the chef.
luuut-fehn sheh-fey
kohm-plee-mahn-lah-rih-mih-zih
ee-leh-tehn
Lütfen şefe komplimanlarımızı iletin.

This food is ...	buu yeh-mahk ...	Bu yemek ...
brilliant	muuu-kehm-mehl	mükemmel
burnt	yah-nihk	yanık
cold	sohh-uuk	soğuk
spoiled	boh-zuul-muush	bozulmuş
stale	bah-yaht	bayat
undercooked	ahz peesh-meesh	az pişmiş

The bill, please.
heh-sahp luuut-fehn
Hesap lütfen.

You May Hear
Anything else?
bahsh-kah beer-shehy?
Başka bir şey?

At your service!
boo-yoo-roo-nooz!
Buyurunuz!

Come, look!
geh-leen, bah-kihn!
Gelin, bakın!

Family Meals
Bon appétit!
ah-fee-yeht ohl-soon!
Afiyet olsun!

You're a great cook.
sen choke ee-yee ah-chih-sihn
Sen çok iyi ahçısın.

This is brilliant!
buu fehv-kah-lah-deh!
Bu fevkalâde!

Do you have the recipe for this?
buu-nuun sehn-deh
tah-ree-fee vahr-mih?
Bunun sende tarifi var mı?

Is this a family recipe?
buu ayi-leh tah-ree-fee mee?
Bu aile tarifi mi?

I've never had a meal like this before.
buu-nuun gih-bee yeh-mahk
dah-hah ern-jeh yeh-meh-deem
Bunun gibi yemek daha önce yemedim.

Could you pass the (salt) please?
luuut-fehn tuu-zuu veh-rihr
mee-see-neez?
Lütfen tuzu verir misiniz?

Thanks very much for the meal.
yeh-mehk ee-ceen choke
teh-shehk-kyuur-lehr

Yemek için çok
teşekkürler.

I really appreciate it.
ghehr-chehk-tehn
mehm-nuun ohl-duum

Gerçekten
memnun oldum.

Vegetarian & Special Needs

I'm a vegetarian.
behn ve-zheh-tahr-yeh-nihm

Ben vejetaryenim.

I'm a vegan, I don't eat meat or dairy products
behn ve-zheh-tahr-yeh-nihm,
eht vey suut mah-muuul-leh-ree
yeh-mee-yoh-ruum

Ben vejetaryenim,
et ve süt mamülleri
yemiyorum.

Do you have any vegetarian dishes?
ve-zheh-tahr-yehn
yeh-mehk-leh-ree-neez vahr mih?

Vejetaryen
yemekleriniz var mı?

Can you recommend a vegetarian dish, please?
ve-zheh-tahr-yehn yeh-mehh-ee
tahv-see-yeh eh-deh-beel-eh-jehk
mee-see-neez?

Vejetaryen yemeği
tavsiye edebilecek misiniz?

Does this dish have meat?
buu yeh-mehk-teh eht vahr mih?

Bu yemekte et var mı?

Can I get this without the meat?
buu-nuu eht-seez
ah-lah-bee-leer mee-yeem?

Bunu etsiz
alabilir miyim?

I don't eat ...	**behn ... yeh-mehm**	*Ben ... yemem.*
meat	**eht**	*et*
chicken	**ta-vuuk/pee-leech**	*tavuk/piliç*
poultry	**kuuu-mes**	*kümes*
	hahy-wahn-lah-rih	*hayvanları eti*
	eh-tee	
fish	**bah-lihk**	*balık*
seafood	**deh-neez**	*deniz mahsülleri*
	mah-suuul-leh-ree	
pork	**doh-muz**	*domuz*
cured/processed meats	**eht uuu-ruuun-leh-ree**	*et ürünleri*

I don't even eat meat juices.
eht soo-yoo bee-leh
yeh-mee-yoh-room

Et suyu bile yemiyorum.

Does it contain eggs/dairy products?
buun-lahr-dah suut/yuu-muur-tah
mah-muul-leh-ree vahr mih?

Bunlarda süt/yumurta
mamulleri var mı?

Does this dish have gelatin?
buu yeh-mehk-teh *Bu yemekte jelatin var mı?*
zhey-lah-teen vahr mih?

I'm allergic to ...
beh-neem ... ah-lehr-zheem vahr *Benim ... alerjim var.*

Is this organic?
buu ohr-ghah-neek mee? *Bu organik mi?*

Is it ...?	**buu ... mee/mih/muuu/muu?**	*Bu ... mi/mı/mü/mu?*
gluten-free	**gluu-tehn-seez**	*glutensiz*
lactose-free	**suuut sheh-kehr-seez**	*süt şekersiz*
wheat-free	**buu-dahy-sihz**	*buğdaysız*
salt-free	**tuuz-suuz**	*tuzsuz*
sugar-free	**sheh-kehr-seez**	*şekersiz*
yeast-free	**mah-yah-sihz**	*mayasız*

I'd like a kosher meal.
tuur-fah ohl-mah-yahn (muus-eh-wee) *Turfa olmayan (Musevi)*

Is this kosher?
tuur-fah-lih ohl-mah-yahn mih *Bu turfalı olmayan mı (Musevi)?*
(muus-eh-wee)?

At the Market

Where's the nearest market?
ehn yah-kihn mahr-keht *En yakın market*
neh-reh-deh? *nerede?*

How much?
neh kah-dahr? *Ne kadar?*

Can I have a ...?
... ah-la-bee-leer mee-yeem? *... alabilir miyim?*

I'd like some ...
bee-rahz ... ees-tee-yoh-ruum *Biraz ... istiyorum.*

Can I taste it?
tah-dih-nah bah-kah-bee-leer *Tadına bakabilir miyim?*
mee-yeem?

Give me (half) a kilogram, please.
(yah-rihm) kee-loh veh-reen *(Yarım) kilo verin, lütfen.*
luuut-fehn

I'd like (six slices of ham).
(ahl-tih dee-leem zham-bohn) *(Altı dilim jambon)*
ees-tee-yoh-ruhm *istiyorum.*

How much is a kilogram of cheese?
pehy-neer-een kee-loh-suh *Peynirin kilosu ne kadar?*
neh kah-dahr?

Do you have anything cheaper?
dah-hah uu-juuz beer
shey-yee-neez vahr mih?

Daha ucuz bir
şeyiniz var mı?

Is this the best you have?
eh-lee-neez-deh oh-lahn
ehn ee-yee buu muu?

Elinizde olan
en iyi bu mu?

What's the local speciality?
yer-reh-neen er-zehl-leee-ee
neh-deer?

Yörenin özelliği nedir?

Will this keep in the fridge?
buu-nuu buuz-doh-lah-bihn-dah
tuu-tah-bee-leer mee-yeem?

Bunu buzdolabında
tutabilir miyim?

Where can I find the (sugar)?
(sheh-keh-ree) neh-reh-deh
buu-lah-bee-leer-eem?

(Şekeri) nerede
bulabilirim?

At the Bar

Shall we go for a drink?
eech-kee eech-meh-yeh
gee-deh-leem mee?

İçki içmeye
gidelim mi?

I'll buy you a drink.
sah-nah eech-kee ah-lah-jahh-ihm

Sana içki alacağım.

You can get the next one.
buun-dahn sohn-rah sehn ah-lihr-sihn

Bundan sonra sen alırsın.

Thanks, but I don't feel like it.
te-shehk-kyuur-lehr, fah-kaht
jah-nihm ees-teh-mee-yohr

Teşekkürler, fakat
canım istemiyor.

I don't drink (alcohol).
ahl-kohl ahl-mih-yoh-ruum

Alkol almıyorum.

What would you like?
neh ees-tehr-seen?

Ne istersin?

It's on me.
behn-dehn ohl-suun

Benden olsun.

OK.
peh-kee

Peki.

I'm next.
ghe-leh-jehk sih-rah-dah-yihm

Gelecek sıradayım.

Excuse me.
ahf-feh-dehr-see-neez

Affedersiniz.

I'll have (a) ...	behn ... ah-leem	Ben ... alayım.
beer	bee-rah	bira
brandy	kohn-yahk/kahn-yahk	konyak/kanyak
champagne	shahm-pahn-ya	şampanya
cider	ehl-mah shah-rah-bih	şarabı
cocktail	kohk-teyl	kokteyl
liqueur	lee-ker	likör
rum	rohm	rom
whiskey	wihs-kee	viski

No ice.
buuz-suuz   *Buzsuz.*

Can I have ice, please?
buuz ah-lah-bee-leer mee-yeem,   *Buz alabilir miyim, lütfen?*
luuut-fehn?

Same again, please.
ahy-nih-sih luuut-fehn   *Aynısı lütfen.*

Do they serve food here?
buu-rah-dah yee-yeh-jehk vahr mih?   *Burada yiyecek var mı?*

Where's the toilet?
tuu-wah-leht neh-reh-deh?   *Tuvalet nerede?*

Cheers!
sheh-reh-feh!   *Şerefe!*

This is hitting the spot.
buu choke ee-yee gehl-dee   *Bu çok iyi geldi.*

I'm a bit tired, I'd better get home.
bee-rahz yohr-ghuu-nuum,   *Biraz yorgunum,*
eh-veh geet-meh-lee-yeem.   *eve gitmeliyim.*

I'm feeling drunk.
kehn-dee-mee sahr-hohsh   *Kendimi sarhoş*
hihs-seh-dee-yoh-ruum   *hissediyorum.*

I feel ill.
kehn-dee-mee hahs-tah   *Kendimi hasta*
hihs-seh-dee-yoh-ruum   *hissediyorum.*

I'm hung over.
ahk-shahm-dahn kal-mah-yihm   *Akşamdan kalmayım.*

Wine
May I see the wine list, please?
shah-rahp lees-teh-nee-zee   *Şarap listenizi*
ger-reh-bee-leer mee-yeem,   *görebilir miyim, lütfen?*
luuut-fehn?

What's a good year?
hahn-ghee seh-neh shah-rah-bih ee-yee?   *Hangi sene şarabı iyi?*

May I taste it?
tah-dih-nah bah-kah-bee-leer mee-yeem?   *tadına bakabilir miyim?*

Can you recommend a good local wine?
guuu-zehl yer-reh shah-rah-bih tahv-see-yeh eh-dehr mee-seen?   *Güzel yöre şarabı tavsiye eder misin?*

Which wine would you recommend with this dish?
bu yeh-mahk-leh han-ghee shah-rah-bih tahv-see-yeh eh-dehr-seen-eez?   *Bu yemekle hangi şarabı tavsiye edersiniz?*

I'd like a glass/ bottle of … wine.	**kah-deh/shee-sheh … shah-rahp ees-tee-yoh-ruum**	*Kadeh/Şişe … şarap istiyorum.*
red	**kihr-mih-zih**	*kırmızı*
white	**beh-yahz**	*beyaz*
rose	**roh-zeh/pehm-beh**	*roze/pembe*

This is brilliant!
buu myuuu-kehm-mehl!   *Bu mükemmel!*

This wine has a pleasant/bad taste.
buu shah-rah-bihn tah-dih gyuuu-zehl/ker-tuu   *Bu şarabın tadı güzel/kötü.*

This wine has a good/bad colour.
buu shah-rah-bihn rehn-ghee gyuuu-zehl/ker-tuu   *Bu şarabın rengi güzel/kötü.*

This wine is corked.
buu shah-rahp ah-chihl-mihsh   *Bu şarap açılmış.*

A

acid	*ah-seet*	asit
acidity	*ehk-shee-leek/ehk-shee-meh/ ah-see-dee-teh*	ekşilik/ekşime/ asidite
allspice	*yeh-nee-bah-hahr*	yenibahar
almond	*bah-dehm*	badem
anchovy	*hahm-see, ahn-chuu-wehz*	hamsi, ançüvez
angelica	*meh-leh-koh-tuu*	melekotu
angler fish	*feh-nehr bah-lih-ih*	fener balığı
anise	*ah-nah-sohn*	anason
antacid	*ah-seet-leh-ree ghee-deh-ree-jee*	asitleri giderici
aperitif	*ah-pehr-ah-teef*	aperitif
appetiser	*ohr-derv, meh-zeh*	ordövr, meze
apple	*ehl-mah*	elma
apricot	*kahy-ih-sih*	kayısı
artichoke	*ehn-ghee-nar*	enginar
ashtray	*kuul tah-blah-sih*	kül tablası
asparagus	*kuhsh-kohn-mahz*	kuşkonmaz
aubergine	*paht-lih-jahn*	patlıcan
avocado	*ah-vah-kah-doh (ahr-muut)*	avokado (armut)

B

bacon	*behy-kohn*	beykon
bag	*tohr-bah*	torba
bake	*fih-rihn-dah pee-sheer-mehk*	fırında pişirmek
bakery	*fih-rihn*	fırın
baking soda (powder)	*kah-bahrt-mah toh-zuu*	kabartma tozu
banana	*muuz*	muz
barbeque/barbecue	*ihz-ghah-rah*	ızgara
barbeque grill	*ihz-ghah-rah/mahn-ghahl*	ızgara/mangal
barley	*ahr-pah*	arpa
bass	*lehv-rehk*	levrek
(sea) bass	*deh-neez lehv-rehk*	deniz levreği
batter	*suu-luu hah-muur*	sulu hamur
bay	*kohy; kuu-chuuk ker-fehz.*	koy; küçük körfez
bean	*fah-suul-yeh*	fasulye
(broad) bean	*bahk-lah*	bakla
(small, red) bean	*bahr-buhn-yah*	barbunya
beef	*sihh-ihr eh-tee*	sığır eti
beef broth	*eht suu-yuu*	et suyu
beer	*bee-rah*	bira
beetroot	*pahn-jahr*	pancar
berries	*eht-lee veh zahr-lih kah-buhk-suuz mehy-veh*	etli ve zarlı kabuksuz meyve
bill	*heh-sahp*	hesap

bird chilli	*kuush bee-beh-ree*	kuş biberi
black bean	*see-yah fah-suul-yeh*	siyah fasulye
black olive	*see-yah zehy-teen*	siyah zeytin
black pepper	*kah-rah bee-behr*	kara biber
blackberry	*ber-uuut-lehn*	böğürtlen
black-eyed bean	*ber-uuul-jeh*	börülce
(to) blend	*kah-rihsh-tihr-mahk*	karıştırmak
blueberry	*chahy-uuu-zuuu-muuu*	çayüzümü
blue fish	*lyuu-fehr, chee-neh-kohp*	lüfer, çinekop
(large) bluefish	*koh-fah-nah*	kofana
boil	*kahy-naht-mahk*	kaynatmak
bottle	*shee-sheh*	şişe
bottle opener	*shee-shey ah-chah-jah-ih*	şişe açacağı
bowl	*tahs*	tas
box	*kuu-tuu*	kutu
bran	*keh-pehk, buu-dahy keh-peh-ih*	kepek, buğday kepeği
brandy	*kahn-yahk/brehn-dee*	kanyak/brendi
bread	*ehk-mehk*	ekmek
breadstick	*gah-leh-tah*	galeta
breakfast	*kah-vahl-tah*	kahvaltı
(Red Sea) bream (fish)	*mehr-jahn*	mercan
breast	*ger-uus*	göğüs
brill	*dee-kehn-seez kahl-kahn*	dikensiz kalkan
brisket	*dersh*	döş
broad bean	*bahk-lah*	bakla
broccoli	*broh-koh-lee*	brokoli
broth (beef/chicken)	*(eht/tah-vuhk) suu-yuu*	(et/tavuk) suyu
brown lentil	*merh-jee-mehk*	mercimek
brown rice	*ehs-mehr pee-reench*	esmer pirinç
brown sugar	*ehs-mehr-sheh-kehr*	esmerşeker
buckwheat	*kah-rah-buu-dahy*	karabuğday
bunch (of greens/herbs)	*deh-meht*	demet
burnet	*sah-lah-tah-lihk sehb-zeh, meh-see-neh*	salatalık sebze, mesine
(the) butcher	*kah-sahp*	kasap
butter	*teh-reh-yah*	tereyağ
butter bean	*lee-mah-fah-suul-yeh-see*	limafasulyesi
button (mushroom)	*mahn-tar bah-shih*	mantar başı

C

cabbage	*lah-hah-nah*	lahana
cake	*kehk*	kek
can	*teh-neh-keh/kuu-tuu*	teneke/kutu
can opener	*kohn-sehr-veh ah-chah-jah-ih*	konserve açacağı

English	Pronunciation	Turkish
candy	*sheh-kehr/bohn-bohn*	şeker/bonbon
cantaloupe	*kah-vuhn*	kavun
capers	*keh-beh-reh, gehb-reh-oh-tuh*	kebere, gebreotu
caramel	*kah-rah-meh-lah*	karamela
caraway seed	*kah-rah-mahn kihm-yohn*	karaman kimyonu
cardamom	*kah-kuu-leh*	kakule
cardoon	*kehn-ghehr/kehn-ghel/ yah-bah-nehghee-nah-rih*	kenger/kengel/ yabanenginarı
carrot	*hah-vuhch*	havuç
(to) carve	*kehs-mehk*	kesmek
cauliflower	*kahr-nah-bah-hahr*	karnabahar
caviar	*hawv-yahr*	havyar
cayenne	*ahr-nah-vuht-bee-beh-ree*	arnavutbiberi
celeriac	*keh-reh-weez*	kereviz
celery	*sahp keh-reh-wee-zee*	sap kerevizi
celery root	*keh-reh-weez (ker-kuuu)*	kereviz (kökü)
celery seed	*keh-reh-weez toh-huh-muu*	kereviz tohumu
cereal	*tah-hihl*	tahıl
champagne	*cham-pahn-yah*	şampanya
chanterelle	*hoh-rohz-mahn-tah-rih*	horozmantarı
cheese	*pehy-nihr*	peynir
blue	*mah-vee pehy-neer*	mavi peynir
white	*beh-yahz pehy-neer*	beyaz peynir
feta	*beh-yahz pehy-neer*	beyaz peynir
cottage	*cher-keh-lehk pehy-nee-ree*	çökelek peyniri
cream	*rehm pehy-nee-ree*	krem peyniri
goat's	*keh-chee pehy-nee-ree*	keçi peyniri
hard	*sehrt pehy-neer*	sert peynir
semi-firm	*yah-rih-sih pehy-neer*	yarısı sert peynir
soft	*yuu-muu-shak pehy-neer*	yumuşak peynir
chef	*shehf, ah-chih*	şef, ahçı
cherry	*kih-rahz/veesh-neh*	kiraz/vişne
bing cherry	*nah-pohl-yohn kih-rah-zih*	Napolyon kirazı
Cornelian cherry	*kih-zihl-jihk*	kızılcık
sour cherry	*veesh-neh*	vişne
wild cherry	*kuush kih-rah-zih*	kuş kirazı
cherry tomatoes	*kih-rahz doh-mah-teh-see*	kiraz domatesi
chervil	*frehnk-mahy-doh-noh-zuu*	frenkmaydonozu
chestnut	*kehs-tah-neh*	kestane
chickpea	*noh-huht*	nohut
chicken	*tah-vuhk/pee-leech*	tavuk/piliç
chicory	*heen-dee-bah/gyuu-neh-ghit*	hindiba/günegik
chilli	*kih-rih-mih-zih-bee-behr*	kırmızıbiber
chips (French fries)	*kih-zahr-mihsh pah-tah-tehs*	kızarmış patates
potato chips	*chihpz*	çips
chive	*frehnk-soh-ah-nih*	frenksoğanı

chocolate	*chee-koh-lah-tah*	çikolata
chopping board	*kuuu-tuuuk*	kütük
to chop	*doh-rah-mahk*	doğramak
(lamb) chops	*peer-zoh-lah*	pirzola
cider	*ehl-mah shah-rah-bih*	elma şarabı
cinnamon	*tahr-chihn*	tarçın
citrus fruit	*tuh-ruhnch-ghee-lehr-dehn beer mehy-veh*	turunçgillerden bir meyve
clam	*deh-neez tah-rah-ih*	deniz tarağı
clove (seasoning)	*kah-rahn-feel*	karanfil
clove (of garlic)	*(sah-rihm-sahk-tah) dihsh*	(sarımsakta) diş
cockle	*deh-leh-jeh*	delice
cocktails	*kohk-tehyl*	kokteyl
cocoa	*kah-kah-oh*	kakao
coconut	*heen-dee-stan-jeh-wih-zee*	hindistancevizi
cod	*moh-rih-nah*	morina
coffee	*kah-veh*	kahve
coffee grinder	*kah-veh er-ruut-meh mah-kee-neh-see*	kahve öğütme makinesi
coffee-making machine	*kah-veh yahp-ma mah-kee-neh-see*	kahve yapma makinesi
cold	*soh-uuk*	soğuk
condiments	*yeh-meh-eh chesh-nee veh-rehn shey-lehr*	yemeğe çeşni veren şeyler
conserve	*kohn-sehr-veh*	konserve
consomme	*kohn-soh-meh; eht suu-yuu*	konsome; et suyu
contents	*ee-cheen-deh-kee-ler*	içindekiler
cookie (biscuit)	*kuu-rah-bee-yeh*	kurabiye
coriander	*kihsh-nihsh*	kişniş
corn	*mih-sihr*	mısır
corn flakes	*mih-sihr ghev-reh-ee*	mısır gevreği
cornmeal	*mih-sihr uu-nuu*	mısır unu
courgette	*sah-kihz-kah-bah-ih*	sakızkabağı
couscous	*kuus-kuus*	kuskus
crab	*yehn-ghehch*	yengeç
cracked wheat	*buuhl-ghuur*	bulgur
crayfish (crawfish)	*keh-reh-veet*	kerevit
cream	*krehm*	krem
clotted cream	*kahy-mahk*	kaymak
sour cream	*ehk-shee-meesh krehm*	ekşimiş krem
whipping cream	*krehm-shan-tee*	kremşanti
cress	*teh-reh*	tere
croissant	*ahy-cher-reh-ee*	ayçöreği
croquette	*kerf-teh/kohk-tehyl kerf-teh-see*	köfte/kokteyl köftesi
cucumber	*sah-lah-tah-lihk*	salatalık

English	Pronunciation	Turkish
cube	*kyuup*	küp
cumin	*kihm-yohn*	kimyon
cup	*feen-jahn*	fincan
currant	*kuu-shuuu-zuuu-muuu*	kuşüzümü
curry (powder)	*ker-ree (toh-zoh)*	köri (tozu)
to cut	*kehs-mehk*	kesmek
cutlery	*chah-tahl bih-chahk tah-kih-mah*	çatal bıçak takımı
cutlets	*koht-leht*	kotlet

D

English	Pronunciation	Turkish
a dab	*doh-kuhn-mah; hah-feef vuu-ruush*	dokunma; hafif vuruş
date	*huhr-mah*	hurma
deep-fry	*bohl yah-dah kih-zahrt-mahk*	bol yağda kızartmak
dessert	*taht-lih*	tatlı
dessert spoon	*taht-lih kah-shih-ih*	tatlı kaşığı
dewberry	*ber-uuurt-lehn*	böğürtlen
dill	*deh-ree-oh-toh*	dereotu
dinner	*ahk-shahm yeh-meh-ee*	akşam yemeği
dried fruit	*kuu-ruu-tuul-muush mehy-veh*	kurutulmuş meyve
drinks	*eech-kee-lehr*	içkiler
duck	*er-dehk*	ördek
dumplings (sweet)	*hah-muur tat-lih-sih*	hamur tatlısı
dumplings (in soup)	*(kahy-nahr chohr-bah ee-cheen-deh pee-shehn kuu-chuuk) hah-muhr pahr-chah-sih*	(kaynar çorba içinde pişen küçük) hamur parçası

E

English	Pronunciation	Turkish
eel	*yih-lahn-bah-lih-ih*	yılanbalığı
egg(s)	*yuu-muur-tah-(lahr)*	yumurta(lar)
hard boiled egg	*hahsh-lahn-mihsh kah-tih yuu-muur-tah*	haşlanmış katı yumurta
eggplant	*paht-lih-jahn*	patlıcan
endive	*ah-jih-mah-ruhl, yah-bah-nee-mah-ruhl heen-dee-bah*	acımarul, yabanimarul, hindiba
entrée	*bahsh yeh-mehk*	baş yemek

F

English	Pronunciation	Turkish
fennel (seed)	*reh-zeh-neh (toh-huu-muu)*	rezene (tohumu)
fenugreek	*cheh-mehn-oh-toh*	çemenotu
fig	*een-jeer*	incir

fillet	*fee-leh-toh*	fileto
first course	*ohr-dervr/meh-zeh*	ordövr/meze
fish	*bah-lihk*	balık
flageolet bean	*flah-gheh-oh-leht fah-suul-yeh-see*	flageolet fasulyesi
flank	*ber-uuur*	böğür
flavour	*taht/lehz-zeht*	tat/lezzet
flounder	*deh-reh-pee-see-see*	derepisisi
flour	*uun*	un
fork	*chah-tahl*	çatal
free-range (oven-range)	*oh-jahk*	ocak
fresh	*tah-zeh*	taze
fresh garden pea	*tah-zeh bah-cheh beh-zehl-yeh-see*	taze bahçe bezelyesi
frog	*kuhr-bahh-ah*	kurbağa
fruit	*mehy-veh*	meyve
fruit cake	*mehy-veh-lih kehk*	meyvalı kek
fruit juice	*mehy-veh suu-yuu*	meyve suyu
fruit knife	*mehy-veh bih-chah-ih*	meyve bıçağı
fruit punch	*mehy-vah-lih eech-kee*	meyvalı içki
fruit salad	*mehy-veh sah-lah-tah-sih*	meyve salatası
fry	*kih-zahrt-mahk*	kızartmak
frying pan	*tah-vah*	tava

G

game (bird)	*ahv kuu-shuu*	av kuşu
garlic	*sah-rihm-sahk/sahr-mih-sahk*	sarımsak/sarmısak gel-
atin	*zheh-lah-teen*	jelatin
gherkin	*kohr-nee-shohn*	kornişon
gin	*jeen (eech-kee)*	cin (içki)
ginger	*zehn-jeh-feel*	zencefil
glass	*bahr-dahk*	bardak
goatfish	*teh-keer*	tekir
goby (fish)	*kah-yah bah-lih-ih*	kaya balığı
goose	*kahz*	kaz
gooseberry	*behk-tah-shee-uuu-zuuu-muuu*	bektaşiüzümü
grapefruit	*grehy-fruut*	greyfrut
grape(s)	*uuu-zuuum(lehr)*	üzüm(ler)
to grate	*rehn-deh-leh-mehk*	rendelemek
grater	*reh-deh*	rende
gravy	*sohs (eht veh-yah tah-vuhk suu-yuu)*	sos (et veya tavuk suyu)
grayling (fresh water fish)	*kuur-shuu-nee taht-lih suu bah-lih-ih*	kurşuni tatlı su balığı
grease	*yah*	yağ

green capsicum (pepper)	yeh-sheel bee-behr	yeşil biber
green lentil	yeh-sheel mehr-jee-mehk	yeşil mercimek
green olive	yeh-sheel zehy-teen	yeşil zeytin
grill	ihz-ghah-rah/mahn-ghahl	ızgara/mangal

H

haddock	mehz-ghiht	mezgit
hake (like cod fish)	bahr-lahm/mehr-lohs	barlam/merlos
halibut	kahl-kah-nah behn-zeh-yehn beer bah-lihk	kalkana benzeyen yassı bir balık
ham	zham-bohn	jambon
hamburger (sandwich)	hahm-buur-ger	hamburger
hare	tahv-shahn	tavşan
haricot bean	kuu-ruu fah-suul-yeh	kuru fasulye
hazelnut	fihn-dihk	fındık
heart	yuuu-rehk	yürek
herring	reen-ghah	ringa
honey	bahl	bal
horseradish	bah-yihr-tuhr-puu	bayırturpu
hors d'oervre	ohrderv/cheh-rehz/meh-zeh	ordövr/çerez/meze
hot (spicy)	ah-jih	acı
hot (temperature)	sih-jahk	sıcak

I

ice	buuz	buz
ice cream	doh-duhr-mah	dondurma
icing sugar	krehm-shahn-tee; sheh-kehr poo-drah-sih	kremşanti; şeker pudrası
ingredients	gheh-rehch-lehr, mahl-zeh-meh-lehr	gereçler malzemeler

J

jam	reh-chehl, mahr-meh-laht	reçel, marmelat
jelly	zher-lee	jöle
Jerusalem artichoke	kuu-duuus ehn-ghih-nahr	Kudüs enginarı
juice (fruit, vegetable or meat)	(meh-veh, sehb-zeh veh-yah eht) suu-yuu	(meyve, sebze veya et) suyu
juniper	ahr-dihch	ardıç

K

kettle	chahy-dahn-lihk	çaydanlık
kidney	ber-brehk	böbrek
kipper	chee-rohz	çiroz

kitchen	muut-fahk	mutfak
kiwi	kee-wee	kivi
knife	bih-chahk	bıçak
knives	bih-chahklahr	bıçaklar
knuckle	pahr-mah-ihn ohy-nahk yeh-ree	parmağın oynak yeri
kosher	tuur-fah ohl-mah-yahn (muus-eh-wee)	turfa olmayan (Musevi)
kumquat	kuum-kaht	kumkat

L

ladle	kehp-cheh	kepçe
lager	hah-feef beer ahl-mahn bee-rah-sih	hafif bir Alman birası
lamb	kuu-zuu	kuzu
lard	doh-muuz yahh	domuz yağı
leek	pih-rah-sah	pırasa
leer fish	ahk-yah (kuu-zuu bah-lih-ih	akya (kuzu balığı)
leg	bah-jahk	bacak
legumes	bahk-lah-gheel-lehr	baklagiller
lemon	lee-mohn	limon
lemonade	lee-moh-nah-tah	limonata
lime	mees-keht lee-moh-nuu	misket limonu
liqueur	lee-ker	likör
liquorice	meh-yahn/meh-yah-ker-kyuu	meyan/meyankökü
liver	jee-ehr/kah-rah-jee-ehr	ciğer/karaciğer
lobster	ees-tah-kohz	istakoz
loin	eh-teen fee-leh-toh kihs-mih	etin fileto kısmı
(young) lufer fish	chee-neh-kohp	çinekop
(large) lufer fish	koh-fah-nah	kofana
lovage	seh-lahm oh-toh; yah-bahn keh-reh-wee-zee	selam otu; yaban kerevizi
lunch	er-leh yeh-mehh-ee	öğle yemeği

M

macadamia	mah-kah-dehm-yah fihn-dih-ih	makademya fındığı
mackerel	uus-kuum-ruu	uskumru
mackerel, horse	ees-tahv-reet	istavrit
mackerel, salted dried	chih-rohz	çiroz
Madeira (wine)	mah-deh-ee-rah shah-rahp	Madeira şarap
main course	bahsh yeh-mehk	baş yemek
mandarin	mahn-dah-lee-nah	mandalina
mangetout pea	manzh-tuu beh-zehl-yeh-see	manjtu bezelyesi
mango	heent-kee-rah-zih, mahn-goh	Hintkirazı, mango
margarine	mahr-ghah-reen	margarin

marinade	*eht sah-lah-muh-rah*	et salamura
marjoram	*mehr-jahn-kersk*	mercanköşk
	mehr-zehn-ghuush; shee-leh	merzenguş; şile
marmalade	*mahr-meh-laht*	marmelat
marrow (bone)	*ee-leek (keh-mee-ee)*	ilik (kemiği)
marrow (vegetable)	*sah-kihz kah-bah-ih*	sakız kabağı
marzipan	*beer cheh-shiht*	bir çeşit acıbadem
	ah-jih-bah-dehm	kurabiyesi
	kuu-rah-bee-yeh-see	
mayonnaise	*mah-yoh-nehs*	mayones
meal	*yeh-mehk*	yemek
medium (cooked)	*ohr-tah peesh-meesh*	orta pişmiş
melon	*kah-vuun*	kavun
menu	*meh-nuu*	menu
milk	*suuut*	süt
skimmed milk	*yah-sihz suuut/ahz yah-lih*	yağsız süt/az yağlı
	suuut	süt
millet	*dah-rih*	darı
to mince	*kihy-mahk, een-jeh een-jeh*	kıymak, ince ince
	doh-rah-mahk	doğramak
mincer	*kihy-mah mah-kee-neh-see*	kıyma makinesi
mineral water	*mah-dehn suu-yuu*	maden suyu
mint	*nah-neh*	nane
to mix	*kah-rihsh-tihr-mahk*	karıştırmak
mixing bowl	*kah-rihsh-tihr-mah*	karıştırma kâsesi
	kah-seh-see tah-sih	tası
monkfish	*keh-lehr*	keler
morel	*see-yah*	siyah
mortar (stone or wooden)	*dee-behk*	dibek
muesli	*myuus-lee*	muesli
mulberry	*duut*	dut
mullet (red)	*bahr-buun-yah/teh-keer*	barbunya/tekir
mussel	*meed-yeh*	midye
mustard	*hahr-dahl*	hardal
mutton	*kuu-zuu*	kuzu

N

napkin	*peh-cheh-teh*	peçete
neck	*boh-yuhn/ghehr-dahn*	boyun/gerdan
noodles	*(sheh-reet hah-lihn-deh-kee)*	(şerit halindeki)
	mah-kahr-nah	makarna
nougat	*kohz hehl-vah-sih*	koz helvası
nutcracker	*fihn-dihk-kihr-rahn*	fındıkkıran
nutmeg	*kuuu-chuuuk-heen-dee-stahn-*	küçükhindistan-
	cheh-wee-zee	cevizi

O

oatmeal	yuu-lahf ehz-meh-zee	yulaf ezmesi
octopus	ah-tah-paht	ahtapot
offal	sah-kah-taht	sakatat
oil	yah	yağ
okra	bahm-yah	bamya
olives	zehy-teen	zeytin
black	see-yah	siyah
green	yeh-sheel	şil
stuffed	dohl-duur-muush	doldurmuş
olive oil	zehy-teen-yahh-ih	zeytinyağı
omelette	ohm-leht	omlet
oregano	keh-kee-koh-tuu	kekikotu
organic	ohr-ghah-neek/er-ghen-sehl	organik/örgensel
oven	fih-rihn	fırın
oxtail	er-kyuuz kuhy-ruu-uu	öküz kuyruğu
ox tongue	sihh-ihr dee-lee	sığır dili
oyster	is-tih-reed-yeh	istiridye

P

packet	pah-keht	paket
papaya	kah-vu-nah-ah-jih-nihn mehy-weh-see	kavunağacının meyvesi
paprika	(taht-lih beer tuur) kih-rih-mih-zih bee-behr toh-zoh	(tatlı bir tür) kırmızı biber tozu
parasol (sun protector)	gyuu-nehsh shehm-see-yeh-see	güneş şemsiyesi
parsley	mahy-doh-nohz	maydanoz
parsnip	yah-bahn-hah-vuu-juu	yabanhavucu
pasta	mah-kahr-nah	makarna
pastrami	sihh-ihr pahs-tihr-mah-sih, pahs-tihr-mah	sığır pastırması, pastırma
pastry	hah-muhr taht-lih-sih	hamur tatlısı
(black eye) pea	ber-ruuul-jeh	börülce
peach	shehf-tah-lee	şeftali
peanut	yehr-fihs-tihh-ih, ah-meh-ree-kahn fihs-tihh-ih	yerfıstığı, Amerikan fıstığı
pear(s)	ahr-muut(lahr)	armut(lar)
pecan	jeh-wihz gih-bee kah-buuk-luu beer yeh-meesh	ceviz gibi kabuklu bir yemiş
peeler	kah-buuk soh-yuu-juu	kabuk soyucu
pepper	bee-behr	biber
pepper (black)	kah-rah-bee-behr	karabiber

English	Pronunciation	Turkish
pepper (red)	*kihr-mih-zih bee-behr*	kırmızı biber
peppercorn	*cheh-keel-meh-meesh bee-behr*	çekilmemiş biber
peppermint	*nah-neh, nah-neh-sheh-keh-ree*	nane, naneşekeri
pepperoni (sausage)	*ee-tahl-yahn soh-sihs*	italyan sosis
persimmon	*trahb-zohn-huhr-mah-sih, jah-pohn-huhr-mah-sih*	trabzonhurması, japonhurması
pestle	*hah-wah-neh-lee*	havaneli
pheasant	*suuu-luuun*	sülün
pickerel (fish)	*ihz-mah-reet bah-lih-ih*	izmarit balığı
pickle	*tuur-shuu*	turşu
pickled	*tuur-shuu hah-lee-neh gheh-tee-reel-meesh seb-zeh/mehy-veh*	turşu haline getirilmiş (sebze/meyve)
picnic	*peek-neek*	piknik
pigeon	*gyuuu-vehr-jeen*	güvercin
pike	*tuur-nah-bah-lih-ih*	turnabalığı
pine nut	*chahm-fihs-tih-ih*	çamfıstığı
pineapple	*ah-nah-nahs*	ananas
pinto bean	*bahr-buhn-yah, beer jeens beh-nehk-lee fah-suul-yeh*	barbunya, bir cins benekli fasulye
pistachio	*fihs-tihk, shahm fihs-tihk, ahn-tep-fihs-tih-ih*	fıstık, şam fıstık, antepfıstığı
plaice	*pee-see-bah-lihh-ih*	pisibalığı
plain flour	*duuuz uun, sih-rah-dahn uun*	düz un, sıradan un
plate	*tah-bahk*	tabak
plum	*eh-reek*	erik
plum tomatoes	*eh-reek byuuu-yuuuk-luuu -uuun-deh beer doh-mah-tehs*	erik büyüklüğünde bir domates
(to) poach	*(beer shehy) (kahy-nah-mah deh-reh-jeh-see-neen bih-rahz ahl-tihn-dah-kee beer sih-vih-dah) pee-sheer-mehk*	(bir şeyi) (kaynama derecesinin biraz altındaki bir sıvıda) pişirmek
pomegranate	*nahr*	nar
popcorn	*paht-lah-mihsh mih-sihr; pohp kohrn*	patlamış mısır; pop korn
poppy	*ghe-leen-jeek-gheel-lehr hehr-hahn-ghee beer biht-kee*	gelincikgillerden herhangi bir bitki
poppy seed	*hahsh-hahsh toh-huu-muu*	haşhaş tohumu
pork (sausages)	*doh-muuz (soh-sih-sih)*	domuz (sosisi)
port (wine)	*pohr-toh shah-rah-bih*	porto şarabı
pot (clay)	*cherm-lehk*	çömlek
potatoes (mashed)	*pah-tah-tehs (pyuuu-reh-see)*	patates (püresi)

poultry (animal, animal meat)	kyuuu-mehs hahy-wahn-lah-rih; kyuuu-mehs hahy-wahn-lah-rih eh-tee	kümes hayvanları; kümes hayvanları eti
(to) pour	derk-mek	dökmek
prawn	kah-ree-dehs	karides
preservative	koh-ruu-yuu-juu mahd-deh	koruyucu madde
pressure cooker	duuu-duuuk-luuu tehn-jeh-reh	düdüklü tencere
prune	kuu-ruu-tuul-muush eh-reek	kurutulmuş erik
pulses	bahk-lah-gheel-lehr	baklagiller
pumpkin	bahl-kah-bah-ih	balkabağı

Q

| quail | bihl-dihr-jihn | bıldırcın |
| quince | ahy-wah | ayva |

R

rabbit	tawv-shahn	tavşan
radicchio	rah-dee-kah	radika
radish	kihr-mih-zih-tuurp	kırmızıturp
raisin	kuu-ruu uuu-zuuum, suul-tah-nee	kuru üzüm, sultani
rare (cooked)	ahz peesh-meesh	az pişmiş
raspberry	ah-hu-duu-duu	ahududu
ray (skate-like fish)	tihr-pah-nah	tırpana
receipt	feesh	fiş
red cabbage	kihr-mih-zih lah-hah-nah	kırmızı lahana
red capsicum (pepper)	kihr-mih-zih bee-behr	kırmızı biber
red kidney bean	kihr-mih-zih bahr-buun-yah,	kırmızı barbunya
red lentil	kihr-mih-zih mehr-jee-mehk	kırmızı mercimek
red onion	kihr-mih-zih sohh-ahn	kırmızı soğan
a reservation	reh-sehr-vahs-yohn, yehr ah-yihrt-mah	reservasyon, yer ayırtma
rhubarb	rah-vehnt	ravent
ribs (spare)	kahr-buur-ghah	karburga
rice	pee-reench	pirinç
basmati	bahs-mah-tee	basmati
brown	ehs-mehr	esmer
glutinous	tuut-kah-lah behn-zehr, yah-pihsh yah-pihsh	tutkala benzer, yapış yapış
(rice) flour	pee-reench uu-nuu	pirinç unu
(rice) milk	pee-reench suu-tuu	pirinç sütü
(rice) pudding	(beer cheh-shiht) suut-lahch	(bir çeşit) sütlaç
wild	yah-bah-nee/yah-bahn	yabani/yaban
ripe	ohl-muush; ohl-guun	olmuş; olgun

to roast	*(fih-rihn-dah veh-yah ah-tehsh-teh) kih-zahrt-mahk*	(fırında veya ateşte) kızartmak
to roast coffee	*kah-veh kah-vuhr-mahk*	kahve kavurmak
rocket	*roh-kah*	roka
rockling fish	*gheh-leen-jeek*	gelincik
rolled oats	*yuu-lahf ehz-meh-see*	yulaf ezmesi
rolling pin	*ohk-lah-vah, mehr-dah-neh*	oklava, merdane
rosemary	*bee-beh-ree-yeh*	biberiye
rump (cut of meat)	*buut*	but
runner bean	*chah-lih fah-suul-yeh*	çalı fasulye

S

sachet	*keh-she*	kese
saffron	*sah-frahn*	safran
sage	*ah-dah-chah-yih*	adaçayı
sago	*sah-ghuu*	sagu
salad	*sah-lah-tah*	salata
salad dressing	*sah-lah-tah soh-suu*	salata sosu
salami	*sah-lahm*	salam
salmon	*sohm bah-lihh-ih*	som balığı
salt	*tuuz*	tuz
pepper mills	*bee-behr dehh-eer-meh-nee*	biber değirmeni
salted pork	*tuuz-luu doh-muuz eh-tee*	tuzlu domuz eti
sardine	*sahr-dahl-yah*	sardalya
sauce	*sohs, sahl-chah, tehr-bee-yeh*	sos, salça, terbiye
saucepan	*(uu-zuun sahp-lih) tehn-jeh-reh*	(uzun saplı) tencere
sauté	*soh-teh*	sote
savory/savoury (a food)	*yeh-mehh-een bah-shih-dah veh-yah soh-nuun-dah yeh-nehn sih-jahk beer bah-hah-raht-lih yeh-mehk*	yemeğin başında veya sonunda yenen sıcak bir baharatlı yemek
savory/savoury (a seasoning)	*keh-keee-eh behn-zehr beer neh-vee bah-hah-raht*	kekiğe benzer bir nevi baharat
scad (fish)	*ees-tahv-reet*	istavrit
scales (weighing)	*teh-rah-zee*	terazi
scales (fish)	*bah-lihk puu-luu*	balık pulu
scallop	*deh-neez-tah-rahh-ih*	deniztarağı
scampi	*kah-ree-dehs*	karides
scissors	*mah-kahs*	makas
sea vegetables	*deh-neez sehz-zeh-leh-ree*	deniz sebzeleri
seafood	*deh-neez uuu-ruuu-nuuu*	deniz ürünü
semolina	*eer-meek*	irmik
service	*sehr-vees*	servis
sesame	*suu-sahm*	susam

English	Pronunciation	Turkish
sesame seed	suu-sahm toh-huu-muu	susam tohumu
sesame oil	suu-sahm yahh-ih; tah-heen	susam yağı; tahin
shallot onion	ahr-pah-jihk-sohh-ah-nih	arpacıksoğanı
shallow-fry	(tah-vah-dah) kih-zahrt-mahk	(tavada) kızartmak
shank	een-jeek	incik
shark	ker-pehk bah-lih-ih	köpek balığı
(angel) shark	keh-lehr	keler
sharpening stone	bee-leh-meh tah-shih; bee-leh-yee-jee	bileme taşı; bileyici
shellfish	kah-buuk-luu-lahr	kabuklular
sherry	beh-yahz ee-spahn-yohl sha-rah-bih	beyaz İspanyol şarabı
shin	een-jeek keh-meee-ee	incik kemiği
shrimp	kah-ree-dehs	karides
short-grain rice	kih-sih tah-neh-lee pee-reench	kısa taneli pirinç
shoulder (at butcher)	kyuuu-rehk, kyuuu-rehk eh-tee	kürek, kürek eti
shrimp	kah-ree-dehs	karides
sieve	eh-lehk, kal-buur	elek, kalbur
(flour) sifter	uun eh-lehh-ih	(un) eleği
simmer	(kahy-nah-mah nohk-tah-sih-nihn bee-rahz ahl-tihn-dah beer deh-reh-jeh) pee-sheer-mehk	(kaynama noktasının biraz altında bir derece) pişirmek
sirloin	sihh-ihr fee-leh-toh-suu; bohn-fee-leh	sığır filetosu; bonfile
(a) skewer	sheesh	şiş
(to) skewer	shee-sheh geh-cheer-mehk	şişe geçirmek
skin (outer covering of a fruit or vegetable)	kah-buuk	kabuk
skimmed milk	yah-sihz suuut/ahz yah-lih suuut	yağsız süt/az yağlı süt
(a) slice	dee-leem	dilim
(to) slice	dohh-rah-mahk, dee-leem-leh-mehk	doğramak, dilimlemek
smoke (noun)	duu-mahn	duman
(to) smoke (food)	tuuut-suu-leh-mehk	tütsülemek
snacks	taht-lih, cheh-rehz, mehy-veh ghih-bee hah-feef shehy-lehr yeh-mehk	tatlı, çerez, meyve gibi hafif şeyler yemek
snap peas	beh-zehl-yeh	bezelye
snapper	lehv-rehh-eh behn-zehr beer bah-lihk	levreğe benzer bir balık
soda water	soh-dah, mah-dehn suu-yuu	soda, maden suyu
soft drink	ahl-kohl-suuuz ee-cheh-jehk, mehsh-ruu-baht	alkolsüz içecek, meşrubat

English	Pronunciation	Turkish
sole (fish)	*deel bah-lih-ih*	dil balığı
soup	*chohr-bah*	çorba
soup spoon	*chohr-bah kah-shihh-ih*	çorba kaşığı
sparerib	*kah-buur-gah*	kaburga
sparkling wine	*ker-puuuk-luuu shah-rahp*	köpüklü şarap
spinach	*ih-spah-nahk*	ıspanak
spirits	*ahl-kohl*	alkol
spoon	*kah-shihk*	kaşık
spottail (fish)	*kah-rah-gherz*	karagöz
sprat (fish)	*chah-chah*	çaça
spring onions	*yeh-sheel sohh-ahn, tah-zeh sohh-ahn*	yeşil soğan, taze soğan
squash	*kah-bahk*	kabak
squid	*kah-lah-mahr*	kalamar
star anise	*ah-nah-sohn*	anason
steak	*beef-tehk*	biftek
steam	*buu-hahr*	buhar
steamer	*buu-hahr-lih tehn-jeh-reh*	buharlı tencere
(to) steep (tea)	*chahy dehm-leh-mehk*	çay demlemek
(to) steep (in liquid)	*(sih-vih-yah) bas-tih-rihp behk-leht-mehk*	(sıvıya) bastırıp bekletmek
stew	*tuur-luuu, gyuuu-wetch*	türlü, güveç
still water	*deen-lehn-meesh suu*	dinlenmiş su
stocks (goods)	*sih-tohk, deh-poh-dah-kee mahl-lahr*	stok, depodaki mallar
stout	*tohm-buul*	tombul
straw	*sah-mahn*	saman
strawberry	*chee-lehk*	çilek
stuffing	*eech dohl-ghuu mahd-deh-see*	iç dolgu maddesi
sturgeon	*mehr-seen bah-lih-ih*	mersin balığı
sugar	*sheh-kehr*	şeker
(brown) sugar	*ehs-mehr sheh-kehr*	esmer şeker
sun-dried tomatoes	*gyuuu-nehsh-teh kuh-ruh-tul-muush doh-mah-tohs*	güneşte kurutulmuş domates
surmullet	*teh-keer*	tekir
swede	*shahl-ghahm*	şalgam
sweet basil	*taht-lih fehs-lehh-ehn*	tatlı fesleğen
sweet cicely	*mahy-doh-nohz fah-meel-yah-sihn-dahn beer beet-kee*	maydanoz familyasından bir bitki
sweet potatoes	*taht-lih-pah-tah-tehs*	tatlıpatates
sweetcorn	*taht-lih beer mih-sihr tuuu-tuuu*	tatlı bir mısır türü
swordfish	*kih-litch bah-lih-ih*	kılıç balığı

T

English	Pronunciation	Turkish
tablecloth	*sohf-rah (mah-sah) er-tuuu-suuu*	sofra (masa) örtüsü
tap water	*muuhs-luuk suu-yuu*	musluk suyu
tarragon	*tahr-huun*	tarhun
tartar	*tahr-tahr, keh-feh-kee*	tartar, kefeki
tea	*chahy*	çay
teaspoon	*chahy kah-shihh-ih*	çay kaşığı
tea	*chahy cheh-sheet-leh-ree*	çay çeşitleri
chamomile	*pah-paht-yah chah-yih*	papatya çayı
decaffeinated	*kah-feh-een-seez chahy*	kafeinsiz çay
green	*yeh-sheel chahy*	yeşil çay
herbal	*biht-kee-sehl chahy*	bitkisel çay
lemon	*lee-mohn-luu chahy*	limonlu çay
milk	*suuut-luuu chahy*	sütlü çay
peppermint	*nah-neh-lee chahy*	naneli çay
rose hip	*kuush-buur-nuu chah-yih*	kuşburnu çayı
thyme	*keh-keek*	kekik
tip	*uuch*	uç
toast	*kih-zahr-mihsh ehk-mehk; tohst*	kızarmış ekmek; tost
toaster	*ehk-mehk kih-zahrt-mah mah-kee-neh-see, tohst mah-kee-neh-see*	ekmek kızartma makinesi, tost makinesi
tofu	*toh-fuu*	tofu
tomato	*doh-mah-tehs*	domates
tonic water	*toh-neek (suu-yuu)*	tonik (suyu)
tongs	*mah-shah*	maşa
tongue	*deel*	dil
toothpick	*kyuuur-dahn*	kürdan
topping	*(taht-lih) sohs*	(tatlı) sos
tripe	*eesh-kehm-beh*	işkembe
(speckled) trout	*ah-lah-bah-lihk*	alabalık
tuna	*tohn-bah-lih-ih, ohr-kee-nohs*	tonbalığı, orkinos
(salted) tunny (fish)	*lah-kehr-dah/tohn-bah-lih-ih/ ohr-kee-nohs*	lâkerda/tonbalığı/ orkinos
turbot	*kahl-kahn*	kalkan
turkey	*heen-dee*	hindi
turmeric	*zehr-deh-chal*	zerdeçal
turnip	*shahl-gham*	şalgam
turtle	*kahp-luhm-bahh-ah*	kaplumbağa

V

English	Pronunciation	Turkish
vanilla	*wah-neel-yah*	vanilya
veal	*suut dah-nah-sih; dah-nah eh-tee*	süt danası; dana eti

vegetable(s)	*sehb-zeh(lehr)/beet-kee(lehr)*	sebze(ler)/bitki(ler)
vegetable marrow	*sah-kihz-kah-bahh-ih*	sakızkabağı
vegetable oil	*beet-kee-sehl yahh*	bitkisel yağ
vegetarian	*veh-zheh-tahr-yehn/*	vejetaryen/
	eht-yeh-mehz	etyemez
venison	*geh-yeek eh-tee*	geyik eti
vinegar	*seer-keh*	sirke
balsamic vinegar	*bahl-sah-meek seer-keh*	balsamik sirke
cider vinegar	*ehl-mah seer-keh-see*	elma sirkesi
malt vinegar	*mahlt seer-keh-see*	malt sirkesi
rice vinegar	*pee-reench seer-keh-see*	pirinç sirkesi
wine vinegar	*shah-rahp seer-keh-see,*	şarap sirkesi,
	uuu-zuuum seer-keh-see	üzüm sirkesi
vodka	*wot-kah*	votka

W

walnut	*che-weez*	ceviz
water	*dah-hah suu*	daha su
watercress	*teh-reh, suu-teh-reh-see*	tere, suteresi *(see also* rocket*)*
watermelon	*kahr-puuz*	karpuz
well done (cooked)	*choke peesh-meesh*	çok pişmiş
wheat	*buu-dahy*	buğday
(cracked) wheat	*buul-guur*	bulgur
wheatgerm	*buu-dahy toh-huu-muu-nuun*	buğday tohumunun
	ehm-bree-yohn kihs-mih	embriyon kısmı
(to) whisk	*chihrp-mahk*	çırpmak
whisky	*wihs-kee*	viski
white	*beh-yahz, ahk*	beyaz, ak
whitebait	*rihn-ghah yahv-ruu-suu*	ringa yavrusu
white cabbage	*beh-yahz lah-hah-nah*	beyaz lahana
white pudding	*beh-yahz muu-hahl-leh-bee/*	beyaz muhallebi/
	puu-deeng	puding
whiting	*mehr-lah-nos*	merlânos
(made of) whole wheat	*keh-pehk-lee uun-lah*	kepekli unla
	yah-pih-lahn	yapılan
whole wheat flour	*keh-pehk-lee uun*	kepekli un
wild boar	*yah-bahn doh-muu-zuu*	yaban domuzu
wild greens	*yah-bah-nee yeh-sheel*	yabani yeşil
	yahp-rahk-lih sehb-zeh-lehr	yapraklı sebzeler
wild rice	*yah-bah-nee pee-reench*	yabani pirinç
wine	*shah-rahp (shah-rah-bih)*	şarap (şarabı)
red	*kihr-mih-zih*	kırmızı
white	*beh-yahz*	beyaz
wok	*cheen tah-vah-sih*	çin tavası
wooden spatula	*tah-tah kah-sihk*	tahta kaşık

Y

yellow capsicum (pepper)	*sah-rih bee-behr*	sarı biber
(yellow) split pea	*(sah-rih) kuu-ruu-tuu-luup*	(sarı) kurutulup
	kehn-dee-leee-een-dehn	kendiliğinden
	ee-kee-yeh ahy-rihl-mihsh	ikiye ayrılmış
	beh-zehl-yeh tah-neh-see	bezelye tanesi
yoghurt	*yohh-uurt*	yoğurt

Z

zucchini	*sah-kihz-kah-bah-ih*	sakızkabağı (bir tür
		sakızkabağı)

Turkish Culinary Dictionary

Note that in the Turkish alphabet, the letters c, ğ, ş, ö, ü and the undotted ı are listed separately. Alphabetical order is as follows:

a b c ç d e f g ğ h ı i j k l m n o ö p q r s ş t u ü v w x y z

So, for example, when searching for a word with a ü in it, remember that it will appear after all words containing u in the same position. Thus, **küçük** (small), would appear after **kuzu** (lamb) and not after **kucaklama** (hug).

A

abdigör köfte *ahb-dee-gher kherf-teh* **köfte** similar to **içli köfte** (Doğubeyazıt)

abone *ah-boh-neh* regular/habitual

acı *ah-jih* bitter; hot/peppery (to taste); rancid (of butter); sour (of wine)
–**biber** *bee-behr* hot pepper
–**kahve** *kah-vey* coffee with no sugar
–**tatlı** *taht-lih* bittersweet

acıbadem *ah-jih-bah-dehm* bitter almond

acıbadem kurabiyesi *ah-jih-bah-dehm ku-rah-bee-yeh-see* almond cookie

acıkmak *ah-jihk-mahk* to feel hungry

acımsı *ah-jihm-sih* somewhat bitter

acımış *ah-jih-mihsh* rancid

acısız *ah-jih-sihz* lacking in peppery seasoning; mild

acur *ah-jur* gherkin

aç *ahch* hunger; hungry; hungry person

açacak *ahch-ah-jahk* (can/bottle/jar) opener

açış *ah-chihsh* opening; act of opening

açlık *ahch-lihk* hunger

açlıktan gözleri dönmek *ahch-lihk-tahn gerz-leh-ree dern-mehk* to be very hungry; famished

açma *ahch-mah* an opening; a savoury bun

açmak *ahch-mahk* to open

adabımuaşeret *ah-dah-bih-moo-ah-sheh-reht* etiquette

adaçayı *ah-dah-chay-ih* garden sage; sage; sage tea

adale *ah-dah-leh* muscle

Adana kebab *ah-dah-nah keh-bahb* a spicy hot, ground meat patty cooked on a thin flat metal poker over a grill

adatavşanı *ah-dah-tahv-sha-nih* European rabbit

adet *ah-deht* portion/amount; unit

afiyetle *ah-fee-yeht-leh* (eating or drinking) with real pleasure

Afiyet olsun.
ah-fee-yeht ohl-suhn
I hope you enjoy(ed) it.
(Similar in meaning to *bon appétit*.)

ağaç çileği *ahh-ahch chee-leh-ee* raspberry

ağaç kavunu *ahh-ahch kah-voo-noo* citron

ağaç kömürü *ahh-ahch ker-moo-roo* (wood) charcoal

ağda *ahh-dah* lemon & sugar syrup; also grape molasses

ağdalı *ahh-dah-lih* something with a taffy-like consistency; viscous

ağ kabak *ahh kah-bahk* squash

ağır *ahh-ihr* heavy

ağır ağır *ahh-ihr ahh-ihr* very slowly; also (to weigh) at the very most

ağız *ahh-ihz* mouth

ağızlara layık *ahh-ihz-lah-rah lah-yihk* delicious

ağızını ıslatmak *ahh-ih-zih-nih his-laht-mahk* to drink

ağızının tadını bilmek *ah-ih-zih-nihn tah-dih-nih-beel-mehk* to be a gourmet

ağrı mutfağı *ahh-rih moot-fah-ih* Ağrı food kitchen. Ağrı is a city in far eastern Turkey that's known for it's nurtured beef dishes.

ahçı *ah-chih* cook

ahçıbaşı *ah-chih-bah-shih* head cook; chef

ahçılık *ah-chih-lihk* art of cooking; cookery; cuisine

ahlat *ah-laht* wild pear (should be eaten only when well-ripened)

ahtapot *ah-tah-poht* octopus
  –**kavurma** *kah-vuur-mah* fried octopus, simmered in water, with lemon & parsley
  –**lu pilav** *luu pee-lawv* rice pilaf with sliced octopus (Muğla)

ahududu *ah-hoo-doo-doo* raspberry

aileye mahsustur *ay-leh-yeh mah-soos-toor* dining area for families (& single women)

ak(ı) *ahk(ih)* white; also egg white

akasya *ah-kahs-yah* acacia
  –**zamkı** *zahm-kih* acacia gum

akciğer *ahk-jee-ehr* lung

akide şekeri *ah-kee-deh she-keh-ree* kind of hard sweet

akşam *ahk-shahm* evening
  –**yemeği** *yeh-meh-ee* evening meal

akşamdan kalmış *ahk-shahm-dahn kahl-mihsh* to be hungover

akya (kuzu balığı) *ahk-yah (koo-zoo bah-lih-ih)* leer fish

akyabalığı *ahk-yah-bah-lih-ih* large bonito (fish)

akıtma *ah-kiht-mah* type of pancake dessert similar to **yassıkadayıf**

akıtmak *ah-kiht-mahk* to pour liquid slowly

alabalık *ah-lah-bah-lihk* salmon/brown/speckled trout

alacalı *ah-lah-jah-lah* multi-coloured

alacatane *ah-lah-jah-tah-neh* starter, onions with lentils & **bulgur** (Uşak)

alafranga *ah-lah-frahn-gah* European-style

alakart (menü) *ahl-lah-kahrt (meh-nuuu)* à la carte (menu)

alaturka *ah-lah-tur-kah* Turkish-style

âlem yapmak *ah-lehm yahp-mahk* to have a wild party

alet *ah-leht* tool/device/instrument

alev *ah-lehv* flame

alev alev *ah-lehv ah-lehv* flaming

alıcı *ah-lih-cih* customer

alış fiyatı *ah-lihsh fih-yaht-tih* price

alışveriş *ah-lihsh-veh-reesh* shopping
  –**merkezi** *mehr-keh-zee* shopping centre
  –**yapmak** *yahp-mahk* to go shopping

alinazik *ah-lee-nah-zeek* aubergine (eggplant) puree with yoghurt & ground meat **köfte**

alkazar *ahl-kah-zahr* red wine & sweetened lemon juice drink

alkol *ahl-kohl* alcoholic drinks

alkolsüz *ahl-kohl-sooz* non-alcoholic
  –**içkiler/içecekler** *eech-kee-lehr/ee-cheh-check-lehr* non-alcoholic drinks

Allaha ısmarladık. *ahh-lah-hah ihs-mahr-lah-dihk* Goodbye. (said by person leaving)

alt *ahlt* bottom, the lower

alüminyum folyo/kağıdı *ah-loo-meen-yuhm fohl-yoh/kah-ih-dih* aluminium foil

ambar *ahm-bahr* granary; warehouse

Amerikan kahvesi *ah-meh-ree-kahn kah-veh-see* instant coffee

Amerikan salatası *ah-meh-ree-kahn sah-lah-tah-sih* Russian salad (salad topped with mayonnaise, chilli sauce, chopped gherkins)

Amerikan viski *ah-meh-ree-kahn wis-kee* bourbon

ananas *ah-nah-nahs* pineapple
  –**suyu** *suu-yuu* pineapple juice

anason *ah-nah-sohn* anise/aniseed

ana yemekler *ah-nah yeh-mehk-lehr*
main dishes

ançüez *ahn-choo-ehz*
salted or pickled anchovy

Ankara tavası *ahn-kah-rah tah-vah-sih*
lamb with pilaf

Antalya piyazı *ahn-tahl-yah pee-yah-zee* **piyazı** made with dry beans, **tahin**, green pepper & lemon (Antalya)

antepfıstığı *ahn-tehp-fihs-tih-ih*
pistachio (*see also* **şam fıstığı**)

antepfıstığı pilavı *ahn-tehp-fihs-tih-ih pee-lahvv* pilaf with pistachios

antrokot *ahn-troh-koht* beef from the top of the ribs; entrecote

aperetif *ah-pehr-ee-teef* aperitif/appetiser

ara ara *ah-rah ah-rah* a little at a time

Arabaşı çorbası *ah-rah-bah-shi chohr-bah-sih* spicy chicken soup

araka *ah-rah-kah* large peas

arapzamkı *ah-rahp-zahm-kih*
acacia gum

arındırmak *ah-rihn-dihr-mahk* to purify

arınma *ah-rihn-mah* purification

arıpoleni *ah-rih-poh-leh-nee* bee's pollen

arısütü *ah-rih-soo-too* royal (bee) jelly

armut *ahr-muht* pear

Arnavut ciğeri (arnavutciğeri) *ahr-nah-vuht jee-eh-ree* Albanian fried liver

arnavutbiberi *ahr-nah-vuht-bee-beh-ree* Albanian red pepper

arpa *ahr-pah* barley

arpa şehriye *ahr-pah sheh-ree-yeh*
grain-shaped macaroni

arpacıksoğanı *aht-pah-jihk-soh-ah-nih*
shallot

asit *ah-seet* acid (*see* **askorbik asit**)

asitleri giderici *ah-seet-leh-ree gee-dehr-jee* antacid

aslan sütü *ahs-lan soo-too* nickname of **rakı**, the national alcoholic drink

asma *ahs-mah* vine/grapevine
–yaprağı *yahp-rah-ih* grape leaf
–yaprağında sardalya *yahp-rah-ihn-dah sahr-dahl-yah* sardines in grape vine leaves

asmakabağı *ahs-mah-kah-bah-ih*
an edible squash

atardamar *ah-tahr-dah-mahr* artery

ateş gibi *ah-tesh gih-bee* very hot

aş *ahsh* cooked food
–ocağı *oh-jah-ih* soup kitchen

aşçı *ahs-chee* a cook/chef

aşevi *ah-sheh-vee* small restaurant

aşure *ah-shoo-reh* fruit pudding prepared during the first 10 days of the Islamic calendar month **Muharrem**

av *ahv* hunt/hunting/chase;
also game/prey/catch (of fish)
–eti *eh-tee* game meat
–kuşu *koo-shoo* game bird

avcı *ahv-jih* hunter

avuç dolusu *ah-vuhch doh-loo-soo* a handful

ayak *ah-yahk* foot
–bileği *bee-leh-ee* ankle
–parmağı *pahr-mah-ih* toe

ay böreği *ahy ber-rehh-ee*
crescent-shaped **börek**

ayçekirdeği *ahy-cheh-kihr-deh-ee*
sunflower seed(s)

ayçiçeği *ahy-chee-chehh-ee* sunflower
–yağı *yah-ih* sunflower oil

ayçöreği *ahy-choh-reh-ee* croissant

ayıklamak *ah-yihk-lah-mahk* to clean/pick/sort (rice or vegetables); to shell (peas or beans); to bone (meat)

ayırmak *ah-yihr-mahk* to separate

ayran *ahy-rahn* yoghurt drink

ayrı *ahy-rih* (a) separate (something)

ayşekadın (fasulye) *ahy-sheh-kah-dihn (fah-suul-yeh)* string/green bean

ayşe kızın düğün çorbası *ahy-shehy kih-zihn duu-uun chohr-bah-sih* wedding soup made with wheat, meat broth, yoghurt & corn meal. Served with **köfte** & tomato butter sauce. (Uşak)

ayva *ahy-vah* quince
–tatlısı *taht-lih-sih* quince dessert

az *ahz* (a) little

–**pişmiş** (**biftek**) *peesh-meesh (bihf-tehk)* rare (steak)

–**şekerli kahve** *sheh-kehr-lee kah-veh* coffee with a little sugar

azıcık *ahz-ih-jihk* very little; just a bit

azık *ah-zihk* food (to be taken along & eaten while travelling); any food

B

baba hindi *bah-bah heen-dee* turkey cock; gobbler

bacak *ba-jahk* leg

badem *bah-dehm* almond
–**ezmesi** *ehz-meh-see* almond paste; marzipan
–**gibi** *gih-bee* fresh & crisp
–**şekeri** *sheh-keh-ree* sugared almonds

bademli *bah-dehm-lee* with almonds
–**pilav** *pee-lawv* pilaf with almonds

bademyağı *bah-dehm-yah-ih* almond oil

bağ *bah* vineyard; also (a) bunch
–**bahçe** *bah-cheh* vineyards & orchards
–**bozmak** *bohz-mahk* to harvest grapes

bağbozumu *bah-boh-zoo-moo* grape harvest

bağcı *bah-jih* grape grower

bahar *bah-hahr* (a) spice

baharat(lar) *bah-hah-raht(lahr)* spice(s)

baharatçı *bah-hah-raht-chih* spice seller

baharatlı *bah-hah-raht-lih* spiced/spicy

baharatlık *bah-hah-raht-lihk* cruet

bahçe *bah-cheh* garden (see **bağ bahçe**; **çay bahçesi**)

bahçıvan *bah-chih-wahn* gardener

bahşiş *bah-sheesh* tip (gratuity)

bakkal *bahk-kahl* grocer/grocery

bakla *bahk-lah* broad bean; horse bean

baklagiller *bahk-lah-ghee-lehr* family of beans that includes **bakla**

baklava *bahk-lah-vah* a trangular dessert, especially for occasions like weddings – consists of layers of pastry, covered with sweet syrup and stuffed with pistachio & walnuts

bakliyat *bahk-lee-yaht* pulse(s); dried beans; leguminous plants; legumes

baküre *bah-kyuuu-reh* a fruit or vegetable grown outside of season

bal *bahl* honey
–**gibi** *gih-bee* very sweet (like honey)
–**küpü** *kyoop-oo* honey jar

balcan söğürmesi *bahl-jahn ser-er-mey-see* eggplant/aubergine cooked over hot coals (Konya)

balcı *bahl-jih* seller of honey

baldır *bahl-dihr* calf (of the leg); shank

balığı (see **barbunya balığı**)

balık *bah-lihk* fish
–**buğulama** *boo-oo-lah-mah* steamed fish stew
–**çorbası** *chohr-bah-sih* fish soup
–**filetosu tava** *fee-leh-toh-suu tah-vah* fried fillet of fish
–**fırında** *fih-rihn-dah* baked fish
–**köftesi** *kerf-teh-see* fried fish fingers/ balls
–**pazarı** *pah-zah-rih* fish market
–**tavası** *tah-vah-sih* fried fish platter
–**tutmak** *toot-mahk* to fish
–**yağı** *yah-ih* fish oil; cod-liver oil
–**yahni** *yah-nee* ragout of fish
–**yumurtası** *yoo-mer-tah-sih* fish roe; dried & smoked roe of grey mullet

balıkçı *bah-lihk-chee* fishmonger/fisherman
–**dükkanı** *duuu-kah-nih* fishmonger's store
–**gemisi** *geh-mee-see* fishing boat

balkabağı *bahl-kah-bah-ih* pumpkin

ballı *bahl-lih* honeyed; something that contains or is made with honey

balözü *bah-ler-zyoo* nectar

balpeteği *bahl-peh-teh-ih* honeycomb

bamya *bahm-yah* okra/gumbo

bamyalı *bahm-yah-lih* with okra
–**tavuk** *tah-vuhk* chicken with okra

Banvit *bahn-weet* a national brand of ready-to-cook chicken products

barbekü *bahr-beh-kyoo* barbecue

barbunya balığı *bar-buhn-yah bah-lihh-ih* red mullet (fish)

barbunya fasulye *bar-buhn-yah fah-sool-yeh* small reddish kind of a shelled bean; borlotti bean

barbunya pilaki *bar-buhn-yah pee-lah-kee* red bean salad in olive oil (meze)

barbunya tava *bar-buhn-yah tah-vah* fried red mullets

bardak (bardağı) *bahr-dahk (bahr-dah-ih)* glass *(see also* **çay bardağı**)

barmen *bahr-mehn* bartender (male)

barmeyd *bahr-meyd* bartender (female)

barut gibi *bah-ruht gih-bee* very sour

baskül *bahs-kyool* scales (for weighing)

basmavat *bas-mah-vaht* boiled **içli köfte** (Mardin)

bastı *bahs-tih* vegetable stew

bastık *bahs-tihk* sheet of sun-dried mulberry & grape (Malatya)

başgarson *bahsh-gahr-sohn* headwaiter

başka *bahsh-kah* (an)other

başlahana *bahsh-lah-hah-nah* cabbage

başlangıçlar *bahsh-lahn-ghich-lar* *(see* **meze**)

başına *bah-shih-nah* for each

batırmak *bah-tihr-mak* to dunk/sink

baton *bah-tohn* breadstick

battal boy *baht-tahl boy* extra large; oversized

bay *bahy* Mr

bayan *bah-yahn* Ms (Mrs or Miss)

bayat *bah-yaht* stale (of bread); old; aged (of meat)

bayram *bahy-rahm* festival; festivity; religious festival

–arifesi *ah-ree-feh-see* the eve of a **bayram**

–ertesi *ehr-teh-see* the time right after a **bayram**

–etmek/yapmak *eht-mehk/yahp-mahk* to feast; to celebrate a holiday

–günü *goo-noo* a **bayram** day

–havası *hah-vah-sih* holiday spirit

Bayramınız kutlu olsun! *bahy-rah-mih-nihz koot-loo-ohl-suhn* Have a happy bayram!

bazlama *baz-lah-mah* flat baked bread

bedava *beh-dah-vah* free (of cost)

beğendi *beh-ehn-dee* cream sauce made largely of puréed eggplant (aubergine)

beğendili tas kebabı *behh-ehn-dee-lee tahs keh-bah-bih* also known as 'sultan's delight' *(see* **hünkâr beğendi**)

beğendili tavuk *behh-ehn-dee-lee tah-vuhk* chicken with puréed eggplant

beher *beh-her* each

beklemek *behk-leh-mehk* to wait

bekmez *behk-mehz* a food product of grapes, like **pekmez** (Yozgat)

belirli *beh-leer-lee* definite/specific

belirtmek *beh-leert-mehk* to clarify (butter)

bembeyaz *behm-beh-yahz* stark white colour

benekli çorba *beh-nehk-lee chohr-bah* lentil soup (Çorum)

benli pilav *behn-lee pee-lawv* pilaf dish of rice & lentils (Yozgat)

benmari *behn-mah-ree* double boiler

benzer *behn-zehr* similar to; resembling

beraber *beh-rah-behr* together

berbat *behr-baht* spoiled/ruined

berrak *behr-rahk* clear

besili *beh-see-lee* fat; well-fed animal

besin *beh-seen* nutrition/food

besisuyu *beh-see-soo-yoo* sap

besiye çekmek *beh-see-yeh chehk-mehk* to fatten (an animal)

beslemek *bes-leh-mehk* to feed/nourish

beslenme çantası *bes-lehn-meh chahn-tah-sih* lunch box

beslenmek *bes-lehn-mehk* to be fed/ nourished

besleyici *bes-lehy-ee-jee* nutritious

besmele *bes-meh-leh* the blessing **Bismillâhirrahmânirrahîm** 'In the name of God, the Compassionate, the Merciful' is said at religious venues by the most senior community member present to announce the beginning of the meal

beşamel (sos) *beh-shah-mehl* (sohs) bechamel (sauce)

beşinci *besh-een-cheh* fifth

bey *behy* polite term of address (using first names only) for a man (**John bey** means 'Mr John')

beyaz *beh-yahz* white/whiteness
–**ekmek** *ehk-mehk* white bread
–**fıstık** *fihs-tihk* pinenuts
–**peynir** *pehy-neer* white cheese ('feta' cheese is similar)
–**peynirli omlet** *pehy-neer-lee ohm-leht* omelette with white cheese
–**peynirli sandviç** *pehy-neer-lee sahnd-wich* white cheese sandwich
–**şarap** *shah-rahp* white wine
–**toz biber** *tohz bee-behr* white pepper

beyefendi *beh-yeh-fehn-dee* very polite way of saying 'sir'

beyin *beh-yeen* brain
–**haşlama** *hahsh-lah-mah* boiled brain
–**salatası** *sah-lah-tih-sih* sheep's brain salad
–**tava** *tah-vah* fried veal brains platter

beyti (kebab) *behy-tee* (keh-bahb) Adana-style spicy ground meat kebab, rolled in thin bread & sliced

beyzi *behy-zee* oval/elliptical

bez *behz* cloth

bez/beze *behz/beh-zeh* gland

beze *beh-zeh* macaroon; lump of dough

bezelye *beh-zehl-yeh* pea(s)

bezemek *beh-zeh-mehk* to decorate

bıçak *bih-chahk* knife

bıldırcın *bihl-dihr-jihn* quail
–**kebabı** *keh-bah-bih* quail cooked with potatoes, tomatoes, onion, garlic & green pepper (Bilecik)
–**yumurtası** *yoo-mer-tah-sih* quail eggs

bırakmak *bih-rahk-mahk* to leave

biber *bee-behr* pepper (see **acı biber; tatlı biber; çarliston biber; dolmalık biber**)
–**dolması** *dohl-mah-sih* stuffed pepper
–**gibi** *gih-bee* hot/peppery
–**kızartması** *kih-zart-mah-sih* fried peppers
–**tanesi** *tah-neh-see* peppercorn
–**turşusu** *toor-shuu-suu* pickled green pepper

biberiye *bee-beh-ree-yeh* fragrant herb used on grilled meats & seafoods

biberli *bee-behr-lee* peppered/peppery

biberlik-tuzluk *bee-behr-lihk–tuuz-luuk* pepper & salt shakers

bibersiz *bee-behr-sihz* without peppers

biftek *bihf-tehk* steak

bileği taşı *bee-leh-ee tah-shih* whetstone/grindstone

bir *beer* one
–**buçuk** *buu-chuuk* one & a half
–**çift** *chihft* a pair
–**dilim ekmek** *dee-leem ehk-mehk* slice of bread (see also **ekmek**)
–**kaç** *kahch* a few
–**parça buz** *pahr-chah buuz* piece of ice

bira *bee-rah* beer

birahane *bee-rah-hah-neh* pub

biraz *bee-rahz* a small amount

bir bardak su *beer bahr-dahk suu* glass of water

birer *bee-rehr* one each of

birinci *bee-reen-jee* first

bisk *beesk* bisque

bisküvi *beesk-kyuu-vee* biscuit

bitirmek *bee-teer-mehk* to finish

bitiş *bee-teesh* end/finish

bitki *beet-kee* plant/herb
–**çay** *chay* herbal tea

bitkibilim *beet-kee-bee-leem* botany

bitkisel *beet-kee-sehl* vegetable
–**yağı** *yah-ih* vegetable oil

biyoloji *bee-yoh-loh-jee* biology

biyotin *bee-yoh-teen* biotin
bizon *bee-zohn* buffalo/bison
bkz. *(see* **bakınız)**
blander *bih-lahn-dehr* blender
boğa *boh-ah* bull
boğaz *boh-ahz* throat; gullet; neck (of a bottle)
boğazına düşkün *boh-ah-zih-nah doosh-kuun* gourmet
boğazını sevmek *boh-ah-zih-nih sehv-mahk* to enjoy eating
bol *bohl* plentiful/abundant; also claret cup/fruit punch/bowl
bol bol *bohl bohl* amply/abundantly
bolca *bohl-jah* amply/abundantly
boldo *bohl-doh* best category of rice
bonbon *bohn-bohn* candy
bonfile *bohn-fee-leh* sirloin steak
borç *bohrch* debt
Bordo *bohr-doh* claret; Bordeaux wine
boru *boh-ruu* tube/pipe
bostan *bohs-tohn* vegetable garden
bostanpatlıcanı *bohs-tahn-paht-lih-jah-nih* eggplant (aubergine)
boş *bohsh* empty
boşaltmak *boh-shalt-mahk* to empty
boy *boy* size/height/length
boyun *boh-yoon* neck
boyunca *bo-yoon-jah* the whole length of the ...
boyut *boh-yuht* dimension/size
boza *boh-zah* slightly fermented grain-based drink
bozmak *bohz-mahk* to spoil/ruin *(see* **bağ bozmak)**
bozuk *boh-zuhk* spoiled; gone bad
–para *pah-rah* small change
bozulmak *boh-zuhl-mahk* to be spoiled/ ruined
böbrek *ber-brehk* kidney
–ızgara *ihz-ghah-rah* grilled kidney
böğür *boh-uur* side/flank
böğürtlen *boh-uurt-lehn* blackberry
bölmek *berl-mehk* to divide

bölüm *ber-loom* portion/slice/part
bölün *ber-loon* divide (imperative of **bölmek)**
börek *ber-rehk* various types of sweet or savoury pastry dishes with a thin & crispy pastry
–çorbası *chohr-bah-sih* thick soup with mincemeat, bones, tomato paste & mint (Antep)
börekci *ber-rehk-chee* **börek** seller
börülce *ber-ruuul-jeh* black-eyed pea; cow pea
–pilav *pee-lawv* pilaf dish of rice & black-eyed peas (Aydın & Muğla)
–salatası *sah-lah-tah-sih* salad of black-eyed peas, mushrooms, green onion & parsley (Aydın & Muğla)
–teletoru *teh-leh-toh-ruu* black-eyed pea salad with sauce of flour, onion, lemon, olive oil & garlic (Muğla)
brendi *brehn-dee* brandy
Brüksellahanası *brook-sehl-lah-hah-nah-sih* Brussels sprouts
budu *boo-doo (see* **but)**
buğday *boo-dahy* wheat
–ekmek *ehk-mehk* wheat bread
buğu *boo-oo* vapour/steam
buğulama *boo-oo-lah-mah* steaming/ stewing/poaching
buğulama *(see* **balık buğulama)**
buhar *boo-hahr* steam/vapour
–kazanı *kahzah-nih* boiler
buharlaşma *boo-hahr-lahsh-mah* evaporation
buharlaşmak *boo-hahr-lahsh-mahk* to evaporate
buket *boo-keht* bouquet (of flowers)
bulamaç *boo-lah-mahch* batter
–çorbası *chohr-bah-sih* soup made with flour, semolina, water, margarine & salt (Eskişehir)
bulamak *boo-lah-mahk* to roll something or dredge something in flour
bulantı *boo-lahn-tih* nausea
bulaşık *boo-lah-shihk* dirty dishes

–makinesi *mah-kee-neh-see*
dishwashing machine

bulaşıkcı *boo-lah-shihk-jih*
person who washes dishes

bulgur *bool-goor* cracked wheat; boiled & pounded wheat

–pilavı *pee-lah-wee*
cracked wheat pilaf

bumbar *boom-bahr* sausage made of rice & meat stuffed in a large gut

burcu *boor-juu* scent/fragrance

burma kadayıf *buur-mah kah-dah-yihf* shredded wheat bun with pistachios

Bursa kebabı *boor-sah keh-bahb* **döner kebab** with tomato sauce & hot butter, on bed of pita bread (Bursa)

buruk *boo-ruuk* astringent/sour

burun *boo-roon* nose/beak/bill

but (budu) *boot (boo-doo)*
thigh/rump/ leg (of meat)

Buyrunuz! (Buyrun!)
booy-roo-nuuz (booy-roon)
Welcome; Please come in;
May I help you?

buz *buuz* ice (*see also* **bir parça buz**)

–gibi *gih-bee* icy cold

–kesilmek *keh-seel-mehk*
to freeze; to be frozen

buzdolabı *buuz-doh-lah-bih*
refrigerator/ icebox

buzlu *buuz-luu* mixed with ice; freezing compartment; ice cube tray

büfe *buu-fehy* informal counter where food, drink & sundries are sold

bülbül yuvası *buul-buul yuu-wah-sih* shredded wheat with pistachios & syrup

bütan *byuu-tahn* butane

bütün *buu-tuun* whole/complete

büyük *byuu-yuuk* large

büyükbaş *byuu-yuuk-bahsh* cattle

büyükçe *byuu-yuuk-cheh* rather large

büyükhindistancevizi *byuu-yuuk-heen-dee-stahn-jeh-veh-zee* coconut

büyüklüğünde *byuu-yuuk-loo-oon-deh* the size of; as big as (**fındık büyüklüğünde** – as big as a hazelnut)

büyümek *byuu-yuu-mehk* to grow (up)

C

cacık *jah-jihk* cold mixture of yoghurt, garlic, mint, & chopped cucumber, served as a side dish or **meze**

ceviz *jeh-veez* walnut

cevizli bat *jeh-veez-lee baht* salad of fine bulgur, green lentils & tomato paste, sprinkled with crushed walnut & often served with grape leaves (Tokat)

cevizli kek *jeh-vihz-lee kehk*
cake with walnuts

cevizli sucuk *jeh-vihz-lee soo-jook* walnuts on a string dipped in a starchy grape molasses

cezeriye (*see* **Arnavut ciğeri**)

cezve *jehz-veh* coffee pot

cıvarında *jih-vah-rihn-dah*
about/ approximately

cızbız köfte *cihz-bihz kerf-teh*
grilled mincemeat ovals

ciğeri *jee-eh-ree* sweet made with carrots & nuts, served in rectangular slices (Manissa) (*see* **Arnavut ciğeri**)

ciğer tava *jee-ehr tah-vah* fried liver served with onions (meze)

civil *jee-veel*
low-fat string cheese (Erzurum)

Ç

çağanoz *chah-ah-nohz* green crab

çağla badem(ler) *chah-lah bah-dehm (lahr)* green/fresh/unripe almond(s)

çala *chah-lah* seasoned bread & cheese (Mersin, İçel)

çalıbasan *chah-lih-bah-sahn* large kernel wheat, used in making **tarhana**

çalıfasulyesi *chah-lih-fah-sool-yeh-see* string beans

çalkama *chahl-kah-mah* general name for drinks like **ayran** (Sivas)

çam *chahm* pine

çarliston biber *char-lihs-tohn bee-behr* banana pepper (elongated, light-green sweet pepper)

çarşı *char-shih* market

çarşıya çıkmak *char-shih-yah chihk-mahk* to go out shopping

çatal *cha-tahl* fork; also a type of **simit**
—**bıçak** *bih-chahk* silverware/cutlery

çavdar ekmek *chav-dahr ehk-mehk* rye bread

çay *chahy* tea (*see* **bitki çay**)
—**bahçesi** *bah-cheh-see*
tea garden, where tea is served
—**bardağı** *bahr-dah-ih* tea glass
—**fincanı** *fihn-jah-nih* tea cup
—**kaşığı** *kah-shih-ih* teaspoon
—**vermek** *vehr-mehk* to serve tea

çaycı *chahy-jee* tea vendor/grower

çaydanlık *chahy-dahn-lihk*
tea kettle; teapot

çayhane *chahy-hah-neh* teahouse

çekirdek kahve *cheh-keer-dehk kah-veh* coffee beans

çekirdeksiz mandalina (satsuma) *cheh-keer-dehk-seez mahn-dah-lee-nah (saht-suu-mah)* seedless mandarin/tangerine ('satsuma' variety)

çekirdeksiz üzüm *cheh-keer-dehk-seez uu-zuum* seedless grape

çekmece *chehk-meh-jeh* drawer

çemen *cheh-mehn* a pungent 15-spice mix used for **pastırma** which includes cumin, chilli, fenugreek & garlic

çene çarpan çorbası *cheh-neh chahr-pahn chohr-bah-sih* 'jaw bumping' soup made with flour, water, egg, milk & lemon (Tekirdağ)

çerez *cheh-rehz* hors d'oeuvre; appetiser; dried fruit; nuts

çerkez peynir *chehr-kehz pehy-neer* Circassian cheese, similar to **dil peynir**

çerkez tavuğu (çerkeztavuğu) *chehr-kehz tah-vooh-oo* Circassian chicken, made with bread, pounded walnuts, salt, garlic & cayenne pepper (Sakarya & Adapazarı)

çeşit(ler) *che-sheet(lehr)* kind(s), sort(s), variety(ies), assortment(s)

çeşme *chehsh-meh* a water fountain

çevirme *che-veer-meh* eggplant (aubergine), chicken, rice, onion, pistachio nuts & allspice dish. The dish is turned upside down on a serving plate before serving (Antakya); also fondant flavoured with vanilla, bergamot, mastic & cream
—**çorbası** *chohr-bah-sih* soup of flour, egg, rice, yoghurt, butter, salt, pepper & red pepper (Kütahya)

çeyrek *chey-rehk* a quarter
—**ekmek** *ehk-mehk* quarter of (a loaf of) bread – as for a **döner sandwiç**

çıkış *chih-kihsh* exit

çılbır *chihl-bihr* eggs poached in vinegary water topped with yoghurt sauce

çıtırmak *chih-tihr-mahk* boiled honey & roasted sesame seed sweet (Muğla)

çiçek *chee-chehk* flower

çiçekyağı *chee-chehk-yah-ih* sunflower oil

çift (*see* **bir çift**)

çiftçi *cheeft-chee* farmer

çifte kavrulmuş *cheef-teh kahv-ruhl-moosh* Turkish delight, confectionary with a hard consistency

çiftlik *cheeft-leek* farm

çiğ börek *chee ber-ehk* fried **börek** made with ground meat, onions & spices

çiğ köfte *chee kerf-teh* dish made of raw ground lamb, pounded wheat (**bulgur**), onions, clove, cinnamon, salt, black & red pepper

çiklet *cheek-leht* chewing gum

çikolata *chee-koh-lah-tah* chocolate

çikolatalı dondurma *chee-koh-lah-tah-lih dohn-duur-mah* chocolate ice cream

çikolatalı pasta *chee-koh-lah-tah-lih pahs-tah* chocolate cake
çilek *chee-lehk* strawberry
 –reçeli *reh-cheh-lee* strawberry jam
çilekli dondurma *chee-lehk-lee dohn-duur-mah* strawberry ice cream
 –komposto *kohm-pohst-toh* stewed strawberry compote
çimdik *cheem-deek* a pinch (of)
Çin lokantası *cheen loh-kahn-tah-sih* Chinese restaurant
Çin tavası *cheen tah-vah-sih* wok, concave griddle
çinekop *chee-neh-kohp* blue fish or young lufer
çintar *cheen-tahr* mushroom found in the Izmir region
çipura (balığı) *chee-puu-rah (bah-lihh-ih)* gilt-head bream (fish found in the Aegean Sea)
çir hoşafı *cheer hoh-shah-fih* stewed apricot compote (Sivas)
çirli et *cheer-lee eht* dish of seasoned beef chunks & dried apricot (Sivas)
çiroz *chee-rohz* salted, dried thin mackerel (fish)
 –salatası *sah-lah-tah-sih* dried mackerel salad
çoban salatası *choh-bahn sah-lah-tah-sih* shepherd's salad, made with tomatoes, onions, cucumbers & peppers
çoğu *choh-uu* most (of)
çok *chohk* many; much; a lot; very
 –acı *ah-jih* too (spicy) hot
 –az *ahz* a very little
 –fazla *fahz-lah* too much
 –güzel *gyuu-zehl* very nice/beautiful
 –iyi *ee-yee* very good/nice/well
 –kalın *kah-lihn* very thick
 –kötü *ker-tuuu* very bad
 –pişmiş *peesh-meesh* really well done (well cooked)
 –sıcak *sih-jahk* too hot (temperature)
 –soğuk *sohh-uuk* too cold
 –tatlı *taht-lih* too sweet

 –tuzlu *tuuz-luu* very salty
çomak *choh-mahk* stuffed flat bazlama bread (Mersin, İçel)
çorba kaşığı *chohr-bah kah-shih-ih* soup spoon; tablespoon
çorba(lar) *chohr-bah-(lahr)* soup(s)
çorbası *chohr-bah-sih* soup
çortan *chor-tahn* dried çökelek peynir
çökelek (peynir) *choh-keh-lehk (pehy-nihr)* cheese – very similar to cottage cheese though drier
çökelekli biber dolması *cher-keh-lehk-lee bee-behr dohl-mah-sih* dolma dish, made by stuffing large 'bell' peppers with çökelek peynir, parsley, tomatoes, onion, vegetable oil, cumin, black pepper & salt (Antalya)
çökelekli zeytin *cher-keh-lehk-lee zehy-teen* salad of çökelek peynir & seeded green olives with onion, tomatoes, olive oil & parsley (Hatay)
çökertme *cher-kehrt-meh* sliced steak dish served on a bed of fried 'finger' potatoes which have been topped by a garlicky yoghurt sauce (Muğla)
çöp şiş (kebab) *cherp sheesh (keh-bahb)* a meat only kebeb, with small pieces of meat, four or five to a çöp skewer
çörek *cher-rehk* round, ring-shaped or braided biscuit (usually sweet)
çörekotu *cher-rek-oh-tuu* black cumin
çözünmek *cher-zuun-mehk* to dissolve
çubuk makarna *chuu-buuk mah-kahr-nah* medium thin spaghetti
çullama *chuul-lah-mah* dish of sliced quail, butter & flour which looks like a thick fried pancake (Muğla)
çuşka biber *chuush-kah bee-behr* red pepper used for making sauce
çürük yumurta *chuu-ruuk yuu-muur-tah* rotten egg

D

dağ domuzu *dahh doh-muu-zuu* mountain boar

dağ keçisi *dahh keh-chee-see* mountain goat

dağılıncaya kadar haşlanmak *dah-ih-lihn-jah-yah kah-dahr hahsh-lahn-mahk* to cook until (something) falls to pieces or becomes mushy

dakika *dah-kee-kah* minute (time)

dal *dahl* sprig/branch

dalak ızgara *dah-lahk ihz-gah-rah* grilled spleen

damla(lar) *dahm-lah(lahr)* drop(s)

dana (eti) *dah-nah (eh-tee)* veal
  –**ciğer** *jee-ehr* veal liver
  –**rosto** *rohs-toh* roasted veal

davet *dah-veht* invitation
  –**etmek** *eht-mehk* to invite

defne yaprağı *dehf-neh yahp-rah-ih* bay leaf

dekstroz *dek-strohz* dextrose sugar

demet *deh-meht* bunch (of greens)

demir *deh-mihr* iron

demlik *dehm lihk* double boiler for making tea

den çorbası *dehn chorh-bah-sih* soup of **yarma**, beef broth & mint (Erzurum)

deniz ürünleri *deh-neez uuu-ruuun-leh-ree* seafood products
  –**salatası** *sah-lah-tah-sih* seafood salad

dereotu *deh-reh-oh-toh* dill

derepisisi *deh-reh-pee-see-see* flounder

dibekte dövülmüş kahve *dee-behk-teh der-vuuul-muuush kah-veh* coffee that's been ground in a large mortar

dible/diple *dee-bleh/deep-leh* cold vegetable dish, usually with rice, olive oil & often with fresh green beans; also cold dish of roasted onions with beans, salted tomatoes, **karalahana** cabbage & wild herbs (Ordu & Giresun)

didiklemek *dee-deek-leh-mehk* to pull apart; to pick to shreds

diken dutu *dee-kehn duu-tuu* blackberry, another name for **böğürtlen**

dil *deel* tongue

  –**balığı** *bah-lih-ih* sole (fish)
  –**balığı tavası** *bah-lih-ih tah-vah-sih* fried flounder/sole
  –**peynir** *pehy-nihr* mozzarella-like cheese

dilber dudağı *deel-behr duu-dahh-ih* sweet pastry in the shape of a lip

dilim *dee-leem* a slice
  –**dilim doğrayın** *dee-leem dohh-rah-yihn* cut into slices

dilimlemek *dee-leem-leh-mehk* to slice

dilimleyin *dee-leem-leh-yeen* slice (imperative of **dilimlemek**)

dilli sandviç *deel-lee sahnd-which* tongue sandwich

dinlendirme süresi *deen-lehn-deer-meh suuu-reh-see* resting time (for food)

dinlenme tesisleri *deen-lehn-meh teh-sees-leh-ree* roadhouse

dinlenmek *deen-lehn-mehk* to let rest

dinlenmiş *deen-lehn-mihsh* aged (meat)

diş *deesh* clove; tooth

divriği alatlı pilavı *deev-reee-ee ah-laht-lih pee-lah-wih* pilaf dish made with rice, chunks of lamb, bouillon, chickpeas, seedless grapes & butter (Sivas)

diyet *dee-yeht* diet
  –**tatlılar** *taht-lih-lahr* diet desserts; diet sweets

dizmek *deez-mehk* to place/arrange (things) side by side, to line up

doğramak *doh-rah-mahk* to cut in slices/pieces, to carve; to chop to bits

doğranmış *doh-rahn-mihsh* sliced

dolgu *dohl-ghuu* filling/stuffing

dolma(sı) *dohl-mah(sih)* stuffed

dolmalık *dohl-mah-lihk* suitable for stuffing in a **dolma**
  –**biber** *bee-behr* green pepper; sweet pepper; pepper suitable for stuffing
  –**fıstık** *fihs-tihk* nut, usually **antep fıstığı** or **şam fıstığı**, used to season **dolma**

domates(ler) *doh-mah-tehs (lehr)* tomato(s)

–**çorbası** *chohr-bah-sah* tomato soup

–**salatalık salatası** *sah-lah-tah-lihk sah-lah-tah-sih* tomato & cucumber salad

–**suyu** *suu-yuu* tomato juice

domatesli *doh-mah-tehs-lee* with tomato

–**patlıcan çarliston biber kızartması** *paht-lih-jahn chahr-lees-tohn bee-behr kih-zart-mah-sih* fried eggplant (aubergine) with tomatoes & sweet peppers

–**patlıcan kızartması** *paht-lih-jahn kih-zart-mah-sih* fried eggplant (aubergine) with tomatoes

–**pilav** *pee-lawv* tomato pilaf

–**şehriye çorbası** *sheh-ree-yeh chohr-bah-sih* tomato soup with vermicelli

domuz (eti) *doh-muhz (eh-tee)* pork (meat)

dondurma *dohn-duur-mah* ice cream (*see also* **çikolatalı dondurma**; **çilekli dondurma**)

dondurulmuş *dohn-duu-ruul-muush* frozen

–**bakla** *bahk-lah* frozen beans

–**bezelye** *beh-zehl-yeh* frozen peas

–**mısır** *mih-sihr* frozen corn

donmak *dohn-mahk* to freeze

doyum olmamak *doh-yum ohl-mah-mahk* to be extremely delicious

dökmek *derk-mehk* pour

döner *der-nehr* thin slices of meat stacked on a vertical skewer, grilled then shaved off

–**kebab** *keh-bahb* kebab (usually lamb or chicken) cooked on a rotating spit

–**kebabevi** *keh-bahb-eh-vee* döner kebab house

–**li sandviç** *-lee sahnd-which* döner kebab sandwich

dörder *der-dehr* four each of

döş sarması *dersh sahr-mah-sih* stuffed breast

döşemek *der-sheh-mehk* to spread something on or over; to cover

dövme *derv-meh* wheat without husks

dövme etli karalahana sarması *derv-meh eht-lee kah-rah-lah-hah-nah sahr-mah-sih* lamb strips, rice & tomato paste wrapped in **karalahana** leaves (Rize)

dövülmüş *der-vuul-muuush* pounded/beaten/ground (coffee)

dul avrat çorbası *duul ahv-raht chohr-bah-sih* 'widow soup' made with chickpeas, lentils, lamb **but**, tomato paste, peppers & mint (Adana)

dut *duut* mulberry

düdüklü tencere *duu-duuk-luu tehn-jeh-reh* pressure cooker

düğün *duu-uun* wedding

–**çorbası** *chohr-bah-sih* wedding soup made with ground meat, carrots & lemon or vinegar, which gives it a sour flavour. Also known as **ekşili çorba**.

–**pilavı** *pee-lah-wih* wedding pilaf. Made with rice, chickpeas, small fried meat chunks, butter & salt. (Kayseri); or made with chicken, pearled wheat, **yarma** & butter (Sakarya)

dükkan *duuuk-kaahn* shop

dürüm *duuu-ruum* **kebab** rolled in pitta-style bread

düt *duuut* white mulberry

düzine *duuu-zee-neh* dozen

E

ebegümeci haşlaması *eh-beh-ghuuu-meh-jee hahsh-lahn-mah-sih* boiled mallow

ebegümeci haşlaması fasulye çorbası *eh-beh-ghuuu-meh-jee hahsh-lah-mah-sih fah-suul-yeh chohr-bah-sih* boiled mallow bean soup

ekmek *ehk-mehk* bread (*see also* **beyaz ekmek**; **bir dilim ekmek**; **buğday ekmek**; **çavdar ekmek**)

–**böreği** *ber-rehh-ee* oven-baked stale bread & melted **kaşar** cheese (İzmir)

ekmekkadayıf *ehk-mehk-kah-dah-yihf* dessert of baked **kadayıf** bread rusks soaked in thick syrup & layered or topped with **kaymak**

ekşili *ehk-shee-lee* sour

–**çorba** *chohr-bah* (*see* **düğün çorbası**)

–**nohutlu bamya** *noh-huut-luu bahm-yah* mutton stew with okra & chickpeas (Mersin, İcel)

–**patlıcan dolması** *paht-lih-jahn dohl-mah-sih* stuffed eggplant **dolma** (Adana)

–**taraklık tavası** *tah-rahk-lihk tah-vah-sih* sour lamb cutlets with quince

–**ıspanak başı** *ihs-pah-nak bah-shih* spinach & lentil stew (Tarsus)

elbasan *ehl-bah-sahn* open-faced pie made with fried lamb meat chunks, barely cooked eggs & yoghurt – served with hot chips (Manisa)

elma *ehl-mah* apple

–**çayı** *chah-yih* apple tea

–**komposto** *kohm-pohs-toh* stewed apple compote

–**marmeladı** *mahr-mah-lah-dih* apple marmalade

–**suyu** *suu-yuu* apple juice

–**lı pasta** *-lih pahs-tah* apple cake

enginar *ehn-ghee-nahr* artichoke

–**dolması** *dohl-mah-sih* **dolma** made with artichoke, rice, mincemeat, onion, parsley & lemon juice topped with an egg & lemon sauce (Manisa)

erik *eh-reek* plum

–**aşı** *ah-shih* plum dish, of prunes, rice & sugar (Tekirdağ)

–**komposto** *kohm-pohs-toh* stewed plum compote

erikli tavşan *eh-reek-lee tahwv-shahn* rabbit with plums

erikli tavuk dolması *eh-reek-lee tah-vuhk dohl-mah-sih* stuffed chicken with plums

erikli, ekşili biber dolması *eh-reek-lee, ehk-shee-lee bee-behr dohl-mah-sih* pep-pers stuffed with eggplant, tomato paste, bulgur, walnuts, plums, mint & kızılcık (Bilecik)

Erzincan piyazı *ehr-zeen-jahn pee-yah-zih* salad made with cucumber, tomatoes, white cheese, **çökelek** cheese, green pepper, dill, parsley, sweet basil, red pepper, olive oil (Erzincan)

eski *ehs-kee* aged, old

–**peynir** *pehy-nihr* aged cheese

esmer *ehs-mehr* dark brown

–**ekmek** *ehk-mehk* brown bread

–**şeker** *sheh-kehr* brown sugar

espresso *eh-spreh-soh* espresso coffee

et suyu *eht suu-yuu* meat juice; broth; bouillon; stock; gravy

–**(baharatlı)** *(bah-hah-raht-lih)* bouillon

–**(yumurtalı)** *(yuu-muur-tah-lih)* broth with egg

–**hindiba çorbası** *heen-dee-bah chohr-bah-sih* endive broth

et suyuna sebze çorbası *eht suu-yuu sehb-zee chohr-bah-sih* stock (liquid)

et(i) *eht(ee)* meat

etler *eht-lehr* meats

etli *eht-lee* with meat

–**bamya** *bahm-yah* okra with meat

–**biber dolması** *bee-behr dohl-mah-sih* green peppers stuffed with meat

–**bohça böreği** *boh-chah ber-reh-ee* delicate bundle-shaped **börek** filled with seasoned ground beef

–**bulgur pilav** *buul-guur pee-lawv* bulgur pilaf with meat & chickpeas

–**dolma(lar)** *dohl-mah(-lahr)* vegetables stuffed with meat

–**dövme pilavı** *derv-meh pee-lah-vih* pilaf with chickpeas, pounded wheat, & lamb chunks (Mersin, İcel)

–**ekmek** *ehk-mehk* Turkish bread topped with seasoned meat pieces

–**enginar** *ehn-ghee-nahr* a stew of artichoke, mincemeat or lamb chunks, dill, onion, tomatoes & tomato paste, margarine & salt (Aydın)

–enginar dolması *ehn-ghee-nahr dohl-mah-sih* artichokes stuffed with meat

–kabak dolması *kah-bahk dohl-mah-sih* zucchini (courgette) stuffed with meat

–kabak ve biber dolması *kah-bahk veh bee-behr dohl-mah-sih* zucchini (courgette) & pepper stuffed with meat

–kereviz dolması *keh-reh-weez dohl-mah-sih* celery stuffed with meat

–kuru fasulye *kuu-ruu fah-suul-yeh* haricot or butter beans & meat cooked in a crock pot

–lahana dolması *lah-hah-nah dohl-mah-sih* cabbage leaves stuffed with meat

–marul dolması *mah-ruul dohl-mah-sih* lettuce leaves stuffed with rice, onion, tomato, parsley, oil, black pepper, cumin & salt & meat (Edirne)

–nohut *noh-huht* chickpeas in meat sauce

–patlıcan dolması *paht-lih-jahn dohl-mah-sih* eggplant (aubergine) stuffed with meat

–pide *pee-deh* Turkish 'pizza' with ground meat

–sebzeli güveç *sehb-zeh-lee gyuuu-vehch* stewed meat with vegetables

–semizotu *seh-mee-zoh-tuu* purslane with meat

–taze fasulye *tah-zeh fah-suul-yeh* beans with meat

–yaprak dolması *yahp-rahk-dohl-mah-sih* vine leaves with meat stuffing

–yeşil mercimek *yeh-sheel mehr-jee-mehk* lentils with meat, onion, tomato paste, salt & pepper

etsiz *eht-sihz* meatless

–yemekler *yeh-mehk-lehr* meatless dishes

etyemez *eht-yeh-mehz* vegetarian

ev yemekleri *ehv yeh-mehk-lehr-ee* home cooking

ezme lahana *ehz-meh lah-hah-nah* a flat vegetable 'pie' made of karalahana, chard, onion, olive oil, suet, corn flour, tomatoes & red pepper (Rize)

ezme salata *ehz-meh sah-lah-tah* tomato salad or cold tomato soup, similar to gazpacho (Antep)

ezmesi *(see* badem ezmesi)

ezo gelin çorbası *eh-zoh geh-leen chohr-bah-sih* red lentil 'bride' soup

F

fasulye *fah-suul-yeh* dry or fresh beans

fasulye (kuru) *fah-suul-yeh (kuu-ruu)* dry bean(s)

fasulye (taze) *fah-suul-yeh (tah-zeh)* green beans *(see* barbunya fasulye)

–diple *–dee-pleh* green bean, carrot, onion, rice & olive oil salad (Giresun)

–otu *–oh-tuu* fragrant herb used for enhancing the flavour of kuru fasulye & other baklagiller

–pilaki *pee-lah-kee* bean salad

–piyazı *pee-yah-zee* white bean salad *(see* piyazı)

–turşusu kavurması *tuur-shuu-suu kah-vuur-mah-sih* salad made with pickled beans, onion & butter, served either hot or cold (Rize)

fatura *fah-tuu-rah* invoice/bill

fava *fah-vah* mashed broad bean salad

fener balığı *feh-nehr bah-lih-ih* angler fish

fesleğen *fehs-lehh-en* sweet basil

–makarna *mah-kar-nah* basil-based pasta with onion, garlic, tomato, fresh green chilli & eggplant

fındıklı *fihn-dihk-lih* hazelnut

fıstık *fihs-tihk* nut/pistachio/peanut

fincan *fihn-jehn* (a) cup

fındık *fihn-dihk* hazelnut; shape of a hazelnut

fındıkkıran *fihn-dihk-kih-rihn* nutcracker

fırın *fih-rihn* oven/bakery
fırında *fih-rihn-dah* baked
   –sütlaç *suut-lahch* oven-cooked **sütlaç**
   –kuzu (budu) *kuu-zuu (buu-duu)* roast lamb
   –kuzu budu sebzeli *kuu-zuu buu-duu sehb-zeh-lee* leg of lamb & vegetables
   –palamut *pah-lah-muut* baked bonito
   –piliç *pee-leech* baked chicken
   –piliçli bezelye *pee-leech-lee beh-zehl-yeh* oven-cooked chicken with peas
   –sığır kebabı *sihh-ih keh-bah-bih* roasted beef **kebab**
fiks menü *fiks meh-nuuu* fixed menu
fincanı (*see* **çay fincanı**)
firik *fee-reek* boiled, threshed (pounded) fresh wheat (Urfa)
fiş *feesh* receipt
fiyat *fee-yaht* price
folyo (*see* **alüminyum folyo**)
fosul *foh-suhl* kebab of lamb or mutton (Samsun)
frambuaz *frahm-buu-ahz* raspberry (*see* **ahududu**)
francala *frahn-jah-lah* a bread made in a long narrow loaf
Fransız kahvesi *fran-sihz kah-veh-seh* coffee & milk
frenk fesleğeni *frehnk fehs-lehh-eh-nee* (*see* **fesleğen**)
frenk maydanozu *frehnk mahy-dah-noh-zuu* crinkly leaf **maydanoz**
füme *foo-meh* smoked

G

gak hoşafı *gahk hoh-sha-fih* 'crow caw' compote of stewed dried apple
galeta *ghah-leh-tah* breadstick
garnitür *ghahr-nee-tuur* garnish
garson *ghahr-sohn* waiter/waitress
gazino *ghah-zee-noh* bar with food
gazoz *ghah-zohz* clear soft drink; caffeine-free soft drink

gece külübü *gheh-jeh kuu-luu-buu* night club
geçirmez *gheh-cheer-mehz* free from; without; -less
gelin turşusu *gheh-lihn tuur-shuu-suu* bride's pickle, of **çarliston biber**, green pepper with vinegar, garlic & salt (Mersin, İçel)
gelincik *gheh-lihn-jihk* rockling (fish)
gerdan dolması *ghehr-dahn dohl-mah-sih* lamb neck stuffed with onion, rice, mincemeat, almonds, tomato paste & **köfte bahar** (Adana)
gerdaniye *ghehr-dah-nee-yeh* neck of lamb with plum & sugar (Edirne)
gereçler *gheh-rehch-lehr* necessary items; ingredients
geyik eti *gheh-yeek eh-tee* venison
gıda *ghih-dah* food (in an abstract sense); the concept of food or nourishment. **Gıda maddeleri** is used to mean 'food-related materials'.
   –pazarı *pah-zah-rih* food market; supermarket
gileboru *gee-lee-boh-roh* a fruit resembling a miniature cherry
   –şurubu *shuu-ruu-buu* syrup made from gileboru juice & sugar
giriş *gee-reesh* entrance
girişler *gee-reesh-lehr* (*see* **meze**)
glukoz *gih-luu-kohz* dextrose
göbek salata *gher-behk sah-lah-tah* head lettuce; also salad made with head lettuce, tomato, parsley, radish, carrot, cucumber, & black cabbage (İstanbul)
göğüs *gher-ooos* breast (of chicken)
gökkuşağı salatası *gherk-kuu-shahh-ih sah-lah-tah-sih* 'rainbow salad', made with 'pinwheel' macaroni, peppers, olives, dill, mushrooms, pickles, lemon juice & salami strips
gözleme *gerz-leh-meh* filled filo pastry (Tokat)
graten *grah-tehn* au gratin

greyfurt/greyfrut/greypfrut
ghrey-fuurt/ ghrey-fruut/ghreyp-fruut
grapefruit
–reçeli *reh-cheh-lee* grapefruit jam
–suyu *suu-yuu* grapefruit juice
gül reçeli *gyuul reh-cheh-lee* rose jam
gül suyu *gyuul suu-yuu* rose water
gül şerbeti *gyuul sher-beh-tee* non-alcoholic drink made with rosewater,
water & sugar (Sivas)
gül tatlısı *gyuul taht-lih-sih* fried rose-
shaped pastry covered in melted
lemon sherbet
güllaç *gyuul-lahch* thin, dry sheet of
dough; also sweet made from sheets
of **güllaç** soaked in milky syrup, filled
with nuts & flavoured with rose
water.
günün mönüsü *guuun-nuuun mer-*
nuuu-suuu the day's menu
güveç *gyuuu-vehch* earthenware cooking
pot; also food cooked in an earthenware pot
güveçte kurufasulye *gyuuu-vehch-teh*
kuu-ruu-fah-suul-yeh casseroled beans
güveçte kıymalı yumurta *gyuuu-vehch-*
teh kihy-mah-lih yuu-muur-tah
casseroled eggs with minced meat
güveçte türlü (tavuk kanadı ile) *gyuuu-*
vehch-teh toor-loo (tah-vuuk kah-nah-
dih ee-leh) mixed vegetable casserole
with chicken

H

halep işi kebap *hah-lehp ee-shee keh-*
bahp grilled meatballs, onions &
spices
halim aşı *hah-leem ah-shih* thick soup
of chickpeas, meaty bones, wheat **yara-**
ma, tomato & onion
hakiki *hah-kee-kee* 'real', authentic
halal *hah-lahl* the Muslim method of
slaughter. A prayer is said, the animal's throat is cut to ensure rapid
death & the blood is drained from
the body.

hamsi *hahm-see* anchovies
–böreği *ber-rehh-ee* layers of breaded
fried anchovies & seasoned rice
(Giresun)
–buğulaması *buuu-uu-lah-mah-sih*
poached anchovies with tomatoes &
green peppers found throughout the
Black Sea coastal region
–çorbası *chohr-bah-sih*
anchovy & tomato soup (Trabzon)
–ekşilisi *ehk-shee-lee-see* 'anchovy
sour', anchovy, green pepper & tomato salad (Rize)
–ızgara *ihz-ghah-rah* grilled anchovies
served with raw onion & lemon
–kuşu *kuu-shuu* anchovies fried with
thinly chopped tomatoes, green peppers & parsley (Rize, Trabzon)
–li, pazılı pilav *-lee, pah-zih-lih pee-*
lawv mixed anchovy pilaf (Trabzon)
–salamura *sha-lah-muu-rah*
pickled anchovy, rock salt & bayleaf
–tatlısı *taht-lih-sih* jellied sweet whose
main ingredient is anchovy! Other
ingredients include flour, egg, olive
oil, lemon juice, salt; in a jelly made
from pureed banana, orange, raspberry, apple, peach & sugar. Sprinkled
with pistachios & hazelnuts. (Rize)
–tava *tah-vah* fried corn-breaded
anchovies served with thickly sliced
onion & lemon
hamsikoli *hahm-see-koh-lee* bread
made with chard, onion, mint, corn
meal & anchovies (Rize)
hamsili ekmek *hahm-see-lee ehk-mahk*
(see **hamsikoli**)
hamsili pilav *hahm-see-lee pee-lawv*
oven-baked anchovy pilaf, consisting
of tightly arranged layers of anchovies
& seasoned rice with onion, margarine, pistachio nuts, currants (Rize)
hamur işleri *hah-muur eesh-leh-ree*
pastries
hamurlu çorba *hah-muur-luh chohr-*
bah dark soup of **erişte** dough, lentils
& mincemeat (Amasya & Tokat)

hamurlu yeşil mercimek çorbası *hah-muur-luh yeh-sheel mehr-jee-mehk chohr-bah-sih* green lentil soup with small dumplings

hanım göbeği *hah-nihm ger-behh-ih* 'woman's navel', semolina dessert

hanibana *hah-nee-bah-nah* **köfte** cooked with onion, green pepper, carrot, tomato, peas, corn oil, cumin, allspice, parsley & tomato (Kocaeli)

hardal *hahr-dahl* mustard

hardallı patlıcan kızartması *hahr-dahl-lih paht-lih-jahn kih-zahrt-mah-sih* fried eggplant (aubergine) & mustard

hashaşlı *hahsh-hahsh* warm salad made with a mixture of corn flour, pepper sauce, crushed walnuts, chopped **karalahana** & garlic, moulded into a low dome (Artvin)
–tohumu *toh-hoo-moo* opium poppy seed

haşhaşlı ekmek *hahsh-hahsh-lih ehk-mehk* bread with crushed opium poppy seeds

haşhaşlı gözleme *hahsh-hahsh-lih gerz-leh-meh* savoury pancake made from flour & vegetable oil, topped with poppy seed (Eskişehir & Edirne)

haşlama *hahsh-lah-mah* steamed lamb & vegetables in broth

haşlanmış katı yumurta *hahsh-lahn-mihsh kah-tih yuu-muur-tah* hard boiled egg

havuç *hah-wuch* carrot
–kızartması *kih-zahrt-mah-sih* fried carrots
–pane *pah-neh* fried carrots covered with crumbled bread
–salatası *sah-lah-tah-sih* carrot salad

havyar *hawv-yahr* caviar

haydari *hahy-dah-ree* yoghurt with roasted eggplant (aubergine) & garlic (meze)

hayvanı *(see* **av hayvanı**)

hayvansal yağ *hahy-wahn-sahl yahh* animal fat

hazır kahve *hah-zihr kah-veh* instant coffee

hazırlama süresi *hah-zihr-lah-mah suu-reh-see* preparation time

hazırlanışı *hah-zihr-lah-nih-shih* (steps of) preparation

helva *hehl-vah* sweet prepared with sesame oil, cereals & syrup or honey, especially prepared for weddings

helvacı kökü *hehl-vah-jah ker-kyuuu* *(see* **çöğen kökü**)

hesap *heh-sahp* the bill (for a meal)

hırtlama köfte *hihrt-lah-mah kerf-teh* **köfte** of lean veal, corn flour, thyme, butter & salt (Trabzon)

hıyar *hih-yahr* cucumber; also blockhead/arsehole

hibeş *hee-besh* meze spread, made from **tahin**, cumin, red pepper flakes, lemon juice & water (Antalya)

hindi *heen-dee* turkey
–kızartma *kih-zahrt-mah* roasted turkey
–rosto *rohs-toh* roasted turkey

hindiba *heen-dee-bah* endive/chicory

hindistan cevizi (hindistancevizi) *heen-dee-stahn-jeh-wee-zee* coconut; also nutmeg *(see* **hintcevizi**)

hindiba çorbası *heen-dee-bah chohr-bah-sih* endive soup

hingel *heen-ghel* layered dish of thin pastry layers & crumbled cheese, uses **çökelek peyniri** (Yozgat)

hintcevizi *heet-che-vee-zee* 'Indian nut' – nutmeg

hörre *her-reh* soup made of butter, flour, water & tomato paste (Kars)

hoşaf(ı) *hoh-shahf(ih)* (a fruit compote)

hoşmerim *hohsh-meh-reem* classic Anatolian pudding with broken walnuts & pistachios. Stir-fried with cream, it's a real treat for sweet lovers. The name of this dish arises from **Hoş mu erim?** meaning 'Is it good, my brave man?' (Kırklareki)

humus *huu-muus* humus, made with cooked, finely mashed chickpeas blended with sesame oil, lemon & spices. A popular southern Turkish dish, it 'must' be served when **mezes** are taken with **rakı**. A speciality of Mersin, İçel & Hatay.

hurma *huhr-mah* date (fruit)
  –tatlısı *taht-lih-sih*
  semolina & date cake in syrup

hülüklü düğün çorbası *hyuu duu-uun chohr-bah-sih* thick, hearty soup with chopped tripe, meatballs, chickpeas & rice (Adana)

hünkâr beğendi *hyuun-kahr beh-ehn-dee* lamb stew served on puréed eggplant (aubergine)

I

ısırganotu çorbası *ih-sihr-ghah-noh-toh chohr-bah-sih* stinging nettle soup. Wear plastic gloves to protect your hands when cleaning the stinging nettle plant. The dry, crumbled leaves are used to make tea. (Giresun)

ısırganotu ezmesi *ih-sihr-ghah-noh-toh ehz-meh-see* stinging nettle purée (Rize)

ıskorpit (balığı) *ihs-kohr-peet (bah-lihh-ih)* scorpion fish

ıslama *ihs-lah-mah* gravy prepared from beef broth, red pepper & vegetable oil

ıslama köfte *ihs-lah-mah kerf-teh* flattened meat patties on toasted bread & doused in **ıslama** juice (Sakarya)

ıspanak *ih-spa-nahk* spinach
  –çorbası *chohr-bah-sih* spinach soup
  –erişte *eh-reesh-teh* flat spaghetti made with spinach
  –graten *gih-rah-tehn* spinach au gratin
  –krep *kih-rehp* spinach crepe

ıspanaklı börek *ih-spa-nahk-lih ber-rehk* pastry filled with spinach

ıspanaklı mıhlama *ih-spa-nahk-lih mih-lah-mah* spinach & egg dish

ızgara *ihz-ghah-rah* grilled
  –köfte *kerf-teh* grilled meatballs

İ

iç ceviz *eech cheh-wihz* shelled walnuts

iç pilav *eech pee-lawv* rice with onions, nuts & currants

iç(içi) *eech(ee-chee)* stuffing; also batter

içeçek(ler) *ee-cheh-chehk(lehr)* drink(s) (see **sıcak içeçek** & **soğuk içeçek**)

içi dolmuş *ee-chee dohl-muush* thin eggplant slices topped with a mixture of white cheese, onion, tomatoes, parsley, egg, flower, salt & pepper (Balıkesir)

içindekiler *ee-cheen-deh-kee-lehr* ingredients/contents

içki(ler) *eech-kee(lehr)* drink(s) (usually alcoholic)

içli köfte *eech-lee kerf-teh* fist-sized **köfte** with an outer covering of **bulgur** (Antep, Diyarbakır & Adana)

iftar *ihf-tahr* the evening meal that 'breaks the daylight fast' during the month of Ramazan

ikindi *ee-keen-dee* mid-afternoon

ilk *eelk* first

imam bayıldı *ee-mahm bah-yihl-dih* 'the imam, İslamic cleric, fainted' – this famous dish is made of eggplant (aubergine), tomatoes, onion & peppers cooked in olive oil & served cold

imsak *eem-sahk* Ramazam pre-dawn meal

ince erişte *een-jeh eh-reesh-teh* linguine

incir *een-jihr* fig
  –reçeli *reh-cheh-lee* fig jam
  –uyuşturması *uu-yuush-tuur-mah-sih* 'fig narcotic', dessert made of milk, figs & sugar (Sakarya)

indirim *een-dih-reem* discount/reduction

İnegöl köfte *ee-neh-gerl kerf-teh* **köfte** dish made with mincemeat – according to tradition, this famous dish takes about five days to prepare, including a four-day ageing process after the meat has been minced. Seasoning is added just before cooking. (İnegöl, Bursa)

iri kıyılmış *ee-ree kihy-ihl-mihsh* coarsely minced

irmik *eer-meek* semolina
  –helvası *hehl-vah-sih* **helva** with semolina

ishakiye *ees-hah-kee-yeh* traditional Turkish **helva** dessert made of rice flour, almonds & sugar

işkembe *eesh-kehm-beh* tripe
  –çorbası *chohr-bah-sih* tripe soup
  –li nohut yahnisi *lee noh-huut yah-nee-see* chick peas **yahni** with tripe

işkembeci *eesh-kehm-beh-chee* tripe soup eatery

İskender (kebab) *eees-kehn-der (keh-bahh)* **döner kebab** on sliced flat bread, served as a sit-down meal. It's covered with a hot full-flavoured tomato sauce, a hot butter sauce & usually served with yoghurt.

iskoç viski *ees-kohch wihs-kee* whisky

iskorpit (balığı) *ees-kohr-peet (bah-lihh-ih)* scorpion fish

isotreçeli *ee-soh-treh-cheh-lee* unsweetened preserve made of 'Urfa' peppers, cinnamon, ground black pepper, olive oil & eaten with plain slices of Turkish bread (Urfa)

istakoz *ees-tah-kohz* lobster

İstanbul mutfağı *ees-tahn-buul muut-fahh-ih* İstanbul cuisine took shape during the Ottoman centuries, in Topkapı Palace & the mansions of rich merchants. It features very slow cooking, foods heavy in animal fat (mostly lamb & mutton), & endless varieties of hot & cold eggplant (aubergine) dishes. Rice & beans are also important.

istavrit (balığı) *ees-tahv-riht (bah-lih-ih)* horse mackerel; scad (fish)

istavrit tava *ees-tahv-riht tah-vah* fried small mackerels

istiridye *ees-tih-reed-yeh* oyster

iştah *eesh-tah* appetite

ithal *ee-tahl* imported

iyi *ee-yee* good/well
  –pişmiş *peesh-meesh* well done (well cooked)
  –pişmiş biftek *peesh-meesh bihf-tehk* steak that's well done

izmarit (balığı) *ihz-mah-reet (bah-lih-ih)* pickerel; sea bream (fish)

İzmir köfte *eez-meer kerf-teh* **köfte** with coarse mincemeat, egg, breadcrumbs, **köftebahar** & tomatoes (İzmir)

İzmir mutfağı *eez-meer muut-fahh-ih* İzmir regional cuisine featuring dishes such as dry bread or toast with **tarhana** & a meat broth called **kaynarca**, along with toast served with olives, cheese, **sucuk** & sweet preserves. Milk-based soups are popular in winter; while fruits such as watermelon & honey dew melon are favoured in summer. Vegetables, fish & other sea products remain popular all year round.

J

jaji *zhah-zhee (see* **çökelek peynir***)* (Bitlis)

jambon *zham-bohn* ham. Although you won't find ham products everywhere (due to religion & tradition), they're available in upscale city markets. Ham-flavoured poultry is common & you may see this word listed when it is, in fact, a Muslim version of ham made from beef or chicken.

jelatin *zheh-lah-teen* gelatin

jöle *zher-leh* jello/gelatin

K

kabak (kabağı) *kah-bahk (kah-bah-ih)*
squash
  –çekirdeği *cheh-keer-dee-ee*
pumpkin seeds
  –dolması *dohl-mah-sih*
stuffed zucchini (courgette)
  –imambayıldı *ee-mahm-bah-yihl-dih*
zucchini in olive oil & served with
onions (see **imam bayıldı**)
  –karnıyarık *kahr-nih-yah-rihk*
zucchini stuffed with mincemeat
  –kızartması *kih-zahrt-mah-sih*
fried zucchini
  –mücveri *muuj-veh-ree*
fried zucchini patties
  –musakka *muu-sahk-kah*
stewed zucchini moussaka
  –pane *pah-neh* fried zucchini covered
with crumbed bread
  –tatlısı *taht-lih-sih* dessert made with
pumpkin, sweet syrup & walnuts
  –tava *tah-vah* fried zucchini; small
zucchini slices
kabaklı pirinç çorbası *kah-bahk pee-
reench chohr-bah-sih* zucchini & rice
soup
kabuk (kabuğu) *kah-buuk*
skin; rind; husk; shell; crust
kaburga (etleri) *kah-buhr-ghah (eht-leh-
ree)* spareribs; beef ribs; mutton ribs
Kaç?
Kahch?
How many?; How much?
kaç (see **bir kaç**)
kadayıf *kah-dah-yihf* dessert of dough
soaked in syrup & a layer of **kaymak**
as a topping (see **burma kadayıf**)
kadeh *kah-deh* wine/liqueur glass
kadın göbeği *kah-dihn ger-behh-ee*
doughnut in syrup
kadınbudu köfte *kah-dihn-buh-duh
kerf-teh* **köfte** of ground meat mixed
with cooked rice and fried in batter
(İzmir)

kağıdı (see **alüminyum folyo/kağıdı**)
kağıt kebap *kahh-iht keh-bahp* lamb
chunks & vegetables baked in wax
paper (Manisa)
kağıt peçete *kahh-iht peh-cheh-teh*
paper napkin; serviette
kağıtta barbunya *kahh-ihtt-tah bahr-
buun-yah* baked **barbunya** beans
kağıtta pastırma *kahh-ihtt-tah pahs-tihr-
mah* thinly sliced **pastırma** cooked in
aluminium foil with vegetables
kafe/kafeterya *kah-feh/kah-feh-tehr-yah*
café
kahırtlak hamuru *kah-hihrt-lahk hah-
muu-ruu* **kahırtlak** dough; fried
dough used in soup (Adana)
kahvaltı *kah-vahl-tih* breakfast
kahve *kah-veh* coffee (see **acı kahve**;
dibekte dövülmüş kahve)
  –az şekerli *ahz sheh-kehr-lee*
coffee with a little sugar
  –çok şekerli *chohk sheh-kehr-lee*
coffee with a lot of sugar
  –orta şekerli *ohr-tah sheh-kehr-lee*
coffee with medium sugar
  –sade *sah-deh* plain black coffee
  –şekersiz *sheh-kehr-sihz*
coffee without sugar
kahvehane *kah-veh-hah-neh* coffee house
kahverengi şeker *kah-veh-rehn-ghee
sheh-kehr* brown sugar
kahvesi (see **Amerikan kahvesi**)
kakao *kah-kah-oh* cocoa
kakule *kah-kuu-leh* cardamom
kalamar *kah-lah-mahr* squid/calamari
kalamarla makarna *kah-lah-mahr-lah
mah-kahr-nah* noodles with calamari
kalburabastı *kahl-buh-rah-bahs-tih*
baked egg-shaped dessert topped
with lemon syrup
kalkan (balığı) *kahl-kahn (bah-lih-ih)*
turbot (fish)
kalkan tavası *kahl-kahn ta-wah-sih*
fried turbot platter
kanat *kah-naht* wing

kandil kabağı *kahn-deel kah-bah-ih* 'holy night' pumpkin. A sweet made with pumpkin & crushed walnuts prepared for **Miraç**, one of the five holy nights of Islam.

kandil simidi *kahn-deel see-mee-dee* pastry rings sprinkled with cumin & sesame seeds, made for the spring festival (**kandil**) of **Hıdırellez**

kanyak *kahn-yahk* cognac

kap *kahp* pot/container/dish/ plate

kapalı kıymalı pide *kah-pah-lih kihy-mah-lih pee-deh* pocket of **pide** filled with a mixture of mincemeat & tomato (Samsun, Bafra & Giresun)

kapama *kah-pah-mah* basic dish of boiled chicken & rice (Eskişehir)

kapari çiçeği *kah-pah-ree chee-cheh-ee* caper (seasoning)

kapuska *kah-puus-kah* dish (served cool) of onion, tomato paste, cabbage, olive oil & salt (Edirne). Variations include spicy hot peppers & small chunks of meat.

karabiber (siyah biber) *kah-rah-bee-behr (see-yah bee-behr)* black pepper
–**değirmeni** *deh-ehr-meh-nee* black pepper mill

karaca eti *kah-rah-jah eh-tee* venison

karaciğer *kah-rah-jee-ehr* liver

karaçuval helvası *kah-rah-chuu-vahl hehl-vah-sih* sweet potato-shaped pastries served with **pekmez** (Çorum)

karadut *kah-rah-duut* mulberry

kara ekmek *kah-rah ehk-mehk* black bread

karafa *kah-rah-fah* carafe; a type of jug for water or **rakı**

karagöz (balığı) *kah-rah-gerz bah-lih-ih* spottail; black bream (fish)

kara kovanbal *kah-rah koh-wahn-bahl* premium honey from bees that build their own honeycomb (cheaper honey comes from man-made honeycomb)

karalahana *kah-rah-lah-hah-nah* dark-coloured Scotch kale; red cabbage
–**çorbası** *chohr-bah-sih* soup of dark-coloured cabbage, carrots, zucchini (courgette), **çarliston biber**, corn flour, wheat flour & potato (Rize)
–**diple (dible)** *deep-leh (deeb-leh)* salad of **karalahana** cabbage, Albanian red pepper, onion, **barbunya**, rice, butter & salt (Giresun)
–**sarma** *sahr-mah* wrapped **dolma**. Stuffing made with a mixture of thinly sliced veal, cooked rice, & cumin wrapped in **karalahana**. (Rize)

karamel *kah-rah-mehl* caramel

karanfil *kah-rahn-feel* clove

karaş *kah-rahsh* pudding-like dessert made with blackberries, sugar, seedless grapes & hazelnuts

karışık (et) ızgara *kah-rih-shihk (eht) ihz-ghah-rah* mixed grill

karışık dolma *kah-rih-shihk dohl-mah* mixed **dolma** made of stuffed grape leaves, red & green peppers & eggplant (aubergine) (Adana)

karışık meyve *kah-rih-shihk mehy-veh* mixed fruits

karışık pide *kah-rih-shihk pee-deh* Turkish 'pizza' layered with a fine mixture of tomato, onion, parsley & green pepper. The topping is often made with mincemeat, **pastırma sucuk** & **kaşar** cheese.

karışık salata *kah-rih-shihk sah-lah-tah* mixed salad

karışık sebze *kah-rih-shihk sehb-zeh* mixed vegetables

karides *kah-ree-dehs* shrimp (sea)
–**güveç** *gyuu-wech* shrimp casserole
–**kokteyl** *kohk-teyl* shrimp cocktail
–**salatası** *sah-lah-tah-sih* shrimp salad

karnabahar *kahr-nah-bah-hahr* cauliflower
–**kızartması** *kih-zahrt-mah-sih* fried cauliflower

–musakka *muu-sahk-kah*
stewed cauliflower **musakka**

–salatası *sah-lah-tah-sih*
cauliflower salad

karnıyarık *kahr-nih-yah-rihk* 'split belly' – eggplant (aubergine) stuffed with seasoned ground beef

karpuz *kahr-puhz* watermelon

kasadar/kasiyer *kah-sah-daahr/kah-see-yehr* cashier

kasap *kah-sahp* butcher

kase *kah-seh* bowl

kaskaval peynir *kahs-kah-vahl pehy-nihr* variety of cheese

kaşar *kah-shahr* sheep's cheese

–peyniri *pehy-nihr* sheep's milk similar to mild cheddar. Sometimes called **Balkan** cheese.

–peynirli omlet *pehy-nihr-lee ohmlet* omelette with **kaşar peyniri**

–rendesi *rehn-deh-see*
shredded **kaşar peynir**

kaşarlı sandviç *kah-shahr-lih sahnd-wihch* **kaşar peynir** cheese sandwich

kaşer *kah-shehr* kosher

kaşık (kaşığı) *kah-shihk (kah-shih-ih)* spoon

kaşık börek çorbası *kah-shihk ber-rehk chohr-bah-sih* egg, yoghurt, tomato sauce & mint soup (Bilecik)

katıklı aş *kah-tihk-lih ahsh* soup 'salad' made with **bulgur**, water, butter & **süzme yoghurt** (Aksaray)

katkı maddesi içermez *kaht-kih mah-deh-see ee-chehr-mehz* free of additives

katmer böreği *kaht-mehr ber-rehh-ee* flaky, savoury pastry

katmerli pazı böreği *kaht-mehr-lee pah-zih ger-rehh-ee* thin, flat but layered savoury **börek** made with flour, chard, onion, egg yolk, sesame seeds & salt. Served hot or cold. (Edirne)

katmerli sac böreği *kaht-mehr-lee sahj ber-rehh-ee* **börek** of pitta-like bread filled with a mixture of chopped spinach, **çökelek** & onion (Muğla)

kavrulmuş fındık *kahv-ruul-muush fihn-dihk* roasted hazelnuts

kavun *kah-vuun* melon

kavurma eriştesi pilavı *kah-vuur-mah eh-rish-teh-see pee-law-vee* pilaf dish of homemade noodles & rice (Sivas)

kaya balığı *kah-yah bah-lih-ih* goby (fish)

kaya tuzu *kah-yah tuu-zuu* rock salt

kaymak *kahy-mahk* thick clotted cream. Sold in rolls & only eaten with desserts.

kaymaklı dondurma *kahy-mahk-lih dohn-duur-mah* cream-flavoured ice cream; vanilla ice cream

kaymaklı kayısı tatlısı *kahy-mahk-lih kah-yih-sih taht-lih-sih* apricots with thick cream

kaynatmak *kahy-naht-mahk* to boil

kayısı *kah-yih-sih* apricot

–komposto *kohm-pohs-toh*
stewed apricot compote

–marmeladı *mahr-meh-lah-dih*
apricot marmalade

–reçeli *reh-cheh-lee* apricot jam

–yahnisi *yah-nee-see* stew-like dish made from sweet apricots, meat chunks & **pekmez** (Nevşehir)

kaz *kahz* goose

kazan *kah-zahn* cauldron, kettle

–dibi *dee-bee* 'kettle bottom', so-called because it's slightly burned; baked **tavuk göğsü**

KDV (Katma Değer Vergisi) *kah-dehy-veh* Value Added Tax

–dahildir *dah-heel-deer* VAT included

kebab (kebap) *keh-bahb (keh-bahp)* skewered beef, lamb, or poultry & vegetables, cooked on an open fire; also any of a number of meat or chicken concoctions

kebabçı (kebapçı) *keh-bahb-chih (keh-bahp-chee)* kebab seller

keççap *kehch-chuhp*
tomato sauce (tomato ketchup)

keçi *keh-chee* goat
–eti *eht-ee* goat's meat
–sütü *suu-tuu* goat's milk
kef(i) *kehf(ee)* skimmed fat; sediment
kefal (balığı) *keh-fahl (bah-lihh-ih)* grey mullet (fish)
kek *kehk* cake *(see cevizli kek)*
kekik *keh-keek* thyme
kekikotu *keh-kee-koh-tuu* oregano
keklik *kehk-leek* partridge
keler *keh-lehr* monkfish; skate; angel shark
kelle *kehl-leh* sheep's head
–paça çorbası *pah-chah chohr-bah-sih* sheep's head & foot soup
–şekeri *sheh-keh-ree* sugar cone
–tatlısı *taht-lih-sih* sweet pastry
kemik (kemiği) *keh-meek (keh-mee-ee)* bone
kenger otu *kehn-gher oh-too* cardoon (veg)
kepekli bisküvi *keh-pehk-lee bihs-kyuu-wee* bran biscuit
kepekli ekmek *keh-pehk-lee ehk-mehk* wheat bread
kepir dolması *keh-peer dohl-mah-sih* dolma made with kepir & mincemeat wrapped in karalahana & topped with yoghurt (Ordu)
kerbel *kehr-behl* fragrant herb from the parsley family used with fish & salads
kerevit *keh-reh-wiht* crawfish/prawn
kereviz *keh-reh-wihz* celeriac; celery root
kesme çorbası *kehs-me chohr-bah-sih* soup made with black lentils, small köfte & homemade macaroni. (Erzurum); also mincemeat & tomato paste soup (Kayseri); also soup made with eggs flour, onion, butter, ayran & salt (Erzincan)
kestane *kehs-tah-neh* chestnut(s)
–şekeri *sheh-keh-ree* chestnut sweet
–yemeği *yeh-mehh-ee* dish of chestnuts & mincemeat (Sinop)

kestaneli hindi *kehs-tah-neh-lee heen-dee* roast turkey with chestnuts
keşkek *kehs-kehk* coarse ground wheat; also dish of mutton & coarse-ground wheat, especially eaten at weddings (Denizli)
keşkül *kehsh-kyuul* pudding made from ground almonds, coconut & milk
ketçap *keht-chahp* tomato sauce (ketchup)
kete *keh-teh* Danish-style roll with spinach & nuts (Kars)
kevgir *kehw-gheer* perforated ladle
kıkırdak *kih-kihr-dahk* gristle
kılavuz *kih-lah-vuuz* (a) guide
kılçık (kılçığı) *kihl-chihk (kihl-chih-ih)* fishbone
kılıç balığı *kihl-ihch bah-lih-ih* swordfish
kılıç buğulama *kih-lihch boo-ooo-lah-mah* steamed swordfish with a tart sauce on the side
kılıç şiş *kih-lihch sheesh* swordfish on skewers
kımız *kih-mihz* fermented mare's milk
kınalı keklik *kih-nah-lih kehk-leek* rock partridge
kırçın *kihr-chihn* plant used to season soups or roasted/fried meat (Samsun)
kırkambar (balığı) *kihr-kahm-bahr bah-lih-ih* skate (fish)
kırlangıç (balığı) [kırlangıçbalığı] *kihr-lahn-ghihch-bah-lih-ih* swallow fish; red gurnard; gurnard (fish)
kırmızı *kihr-mih-zih* red
–biber (kırmızıbiber) *bee-behr* red pepper
–lahana *lah-hah-nah* red cabbage (veg)
–şarap *shah-rahp* red wine
–turp (salatası) *tuurp (sah-lah-tah-sih)* red radish (salad)
kırmızıbiber salatası *kihr-mih-zih-bee-behr sah-lah-tah-sih* çuşka biber, garlic, lemon & olive oil salad (Adana)

kırıklı mısır *kih-rihk-lih mih-sihr* corn kernels

kısır *kihs-ihr* **bulgur** salad with onion, parsley, olive oil, lemon, cucumbers, tomatoes, garlic, cumin & salt (Adana & Mersin, İçel)

kıtır patlıcan *kih-tihr paht-lih-jahn* crispy eggplant (aubergine)

kıvamında *kih-wah-mihn-dah* the right consistency/thickness; the right degree of density

kıvırcık lahana *kih-vihr-jihk lah-hah-nah* broccoli

kıvırcık salata *kih-vihr-jihk sah-lah-tah* lettuce with very crinkly leaves

kıyma *kihy-mah* ground meat

kıymalı börek *kihy-mah-lih ber-rehk* pastry with ground meat

kıymalı kol böreği *kihy-mah-lih kohl ber-reh-ih* arm-shaped **börek** stuffed with seasoned ground meat

kıymalı makarna *kihy-mah-lih mah-kahr-nah* macaroni with ground meat

kıymalı mercimek *kihy-mah-lih mehr-jee-mehk* lentils with minced meat

kıymalı mıhlama *kihy-mah-lih mih-lah-mah* dish of diced onion, mincemeat, tomato paste, margarine & egg (Sivas) (*see also* **mıhlama**)

kıymalı pide *kihy-mah-lih pee-deh* ground meat 'pizza'

kıymalı semizotu *kihy-mah-lih seh-meez-oh-toh* purslane with minced meat

kızarmış ekmek *kih-zahr-mihsh ehk-mehk* toasted bread

kızarmış patates *kih-zahr-mihsh pah-tah-tehs* fried potatoes

kızartma *kih-zahrt-mah* fried/roasted

kızartmalar *kih-zahrt-mah-lar* fried foods

kızgın *kihz-ghihn* red-hot; very hot

kızılcık *kih-zihl-jihk* cranberry
  –**marmeladı** *mahr-meh-lah-dih* cranberry marmalade/ sauce

–**tarhana çorbası** *tahr-hah-nah chohr-bah-sih* soup of **tahana** mixed with **kızılcık**, onion & garlic (Kastamonu)

kızılkanat (balığı) *kih-zihl-kah-naht (bah-lih-ih)* roach (fish)

kibe *kee-beh* stuffed tripe

kibrit *kee-breet* match (a light)

kilo *kee-loh* kilogram
  –**almak** *ahl-mahk* to gain weight
  –**vermek** *vehr-mehk* to lose weight

kimyon *kihm-yon* cumin

kiraz *kee-rahz* cherry

kiren *kee-rehn* cornel; Cornelian cherry, **kızılcık**; also mixture of **kızılcık**, tomato, beet, yoghurt & milk used to a make a **tarhana** (Kastamonu)

kişilik *kee-shee-leek* serves/portions

kişniş hoşafı *keesh-neesh hoh-shah-fih* raisins, sugar & water drink (Sivas)

kişniş otu *keesh-neesh oh-tuu* coriander (cilantro)

kocakarı gerdanı *koh-jah-kah-rih gehr-dahn-ih* 'old woman's neck' – spiral pastry (Rize)

koç yumurtası *kohch yuu-muur-tah-sih* ram's testicles

kofana *koh-fah-nah* large bluefish (lüfer)

kokoreç *koh-koh-rehch* seasoned grilled lamb/mutton intestines (Tekirdağ)

kokteyl *kohk-tehl* cocktail

kokusu (*see* **ağız kokusu**)

kol böreği *kohl ber-rehh-ee* rolled **börek**

kola *koh-lah* cola-flavoured soft drink

kolay tatlı *koh-lahy tahy-lih* dessert with apricots & sugar water

kolesterol *koh-lehs-teh-rohl* cholesterol
  –**düşük** *duu-shuuk* low in cholesterol
  –**yüksek** *yuuk-sehk* high in cholesterol

kolyoz (balığı) *kohl-yohz (bah-lih-ih)* horse mackerel (fish)

komposto *kohm-pohs-toh* stewed fruit compote (*see also* **çilekli komposto**)

koni *koh-nee* cone

konsome *kohn-soh-meh* consommé

kontrfile *kon-trih-fee-leh*
medium quality cut of beef
konyak *kohn-yahk* cognac
kornişon *kohr-nee-shohn*
gherkin (small pickled cucumbers)
kotlet *koht-leht* cutlet
koyun (eti) *koh-yuhn (eht-ee)* mutton
–**kuşbaşı haşlama** *kuush-bah-shih hahsh-lah-mah* boiled mutton chunks
–**kızartması** *kih-zahrt-mah-sih* roast mutton
köfte *kerf-teh* small mincemeat or bulgur balls (&/or various other shapes). There are many variations of this tasty treat. *(see* **abdigör köfte; cızbız köfte***)*
–**bahar** *bah-har (see* **köfte harcı***)*
–**harcı** *hahr-jih* meatball mix (a general-purpose mix found prepackaged at the market).
köfteci *kerf-teh-jee* **köfte** seller
köftelik bulgur köftesi *kerf-teh-lee buhl-ghur kerf-teh-see* fine **bulgur** *(see* **balık köftesi***)*
köleş *ker-lesh* salad made with cucumber, unripe melon, tomato, green pepper, onion & yoghurt (Eskişehir)
köpek balığı *ker-pehk bah-lih-ih* shark
köpüklü şarap *ker-pook-loo shah-rahp* sparkling wine
köri (tozu) *ker-ree (toh-zuu)* curry (powder)
körpe *ker-peh* young/fresh/tender
kötü *ker-tuuu* bad
közleme biber salatası *kerz-leh-meh bee-behr sah-lah-tah-sih* roasted green pepper salad (Mersin, İçel & Adana)
kraliçe margot *kih-rahl-ih-cheh mahr-goh* Queen Margot (soup)
kredi kart *kreh-dee kahrt* credit card
krem *krehm* cream
–**karamel** *kah-rah-mehl* dessert of baked caramel custard
–**peynir** *pehy-nihr* cream cheese
–**şanti** *shahn-tee* whipped cream

–**şokolade** *shoh-koh-lah-deh* chocolate pudding
krema *kreh-mah* filled with cream
kremalı lazanya *kreh-mah-lih lah-zahn-yah* lasagne in cream sauce
krep *kih-rehp* crepe
kruasan *kih-ruh-ah-sahn* croissant
kruton *kih-ruh-tohn* crouton
kulak çorbası *kuu-lahk chohr-bah-sih* 'ear' soup – meat-filled dumplings boiled in stock
kulaklı çorba *kuu-lahk-lih chohr-bah* 'ear' soup made with chickpeas & meat chunks (Antalya)
kumkat *kuum-kaht* kumquat
kurabiyesi *(see* **acıbadem kurabiyesi***)*
kuu-rah-bee-yeh biscuit (cookie)
kurbağa bacağı *kuur-bahh-ah bah-jahh-ih* frog's legs
kurban kavurması *kuur-bahn kah-wuur-mah-sih* braised lamb (the lamb is from the **Kurban Bayram** sacrifice)
kuru *kuu-ruu* dry; dried
–**erik** *eh-reek* prune
–**fasulye** *fah-suul-yeh* dry beans
–**fasulye pilakisi** *fah-suul-yeh pee-lah-kee-see* haricot bean **pilaki**
–**köfte** *kerf-teh* plain fried meat patty
–**mantı** *mahn-tih* small mincemeat dumplings, served with garlicky yoghurt &/or broth (Çorum)
–**pasta** *pahs-tah* 'dry pastry', such as biscuits & cookies
–**üzüm** *uuu-zuuum* raisin
–**yemişci (kuruyemişci)** *yeh-meesh-jee (kuu-ruu-yeh-meesh-jee)* dried nuts (seller/shop)
kuruluk dolması *kuu-ruu-luuk dohl-mah-sih* dried vegetable **dolma** (Antep)
kurutulmuş hamur *kuu-ruh-tul-muush hah-muur* dried pastry croutons
kuskus *kuhs-kuhs* couscous
kuşbaşı (et) *kuush-bah-shih (eht)* (meat) cut in small chunks

kuşbaşı şiş kebabı *kuush-bah-shih sheesh keh-bah-bih* skewered lamb or beef chunks

kuşburnu *koosh-buur-nuu* rosehip

kuşkonmaz *kuush-kohn-mahz* asparagus

kuşu *(see* **av kuşu**)

kuşüzümü *koosh-ooo-zoo-moo* currant; bird grape

kuyruk yağ *kuuy-ruuk yahh* fatty oil rendered from the tail of a sheep, often used in the preparation of **kokoreç**

kuzu (eti) *kuu-zuu (eh-tee)* lamb
 –**balığı (akya)** *bah-lih-ih (ahk-yah)* leer fish
 –**buğulaması** *buuu-uu-lah-mah-sih* poached lamb
 –**çevirme** *cheh-weer-meh* roast lamb
 –**ciğeri** *jee-eh-ree* lamb's liver
 –**dolması** *dohl-mah-sih* lamb stuffed with rice
 –**etli enginar** *eht-lee ehn-ghee-nahr* artichokes with lamb
 –**etli patlıcan söğürme** *eht-lee paht-lih-jahn ser-uuur-meh* lamb served on mashed aubergine (Antakya)
 –**kapama** *kah-pah-mah* lamb stewed with lettuce (Kocaeli)
 –**kızartması** *kih-zahrt-mah-sih* roasted lamb

küçük *kuu-chuuk* small
 –**küçük** *kuu-chuuk* very small

küçükhindistancevizi *kuu-chuuk-heen-dees-tahn-jeh-wee-see* nutmeg

kül tablası *kyuul tab-lah-sih* ashtray

küme *kyuu-meh* **sucuk** with walnut flavouring (Tokat)

kümes hayvanları *kyuu-mehs hahy-wahn-lah-rah* poultry

künefe *kyuu-neh-feh* sweet shredded pastry with cheese (Hatay, Adana & Mersin, İçel)

küp *kyuup* cube

kürdan *kyuur-dahn* toothpick

Kütahya güveci *kuu-tah-yah gyuu-weh-jeh* **güveç** made with meaty lamb bone, tomatoes, tomato paste & green pepper (Kütahya)

L

labne *lahb-neh* mild cream cheese

lahana *lah-hah-nah* cabbage
 –**dolması** *dohl-mah-sih* stuffed cabbage
 –**turşusu** *tuur-shuu-suu* pickled cabbage (**meze**)

lahmacun *lah-mah-juun* Turkish 'pizza'

laho *lah-hoh* **mezgit** fish (Rize)

lahos (balığı) *lah-hohs (bah-lih-ih)* rock grouper (fish) (Adana)

lahusa şekeri *lah-huu-sah sheh-keh-ree* slabs of sugar flavoured with spices & dyed red. Boiled to make a drink called **lahusa şerbeti**, a sweet & spicy sherbet which is offered at birth feasts.

lahusa şerbeti *lah-huu-sah shehr-beh-tee* sherbet/sorbet. Prepared to celebrate a birth. *(see also* **lahusa şekeri**)

lakerda *lah-kehr-dah* sliced & salted tuna fish (salad) (İstanbul)

lavaş ekmek *lah-vahsh ehk-mehk* thin crispy pitta-like bread

Laz böreği *lahz ber-rehh-ee* **börek** of the Laz people (Black Sea Rize). Made of **yufka** pastry surrounding a mixture of milk, vanilla, sugar & melted butter, & topped with hazelnuts or walnuts.

lazanya *lah-zahn-yah* lasagne

leblebi *lehb-leh-bee* roasted chickpeas

lebeniyeli köfte *leh-beh-nee-yeh-lee kerf-teh* **bulgur köfte** stuffed with meat in a sauce of meat or chicken broth, egg, rice & salt. An exotic dish including sheep's tail oil. (Adana)

levrek (balığı) *lehv-rehk (bah-lih-ih)* sea bass (fish)
 –**fileto ızgara** *fee-leh-toh ihz-ghah-rah* grilled fillet of bass
 –**fırında** *fih-rihn-dah* baked bass

–sultan murat *suul-tahn muu-raht* bass prepared in the way that Sultan Murat liked it

lezzet *lehz-zeht* flavour/taste

lezzetsiz *lehz-zeht-sihz* tasteless/bland

likör *lee-ker* liqueur

limon *lee-mohn* lemon

–şerbet *shehr-beht* lemon sherbet

limon/limonlu dondurma *lee-mohn/lee-mohn-luu dohn-duhr-mah* lemon ice cream

limonata *lee-moh-nah-tah* lemonade

limonlu dana eti *lee-mohn-luu dah-nah -eh-tee* lemon veal

lobi bar *loh-bee bahr* lounge/saloon bar

löbye *lerb-yeh* cold bean salad (İstanbul)

loğusa/lohusa *lohh-uu-sah/loh-huu-sah* sweet made with melted sugar, lemon powder & red food dye *(see also* lahusa şekeri)

lokanta *loh-kahn-tah* basic restaurant

lokma *lohk-mah* yeast fritters with syrup

lokum *loh-kuhm* Turkish delight or sweet pastry

lokum pilavı *loh-kuhm pee-law-vih* dish of square noodles & seasoned mincemeat garnished with parsley (Muğla)

lop *lohp* big, tender & round. Sometimes used to describe a cut of meat like nuar.

lor peyniri *lohr pehy-nih-ree* soft, uncured cheese

lüfer (balığı) *lyuu-fehrn (bah-lih-ih)* bluefish

Lütfen.
lyuut-fehn
Please.

M

Macar gulyas *mah-jahr guul-yahs* Hungarian goulash

macun *mah-juhn* paste; gum-like candy

maden suyu *mah-dehn suu-yuu* mineral water

madımak *mah-dih-mahk* green vegetable (Tokat, Sivas & Amasya)

–yemeği *yeh-mehh-ee* stew-like dish of madımak, pastırma, bulgur, spring onion & salt (Amasya & Tokat)

mafiş tatlısı *mah-fees taht-lih-sih* puff pastry savoury dessert (Balıkesir)

mahallebi/muhallebi (Arabic 'mahallebiye') *mah-hahl-leh-bee* sweet rice flour & milk pudding

mahlep *mahh-lehp* mahaleb; St. Lucie cherry; cordial made from mahaleb

makarna *mah-kahr-nah* pasta

makbuz *mahk-buuz* receipt

malzeme(si) *mahl-zeh-meh(see)* material/supplies/ingredients

manav *mah-nahv* vegetable market

mandalin/mandalina *mahn-dah-leen/mahn-dah-lee-nah* tangerine/mandarin

mandalina suyu *mahn-dah-lee-nah suu-yuu* tangerine/mandarin juice

mangal *mahn-ghahl* barbecue/brazier

mantar *mahn-tahr* mushroom

–(tıpa) *(tih-pah)* cork

–çorbası *chohr-bah-sih* mushroom soup

mantı *(see* kurumantı)

maraska *mah-rahs-kah* sour cherry

Maraş dondurma *mah-rahsh dohn-duur-mah* stringy, chewy & delicious ice cream (Maraş, Kahramanmaraş)

Maraş tarhanası *mah-rahsh tahr-hah-nah-sih* tarhana used in stuffing or toasted & eaten 'as is' in soup (Maraş, Kahramanmaraş)

margarin *mahr-gahr-een* margarine

marmeladı *(see* ayva marmeladı)

marmelat *mahr-meh-laht* marmalade

marul *mah-ruul* lettuce

–göbeği *ger-beh-ee* lettuce heart

–salatası *sah-lah-tah-sih* lettuce salad

masa *mah-sah* table

–örtüsü *er-tuu-suu* tablecloth

maşa *mah-shah* tongs
mayalanma *mah-yah-lahn-mah* fermentation
maydanoz *mahy-dah-noz* parsley
maydanozlu köfte *mahy-dah-noz-loo kerf-teh* meatballs with parsley
mayhoş *mahy-hohsh* agreeably tart; sour
melekotu *meh-leh-koh-tuu* angelica
melisotu *meh-lee-soh-toh* fragrant herb used to flavour salads & fruits
memba su *mehm-bah suu* spring water
Memnum oldum. *mehm-nuum ohl-duum* Glad to meet you.
menemen *meh-neh-mehn* eggs with green peppers, tomatoes & cheese
menü *meh-nyuuu* menu
mercan (balığı) *merh-jahn (bah-lih-h)* Red Sea bream (fish)
mercanköşk *mehr-jahn-kersk* fragrant herb similar to thyme
mercimek *mehr-jee-mehk* lentil
mercimek çorbası *mehr-jee-mehk chohr-bah-sih* strained lentil soup
Merhaba. *mehr-hah-bah* Hello.
merkezi (*see* **alış-veriş merkezi**)
Mersin (balığı) *mehr-sihn (bah-lih-ih)* sturgeon
mertuğa *mehr-tuu-ah* sugarless **helva** of butter, **kaymak** & flour (Hakkari)
mesit (balığı) *meh-seet* (*see* **mezgit**)
meşhur Karadeniz kavurması *meh-shuur kah-rah-deh-neez kah-vuur-mah-sih* plain baked 'pizza' topped with fried meat
meşrubat(lar) *mesh-ru-baht(lahr)* soft drink(s)
mevsim *mehw-sihm* season
–salatası *sah-lah-tih-sih* seasonal salad
mevsimli *mehw-sihm-lee* in season
meyva suyu *mehy-wah suu* fruit juice

meyvalı tart *mehy-wah-lih tahrt* fruit tart
meyvalı turta *mehy-wah-lih tuhr-tah* strudel
meyve *mehy-weh* fruit
–salatası *sah-lah-tah-sih* fruit salad
meyveli dondurma *mehy-weh-lee dohn-duur-mah* fruit ice cream
meyveli kek *mehy-weh-lee kek* cake with fruit
meze(ler) *meh-zeh(lehr)* similar to hors d'oeuvre, served with **rakı**
mezgit buğulama *mehz-geet buuu-uu-lah-mah* steamed **mesgid** fish with green peppers & tomatoes (Trabzon)
mezgit/mesgid/mesit (balığı) *mehz-geet/mehz-gheed/meh-seet (bah-lihh-ih)* whiting or haddock (fish)
mıhlama *mih-lah-mah* dish made with eggs; also dish (originally Syrian) made with **pastırma**, onions & eggs; savoury dish made with grated cheeses mixed with cornmeal & butter (Rize & Trabzon)
mırra *mihr-rah* 'old fashioned' bitter coffee with cardamom (eastern)
mısır *mih-sihr* corn
–cipsi *jihp-see* corn chips
–çorbası *chohr-bah-sih* soup of corn kernels, **barbunya**, meat chunks, onion, margarine & salt (Sinop)
–ekmeği *ehk-meh-ee* corn bread
–gevreği *gewv-reh-ih* corn flakes
–pastası *pahs-tah-sih* corn cake
–unu *uu-nuu* corn flour
mısırunlu baklava *mih-sih-ruun-luu bahk-lah-vah* cornmeal **baklava** (Rize)
midye *meed-yeh* mussel
–çorbası *chohr-bah-sih* mussel, egg & olive oil soup (Balıkesir)
–dolması *dohl-mah* stuffed mussels
–pilavı *pee-law-vih* pilaf dish of rice, mussels, seedless grapes, nuts, olive oil, cumin & allspice (Balıkesir)
–tava *ta-wah* fried mussels

mikrodalga *mee-kroh-dahl-ghah* microwave oven

mikser *meek-sehr* food mixer/processor

milföy *meel-fery* mille-feuille *(see also* **yufka***)*

mini *mee-nee* small

misafir *mee-sah-feer* guest

misket *mees-keht* muscatel grape/fruit
–**elması** *ehl-mah-sih* muscatel apple
–**şarabı** *shah-rah-bih* muscatel wine
–**üzümü** *uuu-zuuu-muuu* muscatel grape

miskotu *mees-koh-tuu* musk. Fragrant herb used with goose, duck & eel. Also used in stews & Vermouth.

mönü *mer-nuu* menu

morina (balığı) *moh-ree-nah (bah-lihh-ih)* codfish

mozzarella (dil peynir benzer) *mohz-zah-reh-lah (deel-pehy-neer behn-zehr)* mozzarella cheese *(see* **dil peynir***)*

muammara *muu-ahm-mah-rah* **meze** or salad made with crushed walnuts, crumbled stale bread, **tahin**, olive oil & lemon juice (Adana)

muayenesi *(see* **alkol muayenesi***)*

muhallebi/mahallebi *muu-hahl-leh-bee/mah-hahl-leh-bee* sweet pudding made with rice flour & milk

muhallebici *muu-hahl-leh-bee-chee* pudding shop

mum *muum* candle

mürdüm eriği *muuur-duuum eh-ree-ee* damson plum

musakka *muu-sahk-kah* vegetable & ground meat pie

muska böreği *muus-kah ber-rehh-ee* triangular-shaped **börek** filled with potato, cheese, mincemeat & onion, often covered in sesame seed (Uşak)

musluk *muus-luuk* tap (faucet)

muşmula *muush-muu-lah* medlar (fruit)

mutfak (mutfağı) *muut-fahk (muut-fah-ih)* kitchen/cuisine

mutfağı *(see* **Ağrı mutfağı***)*

muz *muuz* banana

müskat/muskat *muuus-kaht/muus-kaht* *(see* **hintcevizi***)*

müşteri *muuush-teh-ree* customer

N

nakit para *nah-keet pah-rah* cash

nalburiye *nahl-buu-ree-yeh* hardware & cooking utensils store

nane *nah-neh* mint

naneli *nah-neh-lee* with mint

naneli köfte *nah-neh-lee kerf-teh* **köfte** dish; of mincemeat, mint, onion, tomato paste & stale bread (İzmir)

nar *nahr* pomegranate

nektarin *nehk-tah-reen* nectarine

nem (nemli) *nehm (nehm-lee)* moist/ wet

neskafe sade *nehs-kah-feh sah-deh* black instant coffee (with caffeine)

nevzine *nehv-zee-neh* shallow savoury **börek** cut in squares, of flour, margarine, eggs, **tahin**, vegetable oil, yoghurt, crushed walnuts; often served with lemon sherbet (Kayseri)

Niğde tavası *neee-deh tah-vah-sih* lamb with tomato, peppers, garlic & tomato paste served with rice (Niğde)

nitelik *nee-tee-leek* quality/attribute

niyasin *nee-yah-seen* niacin

nohud/nohut *noh-huud/noh-huut* chickpea; garbanzo bean
–**döğmesi** *der-meh-see* chickpea & parsley salad (Tokat)
–**yahnisi** *yah-nee-see* chickpea stew (Nevşehir)

nohutlu kuskus pilavı *noh-huut-luu kuus-kuus pee-law-vih* couscous with boiled chickpeas & butter (İstanbul)

nokul *noh-kuul* meat pie with a mixture of seasoned mincemeat, parsley & walnuts (Sinop)

nuar *nuu-ahr* a big, tender, round cut of veal, boiled & sliced thinly for sandwiches & cold-cuts
numara *nuu-mah-rah* number

O

o *oh* he/she/it/that/those
ocak *oh-jahk* oven; range; cooking fire
oklava *ohk-lah-vah* rolling pin
oksit giderici *ohk-seet ghee-deh-ree-jee* anti-oxidant
omlet *ohm-leht* omelette (*see* **beyaz peynirli omlet**)
ordövr *ohr-derv* hors d'oeuvre
Ordu mutfağı *ohr-duu muut-fahh-ih* Ordu regional cuisine featuring a vareity of fish products. Anchovies are the staple diet for three to four months of the year. Corn meal & vegetable dishes are also important.
orfoz (balığı) *ohr-fohz (bah-lih-ih)* grouper (fish) (Adana)
orfoz fileto *ohr-fohz fee-leh-toh* filet of grouper garnished with rocket & spread with an olive oil & garlic sauce (Mediterranean)
orkinos *ohr-kee-nohs* tuna
orman kebabı *ohr-mahn keh-bah-bih* roast lamb & onions
orta *ohr-tah* medium
  –**pişmiş biftek** *peesh-meesh bihf-tehk* medium-rare steak
  –**boy** *boy* middle/medium size
  –**derece** *deh-reh-jeh* medium heat (150ºC to 180ºC)
  –**pişmiş** *peesh-meesh* medium-rare
oruç *oh-ruuch* fasting (during the month of **Ramazan**)
ovmak *ohwv-mahk* to knead

Ö

ödeme *er-deh-meh* payment
ödemek *er-deh-mehk* to pay

oğlak (eti) *ohh-lahk (eh-tee)* kid (goat)
öğle yemeği *er-leh yeh-meh-ih* lunch
öğmeç çorbası *er-mehch chohr-bah-sih* soup made with flour, eggs, tomato paste, lemon & parsley (Burdur)
öğütülmüş *er-uuu-tuuul-muuush* ground
öğün *er-uun* meal – only used when referring to time (*see* also **yemek**)
öküz *er-kyuuuz* ox
öküzgözü (üzümü) *er-kyuuz-ger-zuu (uuu-zyuuu-muuu)* 'ox eye' red grape (Elazığ & Malatya)
ölçü (ler) *erl-chuu (lehr)* measurement(s)
ölü gömme-yemek *er-luu gherm-meh* funeral/internment
  –**yüğbaşan** *yuu-bah-shahn* mourning meal
  –**can aşı** *jahn ah-shih* funeral meal (eastern Turkey)
ördek *er-dehk* duck
örgülü makarna *er-gyuuu-luuu mah-kahr-nah* dish with crisscrossing wide noodle-strips with sliced chicken breast, peas, carrots & almonds
örnek *er-nehk* example
örtmek *ert-mek* to cover
Özbek pilav *erz-behk pee-lawv* Uzbek lamb pilaf (Afyon)
özsu *erz-suu* juice/sap

P

paça çorbası *pah-chah chohr-bah-sih* sheep trotter soup
pahali *pah-hah-lih* expensive
palamut (balığı) *pah-lah-muht (bah-lih-ih)* bonito (fish)
  –**balığı pilakisi** *bah-lih-ih pee-lah-kee-see* bonito **pilaki**
  –**tava** *tah-vah* fried bonito
pancar *pahn-jahr* beet (vegetable)
  –**cacığı** *jah-jihh-ih* beet, **bulgur**, yoghurt & garlic **cacik** (Yozgat)

–**suyu** *suu-yuu* beet juice

–**turşusu** *tuur-shuu-suu* pickled beet (meze)

pane *pah-neh* breaded; fried in bread crumbs

papaz yahnisi *pah-pahz yah-nee-see* 'priest's stew'; made of beef, onion, garlic, vinegar & cumin (İzmir)

para *pah-rah* money

parmesan peyniri *pahr-meh-sahn pehy-nihr* parmesan cheese

pasta *pahs-tah* sweet pastry

pastane(si) *pah-stah-neh(-see)* pastry shop

pastırma *pahs-tihr-mah* pressed beef preserved in spices; Turkish pastrami

pastırmalı kurufasulye *pahs-tihr-mah-lih kuu-ruu-fah-suul-yeh* **pastırma** & haricot beans casserole

pastırmalı omlet *pahs-tihr-mah-lih ohm-leht* omelette with **pastırma**

pastırmalı sigara böreği *pahs-tihr-mah-lih see-ghah-rah ber-reh-ee* a savoury rolled pastry of **yufka**, **pastırma**, tomatoes, green peppers, onion, egg, & salt (Kayseri)

paşa pilavı *pah-shah pee-law-vih* 'Sultan's pilaf'; a salad; of potatoes, eggs, onion, lemon juice, black & red pepper, salt (Bolu)

patates *pah-tah-tehs* potato

–**kaygana** *kahy-ghah-nah* large fried potato pancake; mixture of pre-cooked potatoes, garlic, parsley, vegetable oil, salt & red pepper (Kastamonu)

–**köftesi** *kerf-teh-see* **köfte** made from potato, egg & black pepper (Sakarya)

–**kızartması** *kih-zahrt-mih-sih* fried potatoes (meze)

–**musakka** *muu-sahk-kah* stewed potatoes with mincemeat

–**püresi** *pyuu-reh-see* mashed potatoes

–**salataşiç** *sah-lah-tah-sih* potato salad

patlamış, mısır *paht-lah-mihsh mih-sihr* pop corn

patlıcan *paht-lah-jan* eggplant (aubergine)

–**biber tava** *bee-behr tah-vah* fried eggplant & peppers with tomato paste

–**böreği** *ber-rehh-ee* sliced eggplant prepared with mincemeat, egg & onion – topped with a grilled tomato slice (Afyon region); & other varieties, in other regions ...

–**islim kebabı** *ees-leem keh-bah-bih* baked lamb wrapped in eggplant

–**karnıyarık** *khar-nih-yah-rihk* eggplants stuffed with minced meat

–**kebabı** *keh-bah-bih* eggplant kebab

–**kızartması** *kih-zahrt-mah-sih* fried eggplant

–**musakka** *muu-sah-kah* eggplant **musakka**

–**oturtması** *oh-tuurt-mah-sih* eggplant 'oturtma'

–**pane** *pah-neh* fried eggplant covered with crumbled bread

–**reçeli** *reh-cheh-lee* eggplant (sweet) preserves (Adana)

–**salatası** *sah-lah-tah-sih* eggplant salad

patlıcanlı köfte *paht-lih-jan-lih kerf-teh* meatballs with eggplant

patlıcanlı köy dolması *paht-lih-jan-lih kery dohl-mah-sih* mincemeat, bulgur, tomato & onion served on slices of eggplant (Karaman)

patlıcanlı pilav *paht-lih-jan-lih pee-lawv* eggplant pilaf

pavruya *pahv-ruh-yah* hermit crab

payvon *pahy-vohn* night club

pazar *pah-zahr* open air market; bazaar

pazarlıç etmek *pah-zahr-lihk eht-mehk* to bargain

pazı *pah-zih* chard; garden orache

–**cacığı** *jah-jihh-ih* chard mixed with **cacik**

–**kavurma** *kah-vuur-mah (ree-zeh)* fried eggs & chard, with onions & **barbunya** beans, served piping hot (Rize)

–**kavurması** *kah-woor-mah-sih (kahs-tah-moh-nuu)* thinly sliced chard & onion served cold (Kastamonu)

–**pilakisi** *pee-leh-kee-see* a **pilaki** with chard, rice, olive oil, salted anchovy & mint (Trabzon)

peçete *peh-cheh-teh* napkin

Pek iyi! (Peki!)
pehk ee-yee (peh-kee)
Very good!; OK!; That's good!

pekmez *pehk-mehz* a thick syrup commonly made from boiled grape juice; it resembles black treacle

pelte *pehl-teh* a sweet made from cornstarch, sugar, & fruit juice

pelvaze *pehl-vah-zeh* a sweet made from **pekmez** & **nasta** (Uşak)

pelvize *pehl-vee-zeh* sweet made from rose water & **nasta** (Aydın)

pembeleşmek *pehm-beh-lehsh-mahk* to brown food

perdeli pilav *pehr-deh-lee pee-lawv* pilaf covered with crispy pastry

perhiz *pehr-heez* dieting

pestil *pehs-teel* general name for 'thin sheet of sun-dried fruit pulp'

peynir *pehy-neer* cheese

–**helvası** *hehl-vah-sih* **helva** dessert, of cheese, flour, eggs, butter & granulated sugar; also served cold (Tekirdağ); there are other varieties of **helva** in other regions

–**tatlısı** *taht-lih-sih* cheesecake or cheese cookies

peynirli börek *pehy-neer-lee ber-rehk* pastry filled with Turkish cheese

peynirli pide *pehy-neer-lee pee-deh* plain cheese Turkish pizza, in the distinctive flattened canoe shape

picarel (balığı) *pee-jah-rehl (bah-lihh-ih)* a fish (see **izmarit**)

Pınar *pih-nahr* a national brand of quality frozen food products

pırasa *pih-rah-sah* leek

–**çorbası** *chohr-bah-sih* leek soup

–**dolması** *dohl-mah-sih* leeks stuffed with onion, mincemeat, rice, egg, lemon, tomato paste, vegetable oil & parsley (Kastamonu)

–**musakka** *muu-sahk-kah* stewed leeks with ground beef

pıtpıt *piht-piht* **bulgur** flour (Malatya)

pide *pee-deh* very thin pitta-like bread often used to make Turkish-style pizza or **döner kebab**

–**ekmek** *ehk-mehk* flattish unleavened bread, available during the month of Ramazan

pideci *pee-deh-jee*
Turkish-style pizza place

pilaki *pee-lah-kee* cold stew, usually contains beans (or black-eyed peas, sometimes rice) with onion & vegetables; may contain fish.

pilav(lar) *pee-lawv(lahr)* pilaf dish(es); could be rice, bulgur, or lentil pilaf

pilavlı hindi *pee-lawv-lih heen-dee* roast turkey with rice

pilavlı tas kebabı *pee-lawv-lih tahs keh-bah-bih* a 'kebab'; of lamb chunks cooked in butter, salt, & red pepper (Çorum region) – compare with **tas kebapliç pilav**

pili *pee-leech* chicken

–**kızartma** *kih-zahrt-mah* roast chicken

pimpimel *peem-pee-mehl* a type of anise; a fragrant herb

pirinç *pee-reench* rice; also brass

pirinçli *pee-reench-lee* with rice

–**mantı** *mahn-tih* a meatless **mantı** dish (Kastamonu)

pirinç çorbası *pee-reench chohr-bah-sih* rice soup

pirpirim *peer-pee-rihm* purslane (Malatya region), (see also **semizotu**)

–**çorbası** *chohr-bah-sih* chickpea, bean & lentil soup (Malatya)

piruhi/pirohu *pee-ruu-hee/pee-roh-huu* boiled dish of meat, flour, & yoghurt

pirzola *peer-zoh-lah* grilled meat; usually a veal/lamb chop or chicken-leg meat formed into a 'chop'
–(**dana**) *(dah-nah)* grilled veal chop
–(**kuzu**) *(kuu-zuu)* grilled lamb chop

pisibalığı *pee-see-bah-lih-ih* plaice (fish)

pişirme biçimleri *pee-sheer-meh bee-cheem-leh-ree* ways of cooking; suggestions for cooking

pişirme süresi *pee-sheer-meh suu-reh-see* cooking time

pişirmek *pee-sheer-mehk* to cook

pişkin *peesh-keen* (cooked) well-done; *(see iyi pişmiş)*

pişmaniye *peesh-mah-nee-yeh* famous candy made of sugar, flour, & oil with soapwort (Kocaeli)

pişme süresi *peesh-meh suuu-reh-see (see pişirme süresi)*

pişmiş *peesh-meesh* cooked

piyaz *pee-yahz* white bean salad

pizza salonu *peez-zah sah-loh-nuh* Turkish pizza parlour

poğaça *pohh-ah-chah* a variety of buns

portakal *pohr-tah-kahl* orange (either the fruit or the flavour)
–**marmeladı** *mahr-mah-lah-dih* orange-marmalade
–**reçeli** *reh-cheh-lee* orange-jam
–**suyu** *suu-yuu* orange juice

porsiyon *pohr-see-yon* portion, helping, serving (the size/number/amount)

poşet *poh-sheht* plastic bag; plastic (oven safe)

pudra şekeri *pood-rah sheh-keh-ree* powdered sugar

puf böreği *puuf ber-rehh-ee* puffed börek

pul biber/pul kırmızıbiber *puul bee-behr/puul kih-rih-mih-zih bee-behr* red pepper chilli flakes

pürçüklü *pyuur-chuuk-luu* purple carrot (Kırşehir)

püre *pyuuu-reh* mashed potatoes; various vegetable purees

R

radika/radike *rah-dee-kah/rah-dee-keh* herb similar to chicory

radika salatası *rah-dee-kah sah-lah-tah-sih* **radika** salad (İzmir)

rafadan *rah-fah-dahn* soft-boiled (egg)

rakı *rah-kih* Turkish national alcoholic drink made with anise. Transparent when in its natural state but turns white when mixed with water.

(yeni) rakı *(yeh-nee) rah-kih* new or recently produced **rakı**

reçel(i) *reh-chehl(-ee)* fruit preserve; jam

reçeli *(see ayva reçeli)*

reçeller *reh-chehl-lehr* jams/preserves/ marmalades

rehber(i) *reh-behr(ee)* (a) guide

rejim *reh-zheem* diet/regimen

rendelenmiş kaşar *rehn-deh-lehn-mish kah-shahr* grated **kaşar** cheese

rendelenmiş soğan *rehn-deh-lehn-meesh sohh-ahn* grated onion

restoran *rehs-toh-rahn* restaurant

revani *reh-wah-nee* sweet cake made with semolina & vanilla, & topped with clotted cream

reyhan *rehy-hahn* sweet basil *(see also fesleğen)*

rezene *reh-zeh-neh* fragrant herb similar to anise

ringa (balığı) *reen-ghah (bah-lih-ih)* herring

roka *roh-kah* rocket; watercress

rom *rohm* rum

rosto *rohs-toh* roasted meat

rozbif *rohz-bihf* roast beef

roze şarabı *roh-zeh sha-rah-bih* rose wine

rulo *ruh-loh* dish that is 'rolled', such as a rolled **börek**

rumi (üzümü) *ruu-mee (uuu-zyuuu-muuu)* Anatolian white grape (Gaziantep)

Rus salatası *ruus sah-lah-tah-sih* Russian salad

S

saçaklı mantı *sah-jahk-lih mahn-tih* variation on traditional **mantı**, in which chicken is spread over seasoned pastry & sprinkled with black pepper

sade *sah-deh* plain

–**pilav** *pee-lawv* plain rice/pilaf

sadeyağ *sah-deh-yah* plain butter

sağ *sahh* right

sağlık *saah-lihk* good health

Sağol. *saah-ohl* Thanks.

safran *sah-frahn* saffron

sahan *sah-hahn* shallow cooking pan; meat stew cooked with **salça**

sahanda pirzola *sah-hahn-dah peer-zoh-lah* lamb cutlets with tomato sauce cooked in a **sahan**

sahlep *sah-lehp* hot milk & tapioca-root beverage *(see also* **saleb/salep***)*

sahur *sah-huur* meal taken by daytime 'fasters' just before daylight during the month of Ramazan

sakatat *sah-kah-taht* offal/tripe

Sakızlı bakla çorbası *sah-kihz-lih bahk-lah chohr-bah-sih* soup made with **bakla**, onion, flour, egg, yoghurt, margarine & salt (Bolu – originally from the Aegean island of Chios)

sakız *sah-kihz* gummy substance ground with sugar – used in puddings

–**leblebisi** *lehb-leh-bee-see* roasted white chickpea

salam *sah-lahm* salami-like meat product

salamlı sandviç *sah-lahm-lih sahnd-wihch* **salam** sandwich

salamura *sah-lah-muu-rah* brine; also food that's been pickled (in brine)

salata *sah-lah-tah* salad

–**sos** *sohs* salad dressing

salatası *(see* **Amerikan** –; **beyin** –; **börülce** –; **çiroz** –; **çoban** –; **deniz ürünleri** –; **domates salatalık** –; **mevsim** –)

salatalık *sah-ah-tah-lihk* cucumber

–**turşusu** *tuur-shuu-suu* cucumber pickle (meze)

salça(sı) *sahl-chah(-sih)* tomato or pepper purée; tomato paste

salçalı köfte *sahl-chah-lih kerf-teh* meat patties in seasoned tomato sauce

saleb/salepsa'leb *sah-lehb/sah-lehp/ sah'lehb* hot milk & tapioca-root beverage *(see also* **sahlep***)*

salon *sah-lohn* saloon

salonu *(see* **aile salonu***)*

samsa tatlısı *sahm-sah taht-lih-sih* sweet pastry soaked in syrup, similar to **baklava** (Isparta)

Samsun köfte *sahm-suun kerf-teh* meat loaf (**Samsun**)

samut salatası *sah-muut sah-lah-tah-sih* simple salad made with thinly sliced dill, parsley, lemon, olive oil, salt & red pepper

sandviç *sahnd-wihch* sandwich *(see also* **beyaz peynirli sandviç***)*

sap kereviz *sahp keh-reh-weez* celery stalks

saray *sah-rahy* palace

–**usulü pastırmalı yumurta** *uu-suul-yuu pahs-tihr-mah-lih yuu-muur-tah* palace-style eggs with **pastırma**

sardalya (balığı) *sahr-dahl-yah (bah-lih-ih)* sardine *(see* also **asma yaprağında sardalya***)*

sarma(sı) *sahr-mah-(sih)* wrapping/surrounding

sarımsak/sarmısak *sah-rihm-sahk/sahr-mih-sahk* garlic

sarımsaklı/sarmısaklı *sah-rihm-sahk-lih/sahr-mih-sahk-lih* with garlic

–**börülce salatası** *ber-ruuul-jeh sah-lah-tah-sih* black-eyed pea salad (Balıkesir)

–**köfte** *kerf-teh* meatless **köfte** doused with a oil & tomato sauce (Adana)

–**tavuk dolması** *tah-vuuk dohl-mah-sih* stuffed chicken with garlic

sütü *(see* **aslan sütü***)*

süt ve süt ürünleri *suuut veh suuut uuu-ruuun-leh-ree* milk (products)

süzgeç *suuuz-gehch* strainer/colander

süzme yoğurt *suuuz-mah yoh-uurt* yoghurt from which much water has been extracted. Good substitute for sour cream when mixed with **labne**.

Ş

şalak *shah-lahk* unripened melon (Sivas)

şalgam *shal-ghahm* turnip
  –pilavı *pee-law-vih* pilaf dish of turnip, mincemeat & bulgur (Sivas)
  –suyu *suu-yuu* turnip juice (good with Turkish **pide**). A favourite non-alcoholic Turkish drink, also used as an ingredient in making **dolma** stuffing.

şam fıstığı *shahm fihs-tihh-ih* Damascus nut; pistachio nut/tree

şampanya *shahm-pahn-yah* champagne

şarap (şarabı) *shah-rahp (shah-rah-bih)* wine *(see* also **beyaz şarap***)*

şarküteri *shahr-kyuuu-teh-ree* delicatessen

şatobriyan *sha-toh-bree-yan* chateaubriand

şef *shehf* chef

şeftali *shehf-tah-lee* peach
  –komposto *kohm-pohs-toh* stewed peach compote
  –marmeladı *mahr-mah-lah-dih* peach marmalade
  –suyu *suu-yuu* peach juice

şehriye *sheh-ree-yeh* thin noodles usually used in soups *(see* also **arpa şehriye***)*

şeker *sheh-kehr* sugar
  –böreği *ber-rehh-ee* sweet biscuit, taken with lemon sherbet (Niğde)

şekeri *(see* **badem şekeri***)*

şekerleme *sheh-kehr-leh-meh* sweet shops

şekerpare *sheh-kehr-pah-reh* sweet biscuit topped with lemon & sugar syrup

şekersiz *sheh-kehr-seez* without sugar

şerbet *shehr-beht* sherbet/sorbet

Şerefe!
sheh-reh-feh!
Cheers!

şeri şarabı *sheh-ree shah-rah-bih* sherry

şeriden *sheh-ree-dehn* Mardin region **pastırma**

şnitzel/şinitzel *shih-niht-zehl* wiener schnitzel

şiş *sheesh* skewer
  –kebab *keh-bahb* skewered meat/poultry prepared on an open fire
  –köfte *kerf-teh* grilled (usually) meatballs

şişe *shee-shey* bottle
  –açacağı *ah-chah-jahh-ih* bottle opener
  –su *soo* bottled water

şişte kılıç balığı ızgara· *sheesh-teh kih-lihch bah-lah-ih ihz-ghah-rah* grilled swordfish

şor *shohr* soft/fresh cheese (Kars)

şöbiyet *sher-bee-yeht* a butter & sugar cousin of sherbet

şölen çorbası *sher-lehn chohr-bah-sih* feast soup

su *(see* **acı su***)*

şurup (şurubu) *shuu-ruup (shuu-ruu-buu)* syrup

T

(tap) taze *(tahp)-tah-zeh* (very) fresh

tabak (tabağı) *tah-bahk (tah-bah-ih)* plate

tabaka *tah-bah-kah* sheet (of something)

tabla *tahb-lah* ashtray

tahin *tah-heen* sesame seed puree

tahinli lahana sarması *tah-heen-lee lah-hah-nah sahr-mah-sih* cabbage leaves stuffed with rice, crushed chickpeas, **tahin** & tomato paste (Adana)

T

tahinli maydanoz *tah-heen-lee mahy-dah-nohz* salad made with parsley, garlic & **tahin** (Hatay)

tahinli patlıcan *tah-heen-lee paht-lih-jahn* mashed (eggplant salad seasoned with **tahin**) (Hatay)

tahinli soğan *tah-heen-lee sohh-ahn* salad made with onion, mayonnaise, lemon & **tahin**, garnished with tomatoes & olives (Hatay)

tahıl ekmek *tah-hihl ehk-mehk* whole-grain bread

tahıl(lar) *tah-hihl(lahr)* grain(s)

tahta *tah-tah* wooden slab table
–**kaşık (kaşığı)** *kah-shihk (kah-shih-ih)* wooden spoon

talaş böreği *tah-lahsh ber-rehh-ee* puff pastry filled with meat

talaş kebabı *tah-lahsh keh-bah-bih* pieces of meat that are cooked & then baked in pastry

tandır *tahn-dihr* oven in a clay-lined pit; also brazier
–**kebabı** *keh-bah-bih* kebab roasted in an oven in a clay-lined pit

tane *tah-neh* grain/kernel; also single unit of something
–**mısır** *mih-sihr* corn kernel

tantuni kebab *tahn-tuu-nee keh-bahb* a 'kebab' dish of sliced veal & mutton served on **lavaş ekmek**. Often accompanied by the distinctive **şalgam suyu** vegetable juice drink. (Mersin, İçel)

tarak *tah-rahk* cutlet; pilgrim scallop

tarama *tah-rah-mah* fish-roe; red caviar
–**salatası** *sah-lah-tah-sih* fish-roe or red caviar spread (meze)

tarator (sos) *tah-ra-tohr (sohs)* garlic & nut sauce, commonly paired with seafood. May be made with almonds (Aegean), walnuts (Central Anatolia) or hazelnuts (Black Sea).

tarçın *tahr-chihn* cinnamon

tarhana *tahr-hah-nah* dried foodstuff made chiefly of curds & flour

–**çorbası** *chohr-bah-sih* soup made with **tarhana** together with flour, yoghurt, black-eye peas, garlic, meat chunks & herbs (Muğla)

tarhun *tahr-huun* tarragon

tarif(ler) *tah-reef(lehr)* recipe(s)

tart *tahrt* (dessert) tart

tartar börek *tahr-tahr ber-rehk* meat filled **börek**

tarım *tah-rihm* agriculture

tas *tahs* bowl
–**kebabı** *keh-bah-bih* veal & vegetable stew served on rice (Kütahya). Sometimes called **gulaş** (goulash).
–**kebaplı pilav** *keh-bahp-lih pee-lawv* lamb & vegetable stew (Samsun)

tat (tadı) *taht (tah-dih)* taste/flavour

tatlı (see **acı tatlı**)
–**biber** *bee-behr* sweet pepper
–**dürümü** *duuu-ruuu-muuu* rolled dough sweet made of flour, milk, margarine, **yufka**, crushed walnuts, & **pekmez** (Niğde)

tatlı kaşığı *taht-lih kah-shih-ih* tablespoon

tatlı(sı) *taht-lih(sih)* sweet/dessert (see **ayva tatlısı**)

tatlılar *taht-lih-lahr* sweet dishes

tavada *tah-vah-dah* fried

tavşan *tahw-shan* rabbit

tavuk *tah-vuhk* chicken
–**çorbası** *chohr-bah-sih* chicken soup
–**dolması** *dohl-mah-sih* stuffed chicken
–**göğsü** *gerr-uuu-suuu* chicken breast; chicken breast pudding
–**kızartması** *kih-zahrt-mah-sih* roast chicken
–**suyu** *suu-yuu* chicken broth/gravy
–**lu sandviç** *-luu sahnd-wihch* chicken sandwich
–**lu zarf böreği** *-luu zahrf ber-rehh-ee* **börek** shaped like a triangular pocket & stuffed with seasoned chicken

taze *tah-zeh* fresh
 –balık *bah-lihk* fresh fish
 –etli bezelye *eht-lee beh-zehl-yeh*
 diced meat & peas
 –fasulye *fah-suul-yeh*
 green/French beans
 –yeşil biber *yeh-sheel bee-behr*
 fresh green pepper
tekir (balığı) *teh-keer (bah-lihh-ih)*
 striped red mullet
Tekirdağ köftesi *teh-keer-dahh kerf-teh-see* mincemeat cylinders served
 with rice & peppers (Tekirdağ)
tekke çorbası *tehk-keh chohr-bah-sih*
 soup made with flour, mincemeat,
 tomato paste, pepper sauce, grated
 onion & mint (Kütahya)
tel şehriye *tehl sheh-ree-yeh* thin & delicate noodle, similar to vermicelli
tel şehriyeli tavuk çorbası *tehl sheh-ree-yeh-lee tah-vuhk chohr-bah-sih* chicken
 vermicelli soup
telkadayıf *tehl-kah-dah-yihf* dessert of
 baked vermicelli-style **kadayıf** dough,
 soaked in a thick syrup & layered or
 topped with crushed walnuts & **kay-mak**
tencere *tehn-jeh-reh* saucepan *(see*
 düdüklü tencere)
teneke *teh-neh-keh* tinplate; tin; a tin
tepeleme *teh-peh-leh-meh* heaping
tepsi *tehp-see* tray; large, shallow baking tin
 –böreği *ber-rehh-ee* **yufka börek**,
 made in a **tepsi**
terazi *teh-rah-zee* scale; weighing device
terbiye *tehr-bee-yeh* sauce, usually
 made from egg & lemon
terbiye liasyon *tehr-bee-yeh lee-ahs-yohn* egg, flour & lemon sauce
terbiyeli ekşili köfte *tehr-bee-yeh-lee ehk-shee-lee kerf-teh* meatballs with
 egg & lemon sauce
terbiyeli işkembe çorbası *tehr-bee-yeh-lee eesh-kehm-beh chohr-bah-sih* tripe
 soup with **terbiye**

terbiyeli kalkan balığı *tehr-bee-yeh-lee kahl-kahn bah-lihh-ih* turbot with
 sauce
terbiyeli kuzu etli kereviz *tehr-bee-yeh-lee kuu-zuu eht-lee keh-reh-weehz*
 celeriac with lamb in lemon sauce
terbiyeli süt kuzusu kapaması *tehr-bee-yeh-lee soot koo-zoo-soo kah-pah-mah-sih* spring lamb with lettuce
tere *teh-reh* watercress
tere çorbası *teh-reh chohr-bah-sih* cress
 & chicken broth soup (Izmir &
 Aydın)
tereyağı *teh-reh-yah* butter
termos *tehr-mohs* thermos
testi *tehs-tee* earthenware water jug
 –kebab *keh-bahb* kebab in which
 small pieces of lamb or chicken are
 cooked in a mushroom & onion
 sauce. It's prepared in a sealed clay
 pot. (Anatolia)
tıntış çorbası *tihn-tihsh chohr-bah-sih*
 corn meal soup (Zonguldak)
tırpana (balığı) *tihr-pah-nah (bah-lihh-ih)* grayskate (fish)
tirbüşon *teer-buuu-shohn* corkscrew
tiyamin *tee-yah-meen* thiamin
toksin *tohk-seen* toxin
ton balığı *tohn bah-lihh-ih* tuna/tunny
tonik *toh-neek* tonic water
topak *toh-pahk* ball or lump of dough
topik *toh-peek* dish made from chickpeas, pistachios, onion, flour, currants,
 cumin & salt. Topped with a sesame-
 based sauce.
toplam *tohp-lahm* total
toplar(ı) *tohp-lahr(ih)* balls (of dough,
 for example)
torba *tohr-bah* sack
torik (balığı) *toh-reek (bah-lih-ih)* large
 bonito (fish)
tost *tohst* toast
 –makinesi *mah-kee-nee-see* toaster
toyga çorbası *tohy-ghah chohr-bah-sih*
 soup made with of yoghurt, hazelnut,
 rice, egg & mint (Konya)

toz *tohz* granulated/ground
  –karabiber *kah-rah-bee-behr* ground
  black pepper *(see also* **beyaz toz biber**)
  –şeker *sheh-kehr* granulated sugar
  –tarçın *tahr-chihn* powdered **tarçin**
Trabzon peynirlisi *trahb-zohn pehy-neer-lee-see* baked cheese pizza made
  with 'Trabzon' cheese. Served with
  baked egg. (Trabzon & Rize)
trança (balığı) *trahn-chah (bah-lih-ih)*
  sea bream
tulum (peyniri) *tuu-luum (pehy-nee-ree)*
  a variety of sharp & stinky cheese
tulumba tatlısı *tuu-luum taht-lih-sih*
  fluted fried fritters served in sweet
  syrup
turfa *tuur-fah* new/rare/strange thing;
  not kosher
  –olmayan *ohl-mah-yahn* kosher
turfanda *tuur-fahn-dah* out of season
  (of fruit or vegetables)
turfandacı *tuur-fahn-dah-jih* seller of
  out-of-season fruits & vegetables
turna balığı *tuur-nah bah-lih-ih* pike
turp *tuurp* radish
turşu *tuur-shuu* pickled vegetable
  –kavurma *kah-wuur-mah* pickled
  green beans & onions (Rize)
turunç *tuu-ruunch* Seville orange
tutam *tuu-tahm* a few sprigs of; a small
  amount of, a pinch of
tuz *tuuz* salt
tuzlu domates ve fasulye kavurması
  tuuz-luu doh-mah-tehş veh fah-suul-yeh kah-wuur-mah-sih salted tomatoes
  & fresh green beans (Giresun)
tuzluk-biberlik *tuuz-luuk-bee-behr-leek*
  salt & pepper shakers
tüccar *tuuuj-jahr* merchant
tüfeği *(see* **av tüfeği**)
tüfek *tyuuu-fehk* rifle/gun
tüketici *tuuu-keht-chee* consumer
Türk *tuuurk* Turkish person or thing
  –kahvesi *kah-wah-see* Turkish coffee

  –lirası *lee-rah-sih* Turkish lira
  –lokantası *loh-kan-tah-sih*
  Turkish restaurant
  –mutfağı *muut-fahh-ih*
  Turkish cuisine
Türkçe *tuuurk-cheh*
  the Turkish language
Türkiye *tuuuk-ee-yeh*
  Turkey (the country)

U

ucuz *uu-juz* inexpensive/cheap
ufak *uu-fahk* small
  –para *pah-rah* small change
ufalamak *uu-fah-lah-mahk* to crumble; break into small pieces
ufo makarna *uu-foh mah-kahr-nah*
  macaroni; small, curled
un *uun* flour
  –çorbası *chohr-bah-sih* 'flour soup' of
  flour, onion, fried meat bits, olive oil,
  tomato paste, salt, pepper, & red pepper flakes (Muğla)
  –helvası *hehl-vah-sih* 'flour' **helva**
  –kurabiyesi *kuu-rah-bee-yeh-see*
  'flour' cookie, Turkish shortbread
unlanmış *uun-lahn-mihsh* floured
unlanmış bir zemin *uun-lahn-mihsh
  beer zeh-meen* a flat place that has
  been floured
Urfa kebab *uur-fah keh-bahb* grilled
  lamb on skewers
uskumru (balığı) *uus-kuum-ruu bah-
  lih-ih* mackerel
  –ızgara *ihz-ghah-rah*
  grilled mackerel
  –salatası *sah-lah-tah-sih*
  mackerel salad
  –tava *tah-vah* fried mackerel
usulü *uu-suul-uuu* in the style/manner
  of; also methodical, systematic
uyar(ı) *uu-yahr(ih)* warning
uzun *uu-zuun* long, tall

Turkish Culinary Dictionary Ü

Ü

üç *uuuch* three
  –peynirli makarna *pehy-nihr-lee mah-kahr-nah* 'three-cheese' macaroni

üretim tarihi *uuu-reh-teem tah-ree-hee* production date

üvez *uuu-wehz* a variety of **pekmez** 'preserves' made in preparation for winter (Samsun)

üzüm *uuu-zuuum* grape

üzümlü kek *uuu-zuuum-luuu kehk* cake or pie with dried grapes

V

vanilya *wah-neel-yah* vanilla
  –dondurma *dohn-duur-mah* vanilla ice cream

vartabit paçası *wahr-tah-beet pah-chah-sih* dish of seasoned white beans (in sesame oil, garlic, lemon juice, red pepper, salt) served over Turkish bread (**Tarsus**)

vazo *wah-zoh* vase

vejeteryan *weh-zheh-tehr-yahn* vegetarian
  –çorbası *chohr-bah-sih* 'flour soup' of flour, onion, fried meat bits, olive oil, tomato paste, salt, pepper, & red pepper flakes (Muğla)
  –helvası *hehl-vah-sih* 'flour' **helva**
  –kurabiyesi *kuu-rah-bee-yeh-see* 'flour' cookie, Turkish shortbread

vergi *vehr-ghee* tax, see also **KDV**

veznedar *wehz-neh-dahr* cashier

viski *wihs-kee* whisky

vişne *weesh-neh* sour cherry, morello
  –reçeli *reh-cheh-lee* morello-cherry jam

vişneli ekmek tatlısı *weesh-neh-lee ehk-mehk taht-lih-sih* cherry bread pudding

Y

yağ(lar) *yahh(lahr)* cooking oil(s); fat(s); grease; lard; butter; margarine

yağ *(see* **balık yağ; bitkisel yağ**)

yağı *(see* **ayçiçeği yağı**)

yağlı kağıt (kağıdı) *yahh-lih kah-iht (kahh-ih-dih)* grease-proof paper; waxed paper

yağlı kıyma *yahh-lih kihy-mah* full-fat ground beef which is ready-packaged

yağsız *yahh-sihz* fat free; without oil; non-fat; low-fat; lean (meat); greaseless
  –kıyma *kihy-mih* lean ground beef

yahni(si) *yah-nee(-see)* meat & vegetable stew

yahni *(see* **balık yahni**)

yanı sıra *yah-nih sih-rah* together with; along with; beside(s)

yapay (renk) *yah-pahy (rehnk)* artificial (colour)

yaprağı *(see* **yaprak**)

yaprak (yapraklar/yaprağı) *yahp-rahk (yahp-rahk-lahr/yahp-rah-ih)* leaf; layer (leaves) *(see also* **defne yaprağı; asma yaprağı**)
  –dolması *dohl-mah-sih* stuffed grape leaves
  –sarma *sahr-mah* stuffed grape leaves

yârân *yah-rahn* dinner party between friends

yardım etmek *yahr-dihm eht-mehk* to help

yarı(sı) *yah-rih(sih)* (the) half; half of the; half the

yarım *yah-rihm* (a) half; half of a; half a; also, 12.30 pm
  –ekmek *ehk-mehk* half a loaf of bread
  –kilo *kee-loh* half a kilogram (500g)
  –pişecek şekilde *pee-sheh-jehk sheh-keel-deh* half-cooked

yarma *yahr-mah* name given to coarsely ground wheat or barley

yasak(tır) *yah-sahk(-tihr)* prohibited/forbidden

yassıkadayıf *yahs-sih-kah-dah-yihf* dessert of baked **kadayıf** pancakes, soaked in thick syrup & layered or topped with **kaymak**

yaş *yahsh* 'moist; also fresh (fruit)

TURKISH CULINARY DICTIONARY

253

–pasta *pahs-tah* 'moist pastry', such as syrup-soaked cakes & pastries

yavan çorbası *yah-vahm chohr-bah-sih* 'flavourless soup', even though it's made of two kinds of wheat, chickpeas, lentils, dry beans, fried meat chunks, butter, pepper sauce, red pepper flakes, onion & salt! (Malatya)

yayla çorbası *yahy-lah chohr-bah-sih* 'mountain pasture' or 'highland' yoghurt soup with mint

yaz türlüsü *yahz tuur-luu-suu* summer vegetable stew

yemek (yemeği) *yeh-mehk (yeh-meh-ih)* food/meal

–kaşığı *kah-shih-ih* see **çorba kaşığı**

–listesi *lees-teh-see* menu

–odası *oh-dah-sih* dining room

–yemek *yeh-mehk* to eat a meal

yemekler *yeh-mehk-lehr* foods

yemekli vagon *yeh-mehk-lee* train dining car

yemiş *yeh-meesh* dried fruits & nuts

yengeç *yehn-ghech* crab

yeni *yeh-nee* new/again

yenibahar *yeh-nee-bah-hahr* allspice

yer elması *yehr ehl-mah-sih* Jerusalem artichoke

yerfıstığı *yehr-fihs-tihh-ih* peanut

yerli *yehr* local

yermantarı *yehr-mahn-tah-rah* truffle

yeşil *yeh-sheel* green

–biber *bee-behr* green pepper

–mercimekli bulgur pilavı *mehr-jee-mehk-lee buul-guur pee-law-vih* pilaf of green lentils, **bulgur**, margarine & salt (Tokat)

–mercimekli erişteli çorba *mehr-jee-mehk-lee eh-reesh-teh-lee chohr-bah* green lentil & noodle soup (Urfa)

–salata *sah-lah-tah* green salad

–soğan *soh-ahn* green onion, spring onion & chives

–zeytin *zehy-teen* green olives

yeşillik(ler) *yeh-sheel-leek(lehr)* (mixed) greens

yeter *yeh-tehr* enough/sufficient

yıkamak *yih-kah-mahk* to clean/wash

yılanbalığı *yih-lan-bah-lih-ih* eel

yıldönümü *yihl-der-nuuu-muuu* anniversary

yıldız şehriye *yihl-dihz sheh-ree-yeh* star-shaped macaroni (stellini)

yiyecek (yiyeceği) *yee-yeh-jehk (yi-yeh-jeh-ih)* food

–parçalayıcı *pahr-chah-lah-yih-jih* food processor

yoğurt *yoh-uurt* yoghurt

–çorbası *chohr-bah-sih* yoghurt soup – varies according to region

–lu fıstıklı köfte *-luu fihs-tihk-lih kerf-teh* **köfte** dish of bulgur, flour, cumin, yoghurt, garlic, tomato, dry & fresh mint & red pepper flakes (Adana)

–lu patlıcan salatası *-luu paht-lih-jahn sah-lah-tah-sih* eggplant salad with yoghurt

–lu pazı *-luu pah-zih* chard in garlicky yoghurt sauce (Kastamonu)

–tatlısı *taht-lih-sih* yoghurt syrup cake

yöre mutfağı *yoh-reh muut-fah-ih* regional kitchen; regional food style

yöresel *yoh-reh-sehl* local

yörük kebabı *yoh-ruuuk keh-bah-bih* 'nomad's' kebab of lamb, onion, mushroom, green pepper, artichoke, tomato, beans, homemade macaroni, dill & grated **kaşar** (Antakya)

yufka *yuuf-kah* filo pastry (paper-thin sheets of ready-made pastry)

yüksük çorbası *yuuuk-suuuk chohr-bah-sih* chickpea & mincemeat soup (Mersin, İçel)

yüksük makarna *yuuuk-suuuk mah-kahr-nah* macaroni shaped like short, fat sections of a cylinder (*see also* **boncuk makarna**) yüksükotu *yuuuk-suuu-koh-tuu* foxglove; thimble flower

yulaf *yuu-lahf* oat(s)

yulaf ezmesi çorbası *yuu-lahf ehz-meh-see chohr-bah-sih* oat porridge

yumurta *yuu-muur-tah* egg
–akı/beyazı *ah-kih/beh-yahz* egg white
–sarısı *sah-rih-sih* egg yolk

yumurtalılar *yuu-muur-tah-lih-lahr* egg dishes

yumurtalı mezgit *yuu-muur-tah-lih mehz-gheet* **mezgit** fish & eggs (Trabzon)

yumurtalı sandviç *yuu-muur-tah-lih sahnd-wihch* egg sandwich

yumurtalı ıspanak kavurması *yuu-muur-tah-lih ihs-pah-nahk kah-wuur-mah-sih* eggs with spinach

yumurtası (*see* **balık yumurtası**)

yumuşak *yuu-muu-shahk* soft/tender

yürek *yuuu-rehk* heart

yuva *yuu-wah* nest

yuvarlama *yuu-wahr-lah-mah* soup made with chick peas & small mince dumplings (Antep)

yuvarlak *yuu-wahr-lahk* round

yüz *yuuuz* face; one hundred

Z

zamkı (*see* **akasya zamkı**)

zargana (balığı) *zahr-gha-nah (bah-lih-ih)* sea-spike (fish)

zayıflamak *zah-yihf-lah-mahk* to get thin; to lose weight

zeldeli *zehl-deh-lee* wild apricots

zemin *zeh-meen* a low level; flat place

zencefil *zehn-jeh-feel* ginger

zerdali *zehr-dah-lee* wild apricot

zerde *zehr-deh* sweet, gelatinous dessert made with rice, almonds, pistachio & pomegranate that has been coloured & flavoured with saffron. Especially eaten at weddings.

zerdeçal *zehr-deh-chal* turmeric

zerzevatçı *zehr-zeh-vaht-chih* greengrocer

zeytin *zehy-teen* olive
–piyazı avrat salatası *pee-yah-zih ahv-raht sah-lah-tah-sih* salad made with pitted green olives, parsley, onion, coarse ground walnuts, red pepper, sour pomegranate & olive oil (Antep)

zeytinyağı *zehy-teen-yahh-ih* olive oil

zeytinyağlı *zehy-teen-yahh-lih* general name for dishes cooked in olive oil
–ayşe kadın fasulye *ahy-sheh kah-dihn fah-suul-yeh* green beans in olive oil
–bakla (ezmesi) *bahk-lah (ehz-mehs-see)* broad beans in olive oil
–barbunya fasulyesi *bahr-buun-yah fah-suul-yeh-see* borlotti beans in olive oil
–biber dolması *bee-behr dohl-mah-sih* bell peppers stuffed with rice
–dolma içi *dohl-mah ee-chee* seasoned rice that's used for stuffing dishes
–domates dolması *doh-mah-tehs dohl-mah-sih* stuffed tomatoes with rice
–ekşili kabak *ehk-shee-lee kah-bahk* zucchini (courgette) in olive oil & lemon juice
–ekşili patlıcan *ehk-shee-lee paht-lih-jahn* eggplant (aubergine) in olive oil & lemon juice
–ekşili pırasa *ehk-sheh-lee pih-rah-sah* leeks in olive oil & lemon juice
–enginar *ehn-ghih-nahr* artichokes in olive oil
–fasulye pilakisi *fah-suul-yeh pee-lah-kee-see* white beans in olive oil
–iç baklalı enginar *eech bahk-lah-lih ehn-ghih-nahr* artichokes & broad beans in olive oil
–kabak *kah-bahk* zucchini (courgette) in olive oil
–kereviz *keh-reh-weez* celeriac in olive oil
–kış türlüsü *kihsh tuuur-luuu-suuu* mixed winter vegetables in olive oil

–lahana dolması *lah-hah-nah dohl-mah-sih* stuffed cabbage-leaves in olive oil

–patlıcan dolması *paht-lih-jahn dohl-mah-sih* eggplant (aubergine) with rice stuffing in olive oil

–patlıcan imambayıldı *paht-lih-jahn ee-mahm-bah-yihl-dih* stuffed eggplant in olive oil & onions

–patlıcanlı pilav *paht-lih-jahn-lih pee-lawv* pilaf with eggplant (aubergine) in olive oil

–pırasa böreği *pih-rah-sih ber-rehh-ih* leeks pie in olive oil

–pırasa *pih-rih-sah* leeks in olive oil with carrot, rice, sugar, salt & lemon

–pilaki *pee-lah-kee* **pilaki** of black-eyed peas, olive oil, spring onion, carrot, potato, parsley & salt (Aydın)

–taze bakla *tah-zeh bahk-lah* whole broad beans in olive oil

–taze fasulye *tah-zeh fah-suul-yeh* fresh green beans in olive oil

z–yaprak dolması *yahp-rahk dohl-mah-sih* stuffed vine leaves with rice in olive oil

–yaz türlüsü *yahz tuuur-luuu-suuu* mixed summer vegetables in olive oil

–yeşil fasulye *yeh-sheel fah-suul-yeh* green string beans in olive oil

zeytinyağlılar *zehy-teen-yahh-lih-lahr* cold vegetables in olive oil

zırz *zihrz* salad made with fresh onion, spinach, **süzme** yoghurt, olive oil, **çerkez tuzu**, & boiled eggs (Bilecik)

zile pekmezi *zee-leh pehk-mah-zee* pekmez whipped with egg white (Tokat)

ziraat *zee-raht* agriculture

ziyafet *zee-yah-feht* lavish meal; banquet; feast

–vermek *vehr-mehk* to give someone a lavish meal; to hold a banquet in someone's honour

More World Food Titles

Brimming with cultural insight, the World Food series takes the guesswork out of new cuisines and provide the ideal guides to your own culinary adventures. The books cover everything to do with food and drink in each country – the history and evolution of the cuisine, its staples & specialities, and the kitchen philosophy of the people. You'll find definitive two-way dictionaries, menu readers and useful phrases for shopping, drunken apologies and much more.

The essential guides for travelling and non-travelling food lovers around the world, look out for the full range of World Food titles including:

**Italy,
Morocco,
Mexico,
Thailand,
Turkey,
Vietnam,
Spain,
France,
Deep South (USA),
Ireland &
Hong Kong.**

Out to Eat Series

Lonely Planet's Out to Eat series takes its food seriously but offers a fresh approach with independent, unstuffy opinion on hundreds of hand-picked restaurants, bars and cafes in each city. Along with reviews, Out to Eat identifies the best culinary cul-de-sacs, describes cultural contexts of ethnic cuisines, and explains menu terms and ingredients.

Updated annually, new Out to Eat titles include:
Melbourne, Paris, Sydney, London and San Francisco.

Planet Talk

Our FREE quarterly printed newsletter is full of tips from travellers and anecdotes from Lonely Planet guidebook authors. Every issue is packed with up-to-date travel news and advice, and includes:

a postcard from Lonely Planet co-founder Tony Wheeler
a swag of mail from travellers
a look at life on the road through the eyes of a Lonely Planet author
topical health advice
prizes for the best travel yarn
news about forthcoming Lonely Planet events
a complete list of Lonely Planet books and other titles

To join our mailing list, residents of the UK, Europe and Africa can email us at go@lonelyplanet.co.uk; residents of North and South America can do so at info@lonelyplanet.com; the rest of the world can email talk2us@lonelyplanet.com.au, or contact any Lonely Planet office.

The Lonely Planet Story

Lonely Planet published its first book in 1973 in response to the numerous 'How did you do it?' questions Maureen and Tony Wheeler were asked after driving, bussing, hitching, sailing and railing their way from England to Australia. Written at a kitchen table and hand collated, trimmed and stapled, *Across Asia on the Cheap* became an instant local bestseller.

Eighteen months in South-East Asia resulted in their second guide, *South-East Asia on a Shoestring*, which they put together in a backstreet Chinese hotel in Singapore in 1975. The 'yellow bible', as it quickly became known to backpackers around the world, soon became the guide to the region. It has sold well over ¾ million copies and is now in its 10th edition, still retaining its familiar yellow cover.

Today there are over 400 titles, including travel guides, walking guides, language kits & phrasebooks, travel atlases & maps, diving guides, restaurant guides, first time travel guides, condensed guides, illustrated pictorials and travel literature. The company is the largest independent travel publisher in the world.

The emphasis continues to be on travel for independent travellers. Tony and Maureen still travel for several months of each year and play an active part in the writing, updating and quality control of Lonely Planet's guides.

They have been joined by over 120 authors and over 400 staff at our offices in Melbourne (Australia), Oakland (USA), London (UK) and Paris (France). Travellers themselves also make a valuable contribution to the guides through the feedback we receive in thousands of letters each year and on our web site.

The people at Lonely Planet strongly believe that travellers can make a positive contribution to the countries they visit, both through their appreciation of the countries' culture, wildlife and natural features, and through the money they spend. In addition, the company makes a direct contribution to the countries and regions it covers. Since 1986 a percentage of the income from each book has been donated to ventures such as famine relief in Africa; aid projects in India; agricultural projects in Central America; Greenpeace's efforts to halt French nuclear testing in the Pacific.

Lonely Planet Offices

Australia
PO Box 617, Hawthorn, Victoria 3122
☎ 03-9819 1877
fax 03-9819 6459
email:talk2us@lonelyplanet.com.au

USA
150 Linden St, Oakland, CA 94607
☎ 510-893 8555 TOLL FREE: 800 275 8555
fax 510-893 8572
email: info@lonelyplanet.com

UK
10a Spring Place, London NW5 3BH
☎ 020-7428 4800
fax 020-7428 4828
email: go@lonelyplanet.co.uk

France
1 rue du Dahomey, 75011 Paris
☎ 01 55 25 33 00
fax 01 55 25 33 01
email: bip@lonelyplanet.fr